PENGUIN BOOKS

HIGH TIMES IN
THE HIGH COUNTRY

John Kerr, WV's co-author, was born in Oamaru and worked in his teens for WV, a cousin of his father, as a station dogsbody. He recalls being paid £1 a day, which wasn't enough; WV thinks it was more like £1 a week and too much. John's professional life has been centred around books in Australia and New Zealand, as bookseller, editor, publisher, salesman and writer.

HIGH TIMES
IN THE
HIGH COUNTRY

WV: *The Life of a Musterer*

WV Kerr & John Kerr

PENGUIN BOOKS

PENGUIN BOOKS

Penguin Books (NZ) Ltd, cnr Airborne and Rosedale Roads, Albany,
Auckland 1310, New Zealand
Penguin Books Ltd, 27 Wrights Lane, London W8 5TZ, England
Penguin Putnam Inc, 375 Hudson Street, New York, NY 10014, United States
Penguin Books Australia Ltd, 487 Maroondah Highway, Ringwood, Australia 3134
Penguin Books Canada Ltd, 10 Alcorn Avenue, Toronto, Ontario, Canada M4V 3B2
Penguin Books (South Africa) Pty Ltd, 5 Watkins Street, Denver Ext 4, 2094,
South Africa
Penguin Books India (P) Ltd, 11, Community Centre, Panchsheel Park,
New Delhi 110 017, India

Penguin Books Ltd, Registered Offices: Harmondsworth, Middlesex, England

First published by Penguin Books (NZ) Ltd, 2000

1 3 5 7 9 10 8 6 4 2

Copyright © WV Kerr & John Kerr, 2000

The right of WV Kerr and John Kerr to be identified as the authors of this work
in terms of section 96 of the Copyright Act 1994 is hereby asserted.

Designed by Mary Egan
Typeset by Egan-Reid Ltd, Auckland
Printed in Australia by Australian Print Group, Maryborough

Contents

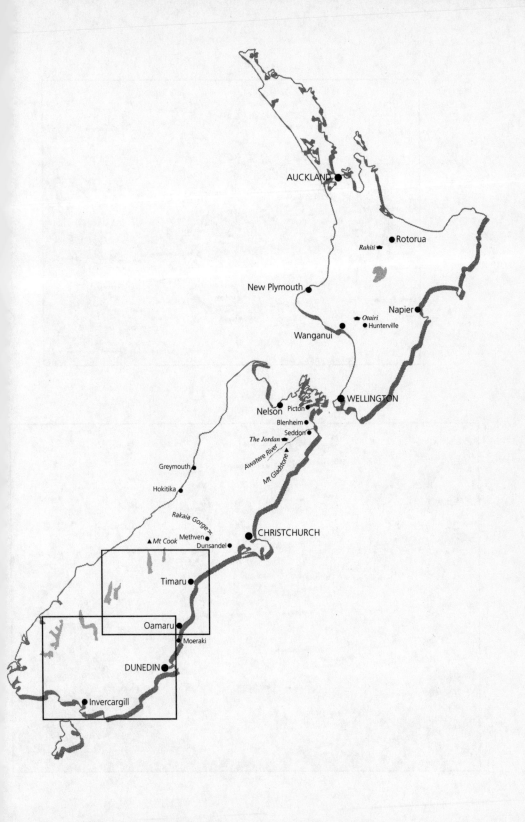

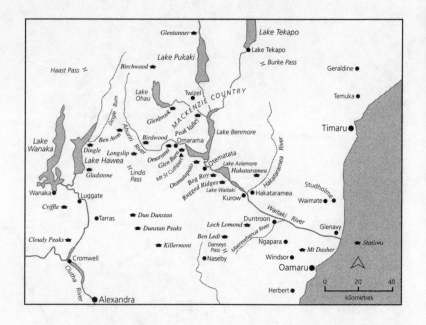

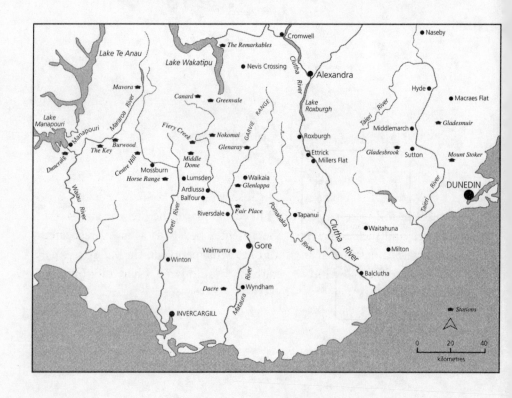

CHAPTER ONE

A Place of My Own?

Home, home on the range
Where the deer and the antelope play
Where seldom is heard
A discouraging word
And the skies are not cloudy all day

Daniel E Kelly and Dr Brewster M Higley,
'Home on the Range'

A S I SAT IN MY CONSUL IN OAMARU ON ONE OF THOSE ANNOYING visits that force you to towns, Jack Tizdell saw me, got in and we had a yarn. He worked for a stock firm and I'd had dealings with him.

'You know, Bill, you ought to take a look at that place Blenheim's advertising.' He outlined it. Sounded interesting: high, wild, sunny, remote country draws me like a merino to a salt lick, always has. But life was sweet in the Upper Waitaki in North Otago in the mid-1960s for me.

I managed Omarama Station, a substantial high-country property, and my years of toil were paying off. I liked the place, the life, the status, the big house and the salary. Even the absentee boss was a man I respected and learned from, though an aloof one. Most people in the valley seemed to like me well enough and I liked them, by and large. I had a lot of good mates. The comradeship of musterers and owners, managers and shepherds, with the irksome exception of boys, was exceptional there. My wife fitted into the life of the station and community and was well respected. She'd never uttered a disparaging word about anyone — except me and that was all right. Nobody could live with me all the time at close range; I tended to be a tiny bit critical and grouchy on the odd occasion. So what was wrong?

I'd even achieved a burning desire: to *own* my own place. Birdwood run was a rough old shingle scree and tussocky nightmare but I loved her. She'd no hope of paying boarding-school fees but earned a few bob, a nice wee salary supplement. Birdwood had emerged from the claws of the banks. I detested and feared debt; I took in stories of foreclosures in the big slump with my rabbit-stew tea as a child. But Jack had sparked my interest.

I checked out the ad for Gladstone Station. The swimming pool and tennis court held no appeal, but the farming did. I rang the Rural Bank to test whether I was wool-gathering in more ways than one, outlined my illustrious career, and explained that I could raise £15 000 from a neighbour who wanted to buy Birdwood, subject to more conditions than Cook Strait weather, but mainly sale of his place. It was nearly true. The bank man assured me I was eligible for the bank's maximum £18 000 loan. An aim of this government-owned bank was to put land under landless young families.

I knew the boss's 'boy', Dick Wardell, wasn't merely able to manage Omarama without me, he was chafing at the bit to do it. My stepson Billy was nearing the end of high school, but son John was about to begin and our unborn child would follow. More boarding-school fees loomed. So, with quiet confidence and raised interest, I rang the bloke in the regional office of National Mortgage, a firm I'd dealt with for four years. He rang the bloke in the city office. They say a man gets the face he deserves by 40, and this local guy's was big and blue with gin blossoms. He said, 'WV Kerr doesn't have enough money for an ice cream.' Oh really? I needed a goad; they were going to pay for that.

I rang his boss. After pleasantries, I measured my words.

'I've been dealing with your company for four years and, it must be said, everything has been quite satisfactory.' No need to apply it with a trowel. 'Recently I wanted to look at a place in Marlborough, but I've had no co-operation from your man here. In fact, I've been quietly insulted.' I rammed the ice cream home. 'In fact, I have £15 000 . . .'

The local man rang me back. What was I doing on Friday?

On Friday, the shortest day of the year, I was flying to Blenheim, courtesy of Blueface's firm. Bill Ross was pilot, the local agent came and I chose Duncan Anderson as my property adviser. He knew land, bragged of pioneering the dropping of phosphorus poison from planes (he did too) and was a mate. Somewhere west of Christchurch we dropped a million feet in a tenth of a second. Stomachs hit tonsils.

'You're not worried, are you, Duncan?'

'Scared stiff!'

The National Mortgage's Marlborough agent was waiting at the landing strip. We toured Gladstone. The local bloke pointed to ugly black clouds glowering over the Tasman. 'I don't envy you flying back in that.' When we returned to his office Duncan took off on urgent business. We had about wound up the matter to hand when Duncan came back, half shickered and with a silly grin. 'Now I can face *anything*!' Bill Ross rang. The weather report was in: we were grounded. Duncan — a dog trial man — befriended publicans everywhere and one lent us toothbrushes. We retired early to earnest discussions of rural land values. Pope's a Hindu, too.

I became a bit infatuated with Gladstone. Skip this if property bores you. It rose to 7000 feet and there was cocksfoot to 5000. Country you walked to muster — too tough for horses — all rocks, cliffs and crags with shingle and tussock high up and good paddocks lower. No bush. Lots of water and Nelson–Marlborough sun. Obvious cattle potential: they had 13 heifers and I planned on 300. I liked the vendor, Bill Rutherford, and he liked me. He had one of those 'genuine reasons for selling': he'd found a place near the coast, nearer to services and the like. And £45 000 was a fair price.

New negotiations with the Rural Bank followed, and I became toey. The bank seemed to be swinging the lead, hoping I'd fade away. It was up to me to keep pressing.

My wife Ima was heavily pregnant with her third child and, on doctor's orders, went to Dunedin's Queen Mary Hospital so they could keep an eye on her. This, on the eve of Omarama's shearing. Johnny was dispatched to my sister Jean at Millers Flat. Billy, home from Waitaki Boys', was staying with the in-laws in Invercargill. The post-Christmas shearing on my run at Birdwood had used up my annual leave. But lack of attention could kill the Gladstone deal. Could I sneak in a trip to Blenheim the moment the shed was cut out, swing back through Millers Flat for a Christmas visit to Johnny, and make Dunedin for Christmas Day and the birth? I drove back on the longest day of the year.

The bank johnnies made assurances with all the substance of flatulence, but they were rattled. I ransacked the cupboards of my mind for the right next move in the New Year as the Mainline ute burned up the miles.

I arrived at Jean's in Millers Flat but the engine didn't cool. 'Better hightail it to Dunedin,' said Jean. Phones at the hospital, my relatives' places and around the Omarama area had been running hot too, looking for WV. My brother John had signed papers authorising a caesarian — why my wife couldn't sign herself is beyond me, but that's how it was done.

I arrived at night on Christmas Eve, already father of a baby girl, Fiona Mary. The mother couldn't talk much; she had an oxygen tube in her mouth. After I'd done all the things you'd imagine a new father would do, she asked, 'What've you been doing?' I kept Gladstone low key: she'd worried herself close to Ulcerland over the debt burden we took on when I bought Birdwood, and Gladstone was much bigger. But I did ask her what she thought. 'Talk about getting a person at a low moment,' she said. She needed rest and I needed a place to stay. And I was high and wide awake. I drove around to my late mother's house out of nostalgia and a sense of continuity. My mother's brother Fred Ferguson, who'd bludged off her all her hard life, was in residence. I'd been Mr Good Guy among her estate's trustees, most of whom wanted to sell the house, and vetoed chucking the old prick out.

'This is a fine time to call on a man!' said Fred.

'Worse than that, I'm staying the night. Can you make me up a bed?'

I told him of my newborn, kept him up from 2 a.m. to 4 a.m., celebrating and earbashing him about work, Gladstone and anything else I felt like.

'Will you be wanting breakfast?' he said wearily.

As I slipped between the sheets I said, 'Yeah. Eggs. Two. Soft boiled.' This has been his breakfast for over 50 years, and I think, from his watery half smile, that he may even have caught the sarcasm.

At a meeting in a National Mortgage office their man didn't look me in the eye. He watched ducks out the window: a bad sign. The £10 000 of promised finance had shrunk to £8000 — head office had said so. 'Sorry you're leaving empty handed,' the man said.

Everything Hazlett, Pinckney and Wardell had taught me came into play. Keep cool. 'Oh, no. You've got it wrong. I've dealt with you for years, and just wanted to give you the chance to do further business with me.' I grinned broadly and extended my hand. (I really wanted to plaster his nose over his face, but had outgrown that.) 'As for going home empty handed, don't worry about it. Thank you for your time.'

I met up with Gladstone owner Bill Rutherford at a men's club. 'How'd it go?' he asked.

'Disaster.'

'Would you talk to my man?'

I'd have sipped sherry with Satan for a deal, but his man turned out to be a quiet, sincere fellow from Dalgety. When the three of us met, he opened with, 'Do you want to buy?'

'Yes,' I said.

'Do you want to sell?' to Bill. Hell, I thought, he's going to marry us!

'Yes,' Bill said.

'It's quite simple. You drop your price to WV. Then you and I go off and see if the bloke who's selling to you will drop his price.'

They did that and came to the Seddon pub, as we arranged, to report it done. We had a daisy chain of three sales: if Rutherford's neighbour sold to Rutherford and Rutherford sold to me and I sold Birdwood to my neighbour, we were all looking sweet. I drove home through the night, excited as a bitch with a bone.

My lawyer rang that night, late. The Rural Bank, despite assurances, wanted out. Its £18 000 was critical; the deal was off.

Next day I went to the Tekapo sales and was approached by Jim Todhunter from Canterbury's Rakaia Gorge. I'd bought rams off Todhunter for Omarama every year. 'Thanks for mentioning me to Bill Rutherford. He wants to get his flock in order and I appreciate the mention. And congratulations, I understand you're buying Gladstone.'

'Was. It's off,' I told him. He got annoyed! He was on the High Country Commission, a body that knew better than I that the job of the recalcitrant Rural Bank was supposed to be to put young blokes on runs. 'Ring your local member of Parliament and if that doesn't do any good, ring me. I'll introduce you to the Minister for Crown Lands . . .' I'd been introduced to Wellington politics, and drove home chest puffed out. It was on again!

Stock agent Graham Shanks rang me on Sunday night on a routine matter. These blokes don't work nine to five. Mugs if they try — before mobile telephones, what sort of a farmer would be available during daylight? We chatted for a while, then he said, 'Have to leave you. Your old friend's come in to see me.' My old friend was Arthur Munro, squire of Dunstan Peaks, a neighbouring property I'd always had my eye on. An hour later Shanks rang me back and said, 'You going to be home tomorrow morning?'

Arthur Munro had broad shoulders and a barrel chest, and wore an elephant-hunter hat — a solar topee — and thick-rimmed round specs. How he came to be squire of Dunstan Peaks I don't know. Some say he got a First World War soldier settlement; others reckon he got it before 1918; still others say from the widow of the previous owner, who'd died in a snowstorm. Arthur was deaf, and so was his brother Cecil. Maybe it was the war, maybe genetic. Arthur spoke in a loud confident monotone. The Scots lass he married would tap on the table — or if he was giving a speech at a race meeting, lower her hand in front of her — to turn down his volume knob. Communication with Arthur was usually easy, though: he was a fluent lip-reader.

What I liked most about Arthur was his outstanding intuition with animals. He loved racehorses, was a superb horseman, and even ran a team of dogs. No amount of keen eyesight will compensate for the inability to hear a dog behind a bluff, but on the hill Arthur once monotoned, of one of my dogs, 'That dog's got a good bark.'

I mouthed, 'How the hell would you know?'

'I can see the way the sheep run off him.' His powers of observation were awesome. One shearer, listening to Arthur's instructions to another, cheekily said, for the benefit of his fellow shearers, 'Silly deaf old bastard.'

Quick as lightning Arthur returned: 'I might be deaf, George, but I'm not silly.' He'd heard him out of the corner of his eye.

Arthur and his astute wife Nell were a unique team who played the complex inter-obligation network of high-country society like Liberace on the piano.

I would come in from Omarama Station's Mount St Cuthbert tired, hot and dirty, and my wife would say, 'You've got to ring Aunt Nell.'

I knew what that was about. 'Aw, no. No, no, no. I can't go. We're flat out. No.'

'Bill, you've *got* to ring her.'

'Hello, Nell.'

'William, how are you?' Her voice was all sweet concern. 'We passed you the other day and you looked *so* tired. Arthur said you work *far* too hard on that property, you're *too* conscientious.' I *was* conscientious, too, I'd think with fatal pride. 'Saw your wee son John in church last Sunday. What a *lovely* little boy! Bill, he's the spitting image of you — a chip off the old block.' Yes, well, Johnny is a good-looking kid, chest puffing out. 'Bill, Arthur's *stuck* for the ram muster. He needs two men and can't get anybody.' Trapped.

'All right.' He already had two Omarama Station men, damn it, but how could you turn Nell down?

'You will? Hold on a minute, Bill.' She'd mouth to Arthur, who would roar in the background. 'Oh, Bill, you want to see the smile on his face. He said, "That's great. I don't need the other man now." So there you are, Bill. Arthur considers you as good as two men.'

Riding over to Arthur's place with Eric Boyle the next day I asked him how Nell had roped him in. Eric said, 'Well, you can't have been much of a gang in the past. Arthur said he didn't need two when I said I could come.' Conned again.

Childless couples with high-country acres weren't exactly thick on the ground and, while the overwhelming likelihood was that a nephew up Mount Cook way would buy them out, as Arthur and Nell had long stated was their intention, there's many a slip twixt cup and lip. It was a fine property and I reckoned no one was going to aid and abet my ambition if they didn't know I was nursing it. As she thanked me for some work I'd done one day, I broached it. 'I'd be interested if you ever felt like selling.'

'Bill, there's nothing I'd like better, but Arthur's given first refusal to his nephew.'

Still, nothing ventured, nothing gained. I was working with Arthur one day while the Marlborough purchase looked like it was on and he asked me about it. I stressed the correspondence school, the remoteness, how my wife wasn't exactly looking forward to it after enjoying our nice possie 300 yards from the primary school and 600 from the store. 'But I want it,' I said.

'Don't be hard, Bill. Think about the children, a young wife, up there.'

'Bugger them. They're getting a helluva sight more than I got. Top boarding schools. You said yourself a man can't depend on a station manager's salary all his life. "Knocking yourself out and nothing to show at the end of it," you said. I want something for them when I die.' If I overplayed the hard man, it should be remembered he'd been handing me out fatherly advice over the 10 years I'd helped him out.

The nephew was Andy Ivy, ex-musterer and stock agent, who'd married a Munro from Rugged Ridges, a place now on the floor of Lake Benmore behind the hydro dam. Glentanner Station, up the side of Mount Cook, was under Andy's management. Arthur's price was £26 000. 'I've given Andy first refusal, and I'll keep my word, but I'll talk him out of it. He's better off where he is.'

Things were looking good. Then Nell rang and told me Andy had been over to talk to Arthur, who'd put the price up to £28 000 to help 'talk him out of it', but Andy still wanted to buy. The flags were down, my dreams squashed. Then I remembered she'd once said they'd insist on a Wright Stephenson sale to a Wright Stephenson client, and I took an educated stab in the dark. I was sure Glentanner was Pyne Gould. 'Well, we've got to accept that, Mrs Munro, but I'm sorry you've changed your mind about Wright Stephenson,' I said.

'We *haven't* changed our mind about Wright Stephenson.'

'Isn't Andy getting his money from Pyne Gould?'

Significant pause.

'Thank you, Bill. *Thank* you.'

Arthur must have checked, because Nell rang a couple of days later: the flags were up again. Arthur was often right about things and he couldn't have been more right in predicting Andy Ivy was better off on Glentanner. Andy was a hard doer, immensely capable and ran Glentanner to the great satisfaction of its owners, Pyne Gould. The negotiations over Dunstan Peaks must have put the frighteners on them, because they offered Andy a quarter share of the place on top of his salary. He ended up owning it outright. The development of the big tourism complex on Glentanner ensured Andy lived well and died, I believe, a very wealthy man.

Graham Shanks turned up at the Omarama Station yards as arranged next morning. Arthur Munro's call on him had had a single, simple purpose: he wanted to sell Dunstan Peaks to WV — nobody else, just WV.

CHAPTER TWO

The Shocking Deeds of Wee Pirate

Ned Kelly: Hands up! We're going to rape all the men and rob all the women on this stagecoach.

Woman: Don't you mean, 'Rape all the women and rob all the men'?

Gay guy: Shut up, you old bag! Who's robbing this stagecoach? You or Mr Kelly?

I SUPPOSE I'D BETTER TELL MY WHAKAPAPA. THEY DO IN THESE books. An Australian bloke once told me that ex-colonials are well advised to leave the ancestor thing alone. 'Shake your family tree and you're bound to find a ratbag or three,' this son of convicts reckoned. Well, happily, the Kerrs are a respectable lot. We're related to the late Diana, Princess of Wales, but I already knew that. When she was out here she rang and wanted to meet me of course, but Ian Anderson and I were going to the dog trials in Methven. Besides, a Pom bloke told me she'd married a dull lad, so the meeting didn't take place.

The connection came through the Cessford Kerrs. But there was another branch from early on, the Ferniehurst Kerrs. The two Kerrs — Kers, Cars, Carrs — didn't care for each other much, apparently.

Sir Walter Scott, no slouch with words, no friend of Kerrs, wrote:

> While Cessford owns the rule of Kerr
> While Ettrick boasts the line of Scots,
> The slaughtered chiefs, their mortal jar,
> The havoc of the feudal war,
> Shall never, never be forgot . . .

And he got to take the minutes! I've read, too:

It's a curious twist of history that the Kerrs, who made their fortune as border reevers, perpetually feuding with the English, were among the greatest beneficiaries of the Union of the Crowns that united the kingdom.

My wife has this two-ton dictionary and 'reevers' means chief officer under the king of a town or district. But the writer could have said 'thievers' and still have been right. Ian Anderson once sent me a postcard from Scotland of a wall in a field said to have been part of the yards the Kerr cattle thieves used.

The Cessford Kerrs were pretty well in with Margaret Tudor, Queen Regent, and the Douglasses. The Ferniehurst lot backed young James V, Scottish independence and the French alliance. They hated one another, so killed one another regularly.

And there were problems with the neighbours: the Elliots and Armstrongs in the east, the Humes and Douglasses in the west, and the Scots over the fence. We were responsible for keeping the thieving English from pinching our sheep, women and cattle. Sir Robert Kerr was attending a meeting and was murdered by three Englishmen — Lyleburn, Starhead and Heron of Ford. They reckon it was in retaliation for rustling. Sir Andrew Kerr was a wee bit unhappy when Henry VIII died and the three killers were let off in a general amnesty. A group of cutthroats went over the border, caught Heron in his nightgown, took his head off and gave it to Sir Andrew, who took it to Edinburgh to show his friends. Henry VIII and James V of Scotland were at odds about what to do about this summary justice, so no one did anything, and the various factions called in favours around the district and met on Melrose Bridge.

The Scots, Sir Walter taking the minutes again, got 300 men there; so did we.

> When first the Scot and Ker were foes
> When royal James beheld the fray
> Prize to the victor of the day
> With Hume and Douglas in the van
> Bored down Vaucluse's retiring clan
> Gallant Cessford's heart blood dear
> Reeked upon Elliot's Border spear.

You can't win 'em all, but you can have a long memory and an eye for opportunity. Scot of Barcoo, half shickered in the streets of Aldreckie, heard a cry for help up an alley. Sir John Hume and a relative of mine slit Scot's throat. They got exiled for that. Should've come here with a few merinos, but Captain Cook hadn't publicised the place back then. They won a pardon — Kerrs tend to attract forgiveness.

Di's and my Cessnock rellies did better than the Ferniehurst Kerrs. The English stormed Ferniehurst Castle and raped every woman and beheaded every man inside. We wrought terrible vengeance on them though, but that'll keep.

Thankfully, this wee pup was born and raised in Millers Flat, Central Otago, New Zealand.

Most Kerrs came from around Roxburgh in the Borders — a bit of a coincidence really, because Roxburgh in Central Otago is about 16 kilometres from Millers Flat, a sort of outer suburb of Millers Flat. And the New Zealand sheepdog is a descendant of the Border collie to boot.

The name 'Kerr' derives from the Gaelic for awkward or the Norwegian for left-handed, depending on whether you go for the Pictish or Viking theory of our origins. The castle in Roxburgh is said to have the only spiral staircase in Europe that screws up so as to free up a southpaw's sword arm. The central column acts as a shield and the wide, open side of the staircase is for cleaving the heads of right-handed attackers coming up the stairs.

Whatever, a John Rennie Kerr, migrant from Scotland to the cold gold-fields of Central Otago, sired a John Alexander Kerr, my father, who married Bertha Ferguson, one of 11 children. Eight were boys and all went to fight for King and somebody's country; two returned. In 1919 Mum and Dad started this country's stock replenishment programme with the birth of Jean (Annie Jean), then Daizie and John Alexander. Dad was 54 years old on the day of his greatest accomplishment, the birth of William Victor.

There was some doubt about my chances of survival after birth, but I pulled through those first critical days. Dad was working hard as always and didn't have a phone to receive news of my condition. A Mrs McDonald had one and when word came through to her that the newborn would make it, as arranged, she hung out a towel on her clothesline so my father too would know. For a New Zealander who must surely be able to claim to be in the top one per cent of the population for distance walked in a lifetime, it is ironic that I didn't walk until two. My mother massaged my thin weak legs with warm olive oil each night before the fire.

When John Rennie Kerr died in 1915, Dad and his brothers Louis and James inherited the family farm. It was too small to support three men and families-to-be, and they couldn't agree on the direction it should take, so Dad and James sold their shares to Louis and made their own ways. Dad purchased a farm settlement block at Pomahaka, near Clinton, then sold it, leaving money on the place as a mortgage. He was working as an agricultural labourer when word came through that the debt could not be repaid, so the family repossessed and occupied the place. But the debt burden and poor prices meant he was forced to auction it off. The sale left just enough, £150, to purchase the house at Millers Flat.

Mum and Dad both fell ill during the influenza epidemic of 1919, which killed 6000 New Zealanders and millions overseas, but pulled through after a tough time of it. A local Irishwoman was kind to them in a general atmosphere of fear, and my sister Daizie's name honours that good woman and the way she pronounced her own name.

Dad thought Michael Joseph Savage was second only to God, as a lot of that generation did. (Although I have served on a rabbit board, the burning sub-committee of a soil conservation outfit and seven years on a school committee, formal politics, Labour or Tory, leaves me unmoved, always has.) Dad was a hard worker, but no amount of effort could suffice when the price of everything fell. His pick and shovel carved out roads around Lake Wanaka in an early work-for-the-dole scheme while he lived in a Ministry of Works camp.

My mother Bertha was probably not a saint — who is? — but her goodness and kindness were hard to fault. She worked hard and never seemed to complain. There was pitiful little money and she always made do.

My Uncle Fred, Mum's brother, was an important influence in the house. I detested him. 'Sssh! Fred's resting,' my mother would say. He was always 'resting'. He came back from the Great War and never worked again, from his early twenties to his seventy-third year. He had a garden little more than six by six, occasionally showing off a giant lettuce to Dad. Dad must have hated Fred's guts. Dad would come home after punching rabbit traps all day for a pittance to see the dapper prick in a shirt Mum had washed and ironed, wanting to argue politics night after night.

Presumably he contributed something from his war pension; he'd been gassed in France. But his afflicted lungs didn't stop him winning a cup for swimming the Molyneaux, what goldminers of the 1870s thereabouts and Mum and Dad and others called the Clutha. He was still going to the St Clair Swimming Baths in Dunedin in his seventies. People said they killed him in hospital out of good taste. He must have died one of the most widely read men in New Zealand.

Mum and Dad were the last generation conditioned to give such unselfish, unrequited care; brother John's wife and mine both thought Fred a parasite. In fact the cruellest thing Ima has said to me this year is that I'm getting to be like Fred.

We were none of us churchgoers, and I was a bit put off religion when a minister came over from Roxburgh and sought the 'advice' of a lady parishioner on a good picnic spot. Between them they decided on Horseshoe Bend on the Molyneaux. Someone saw them settling into a compromising position under the bridge, and the word flashed around. As he had eight kids, I decided at that point 'they' were all 'hypocrites' and never bothered much with religion.

The Kerr house was not one where the terms 'the old country' or 'Home' or 'Hame' were tossed about. None of us had any doubts about what we were: we were New Zealanders. Dad and Mum were not happy about the thing with Mrs Simpson, though; they didn't think that was cricket for a Windsor.

Money was tighter than a flea's arse so I took every opportunity offered for an earner: thinning carrots or swedes, or cleaning poultry sheds for a shilling a day for rabbiters and farmers; catching rabbits with ferret and dog for skins at best price £14 a hundred; milking neighbours' cows.

Despite our circumstances and the times I never went without school clothes. There were always shoes or boots on my feet, and my rabbit-skin money was often used to buy double-breasted suits and the like. We didn't run to a turkey at Christmas but we were perfectly happy with the roast lamb. A bottle of beer would appear in the house then too, but not on the other 364 days; beer was a luxury indeed.

At school I was nicknamed Pirate. I was the shortest bloke at high school until I caught something called puberty. One effect was to shoot me to 6 foot and 11 stone 3 pounds more or less overnight. And that's the way I've stayed.

Millers Flat High School's terms came and went with surprisingly little impact, as I recall. I liked mathematics. I was always second, and Alvery Deans first. She became professor at a Scottish university, I believe.

Mum was understandably sad when war broke out in 1939, with the loss she'd endured during the First World War. Talk of petrol rationing excited me — with no bus, would they close the school? They didn't. When the telegrams starting coming to the mothers, fathers, widows and next-of-kin, as they inevitably must, sadness was in the air. John got in late and saw out the Italian campaign safely. I was too young but had a go at getting into the navy, inappropriately. Life, for under-17s, went on.

Millers Flat was a devious place. The local dance halls were firm about not admitting under-17s, so we hung about outside. After the coy, demure hoopla inside was over, the local footy ground was a colony of seals bobbing up and down.

There wasn't a lot to do in Millers Flat in the 1930s and a nicely tied brown-paper parcel and a bit of string provided some devilment when holidaymakers were travelling to the lakes in summertime. Nowadays New Zealanders are all over tourists like merinos on a salt lick, can't do enough for them. As a child I thought the main purpose of tourists was to provide entertainment. I still do. Back then their cars would pull up to investigate the parcel and we'd yank the string we'd covered in road gravel and take off along our carefully planned line of retreat, yelling, 'Townies! Townies! Have you ever bin had?'

Most would laugh and call us hard little cases, depriving us of the thrill we looked for. We upped the stakes. A fat boy had an old suitcase we reckoned would pull them in, annoy them more. It just needed something more. When Fat Boy was caught short, nothing in the world seemed more natural than to open the suitcase for the purpose . . . A Baby Austin tootled up, a young man in a pressed white shirt motoring with his girlfriend. When he was greeted by a thousand flies, an evil smell, and the taunt, 'Have you ever bin had, you townie?' this townie was unamused — and finely athletic. He jumped the fence and ran after us. My fat mate tripped. Pirate the Coward's hobnailed boot stamped his neck for ever as I passed over him.

We varied the parcel trick on a slat bridge so that when passers-by picked up the parcel we yanked it out of their hands, through the slats.

Little Billie Mudge, the cute small daughter of the local postmaster, was all that was going one day. But her father's wrath could not be avoided: we all had to collect mail on Mondays. This posed the first problem I had with the leadership of men. As leader of the gang, I strongly felt I ought to be the one who went in first. On the other hand, if I was a goner, the gang would be leaderless, all at sea, vulnerable without my mighty problem-solving intellect. But a time comes in every boy's life when he must take his courage in hand.

I sent Fat Boy in first because he was a sap, but he didn't return. I sent Oaf in next. Then the little fella. By the time I looked in, the three of them were lined up looking sorry for themselves and Mr Mudge got me up against the wall too.

We gave up on that one and went back to raiding the odd orchard, pushing the dunny over during Sunday School, and ferreting.

Like all old blokes I remember with pleasure and pride the sporting achievements of my younger days. The school XI was in a fix: the ninth man had been bowled, there was only one ball of the last over to play and we needed 11 runs to win. All seemed lost when I walked to the crease, last man. The crowd was drifting from the field. The bowler sent down a hard, fast, devil-may-care ball with a sneer. I whacked it and split the ball in two. The umpire at the railway end followed the ball's trajectory to the left and called 'six'. The umpire at the Roxburgh end followed the other half to the right and also called 'six'. And the umpires' decisions were final.

My rugby achievements are unique in the annals of the game too. But that happened many years after I grew up and will wait.

In the shooting game I got pretty good at judging lead — the distance between the spot you fire at and the target, to compensate for the target's speed over the distance. I started young, shooting my sister. Daizie was four years older and we didn't get on when I was eight. I made some pointed remark in the garden and she boxed my earhole. Rule one: never hit someone who's carrying a gun. I lined her up. Daizie was a leggy thing, wearing shorts that day, and she was on the concrete steps to the house like a gazelle on the bound. I had six inches' lead and squeezed the trigger. I winged her thigh; the pellet broke the skin and plopped to the ground. The way she screamed and carried on you'd think I'd gutshot her. An irate father confiscated the airgun, but I often think of that as the best shot of my life.

CHAPTER THREE

Drudge and Dogsbody

Hey! I'm depraved on accounta I'm deprived!

Leonard Bernstein's Jet gang member,
West Side Story

I HAVEN'T ALWAYS LIVED IN THE COUNTRY. I SPENT THREE MONTHS in Dunedin in 1941. Today I visit Oamaru 28 kilometres down the road once a month for a haircut, but I find the hustle and bustle of 12 000 people faintly annoying.

But Dunedin in my teens was hell. I'd been a naughty boy at school and the family couldn't afford to keep me there anyway. Whatever the reason, at the age of 16 I was sent off to town to work. The sign outside said:

R.B. DENNISON & CO
Engineers' Supplies & Mining Requisites

People then used grease from tins, four-gallon square-topped tins with round lids. They'd leave the lid off and smear the grease on moving metal parts of cartwheels, automobiles, farm or factory equipment, ships' engines or whatever. I wonder how many users ever considered how the grease got there in the first place. I knew. Boys in cold dark cellars scraped it in with wooden bats from great 44-gallon wooden tubs.

I did deliveries too. For the first month I walked: the country boy had to learn his way around the city, apparently. Then they gave me a big heavy grocer boy's bike with R.B. DENNISON ENGINEERS' etc on the basket in front.

There were no traffic lights in the Exchange but a cop would direct traffic from a stand during rush-hour. He waved me through and I got flustered, riding in front of him, not, as any city kid would know, behind him. He was amazed — and angry. 'What the hell are you coming at, boy?'

Once I forgot to put the bike in the cellar for the night. Next morning it was gone. The manager rang the police, who'd found it and taken it to the station. The wee country boy had to front the desk sergeant to collect it. He asked me where I came from and had a field day: 'Week in jail before you get the bike back.'

I had to light two fires every morning: one for the clerk, secretary and her offsider, another for the boss. One morning the boss tripped over what he said was the kindling I'd chopped, stumbled, dropped a paper-bag parcel which smashed, and gin fumes filled the air. I took off — he was livid with rage — saying to the storeman, 'He drinks booze in the office' in my flight. 'Done it for years,' he replied wearily.

I took a delivery into the bowels of Speight's Brewery once, great smelly vats of beer brewing everywhere like a room in hell. A big pot-bellied man offered me a beer. I was game. He dipped a huge ladle in a billion-gallon vat. I drained it. 'Enjoy that, son?' I drained another. 'Think you'd better get back to work, son.' I wobbled off, DIC of one bicycle. The foreman said, 'What's happened to you, Billy? First time you've smiled since you've been here.'

I stayed with my sister Jean in Maori Hill and paid her 10 shillings a week board and keep out of my 18s 11d wages.

First week I was there I splurged some rabbitskin money I'd saved, on three dozen rabbit traps and a military saddle. On Saturdays, my day off, I would lay out the traps in the back yard and sit on the saddle. The neighbours said I was a caged lion.

I scanned job ads. A Mr Coster of Hyde, back up Central, wanted a rabbiter. I had dogs in Millers Flat, and traps and a saddle. I wrote and found the advertiser was going overseas with the Expeditionary Force, and wanted a youth to take his place with his uncle on their rabbiting block. I travelled to the Wingatui army camp at the racecourse to see the younger Mr Coster. He was playing cards and there was money everywhere — more than I'd seen in my whole life. He took me on.

The foreman at Dennison's had been there 30 years and the traveller

25. Every Christmas the traveller borrowed money from the storeman to buy a new suit. He had to have a presentable suit for sales work. I gave notice to a 64-year-old bloke who'd been there since he was 16. 'I thought you'd stay here,' he said. 'There's room for advancement in this firm. Your hands will drop off out there.' Couldn't see much advancement looking at him, and I knew I could skin three frozen rabbits a minute without hand damage, which he couldn't.

On Saturday I packed my gear, took it to Dunedin Railway Station and consigned it to Hyde. I was going to travel there on Monday. But when I got back to my sister's place, I got the first telegram of my life:

ENGAGEMENT CANCELLED STOP WRITING STOP DAN COSTER

The swine did have the courtesy to write. The letter explained that I was the wrong religion. Why he only trapped Catholic rabbits beats me. I dreamed for days of running that man down in a car, backing over him, and spreading burnt lime over his body until he vanished from the earth.

I was broke, humiliated, had no job, and hated Dunedin. Next stop was the Department of Labour office. Object: escape; assets: three dozen rabbit traps and a 30-shilling saddle. My visit paid off.

I got a casual job at Gladbrook Station on the Taieri Plain, which involved a train trip to Middlemarch first — I thought. Stopped at Sutton I saw a big flash 50-foot-long car by the station. When no one met me at Middlemarch, I explained my predicament to the storekeeper, who got Downs Roberts on the phone. 'You were sa-sa- [pause] sa-p-posed to get off at S-Sutton. Ca-ca-ome out — on the ma-ma-mail coach.' I'd heard a man stutter for the first time, and it wasn't reassuring.

I had silver in my pocket. My mother had always said, 'Pay your way, don't get in debt.' But I was a bit apprehensive when I asked the driver the fare.

'How much have you got?'

'Four and six.'

'That's not enough.'

My stomach turned over. 'I'll have to pay you the rest when I get me wages,' I said, and tendered the 4/6. I put my bag in the bus. People made blankets known as 'woggas' then, using the top half of socks. Maybe he saw my wogga on the top of my bag and took pity.

'Put it in your pocket, son. I drove a team for 7/6 a week in my early days.'

Gladbrook had 13 schoolboys working on it when I arrived and one was deputised to show me around. When I was shown the bathroom he politely gestured, 'You first.' Of course a bucket of water poised on top of the door came down on my head. It was all on. Three days later that boy found a hedgehog in his bed and I didn't let up until well after he cried '*pax*'. Ah, the lack of a classical education! But Pirate, leader of the Millers Flat Gang, had learned a thing or two as well.

Gladbrook Station was a typical sort of Taieri Plain place of the day, raising fat lambs and running wethers on the higher country. Down on the farm it was an all-girls' school that became a maternity ward and postnatal care centre in spring, a butcher's shop for Britain in summer, and a dining hall for destitutes in winter. Wherever it wasn't knee deep in ewes or lambs they grew winter feed crops. I was looking for experience and got it, but I learned little that was useful to me in the real high country.

I worked thinning swedes and acres of turnips with the other boys until they went back to school. One of us had a watch, and we'd remind the overseer fellow, 'It's five o'clock, Frankie.' But his watch always reckoned there was another five or ten to go. The two watches marched in time in the mornings though.

After school started I worked with a single man, a shepherd called Jack, fumigating rabbit warrens. I dug holes, inserted a hose, blocked up the hole again and any rabbit holes likely to be connected to it, then attached the hose to the exhaust pipe. Jack worked a key, ran the engine a while and read wild west magazines. Once he dented the brand-new three-tonner's mudguard on a strainer post. The boss, Downs Roberts, noticed and asked about it. It was my first experience of an adult uttering an out-and-out lie; he said he'd given 'the boy' a drive and I'd hit a post. That afternoon, with his belly full of tucker, he set me digging and nodded off in the cab. Vengeance is mine, saith the preacher. I put the hose in the passenger door and gently closed it.

'Turn 'er on.' After a few minutes he stumbled out, hacking, spitting, coughing, retching. He recovered and chased me, but the warthog doesn't outrun the cheetah.

'Why'd you do that?' There was 50 metres between us.

'You lied. Put my weights up with the boss.'

Nor was I finished with Jack. He had to be at one end of the place the next morning, at an isolated lonely hut. He refused to go on his own, and, as I was the only other one who could ride a horse, I had to go with him. On the fenceline little would progress whenever I wasn't there. Jack'd send me to the hut to peel spuds, chop wood and any other dirty work going. He used the time to round up some sheep and work his dogs, something I understand better now than I did then.

Various clues he dropped had led me to judge Jack to have great respect for supernatural forces. So ghosts he'd get. I rigged up a string under our beds in the tin hut we bunked in. A convenient hole on his side took the string outside, where I'd looped an old horseshoe on it. That night I pulled the string tight and a fearsome *Eee-eee-eee* was heard outside.

'You hear that?' He was bolt upright, his hair standing out from his head.

'No.' Silence. He lay down again.

Eee-eee-eee.

But eventually he sent *me* out in the cold to investigate, so I cut the string and reeled it back into my bunk. The sound-effects department closed for the night.

Little good comes of comparing the 1930s and early 1940s with the 1990s because so much has changed, but those decades were economically hard on a lot of people, young people especially. Back then there seemed to be *some* work for a strong back, though. Wages of six shillings a day didn't buy a lot, even for a frugal 16-year-old. Our hands were blistered after days of harvesting oats under a pitiless February sun. Our only ally against the heat and dust was a swig of oatmeal and water, said to be the thing to quench thirst. Maybe it was, but it was cheap and convenient too.

I'd been grateful for the 30 shillings a week, but I was glad to leave Gladbrook too.

Gladesmuir was different from Gladbrook and more to my taste. I was 16, a good age to be if you don't count the feelings of older people, and 16-year-olds don't. Older men were enjoying Cairo and fighting the Afrika Korps, but the fighting forces had no use for 16-year-olds.

I was Gladesmuir's cow boy, which described my first and last task of the day, milking my three cows and separating the cream before seven o'clock, seven days a week, with a fortnight a year off. We four got on fabulously and I never heard a murmur of complaint from those patient, tolerant creatures. I heard that wax matches inserted in the teats made the milk flow faster. So when I found a golf tee while mowing the lawns . . . The experiment was approached with some trepidation, but it didn't hurt me one bit. It worked, and I swear they were pleased and grateful too.

Females of another species were also taking an increasing share of my attention and I'd left a good sort and fine prospect at Gladbrook, Elizabeth. Gladesmuir was halfway between Middlemarch and Macraes Flat with Gladbrook way across the plain, but what's 14 miles cross country on a lady's bike to Romeo? Elizabeth was expecting me, so I was delighted when I found we were alone. She was ironing when I arrived. When she offered a cup of tea I thought I'd be in like Flynn, but she did it one handed. The iron obviously wasn't going to leave her mitt, so I plugged away home. The chain broke and my testicles, for whose future I'd nursed high hopes, hit the seat hard. I walked the last three miles in agony, carrying bike and chain. Next morning I came in to breakfast yawning. 'Did you not sleep very well, William?' I greeted this breathtaking understatement with a quiet, 'No.'

I purchased a motorbike at the foolish age of 17. My mates reckon we pushed it further than I ever rode it: disastrous buy. I picked up a girl on it once but she burned her leg on the exhaust pipe and when I pulled up at the pub she escaped to the ladies' for repairs. Next thing I knew she'd fastened on to a bloke with a car.

Didn't have much interest in bike paraphernalia but I bought a sou'wester hat and a coat for a trip from Gladesmuir to Millers Flat. When the bike wouldn't start, a Harley owner I knew pushed until I got going. The sou'wester came off but I kept the bike ticking over all the way. Gave the bloody things away a bit after that — for 30 years.

I had more luck on horseback. I rode around old Charlie Patterson's remote place every three days, keeping his ewes on their feet — a most pleasant task in good weather. One day I saw a girl on the other side of the boundary doing the same thing. I gave her a wave. Second day we had a wee yarn, and smoko together the third. It was a bright, beautiful day the last time we met, sun shining and dry underfoot. I crossed the fence. And that was the last time my skinny white legs saw the sun.

Charles Patterson gave me care of three old brood bitches when I took the job, so I could do simple dog jobs like cutting out the mutton or dog tucker culls, and simple shepherding tasks. Patterson bred working collies and sold bitch pups. These three he'd bought back for breeding when their working lives were winding down. They belonged to the station. I learned a lot from these three; they knew more than I did. You can't teach an old dog new tricks, but an old dog can teach a young boy a very great deal.

The living set-up was of a kind that no longer exists, and it shouldn't either. There is now no excuse for it. But for the standards and constraints of the day it was quite good and I had little cause for complaint. There was a war on, after all.

Hired help went to the house to get the meals cooked by Mrs Patterson, whose pikelets heralded the era of plastics but who was otherwise an okay cook and a pleasant woman. I would take my meals in the kitchen with Mr and Mrs Patterson, then it was back to the old hut under the pine trees. There was no running water and in winter we washed in a basin of cold water after breaking the ice. A bath could be effected, usually on fine Sundays, by filling a copper tub with water from the rainwater drum fed by the spouting and drainpipe. We boiled it over a wood fire. The bath itself stood under the pines. One way and another it was often a long haul between baths. We had an open fire, and read by candlelight. Social life was pretty well non-existent; I didn't go to church.

Old Charlie Patterson and his wife once kindly took the shy gawky 16-year-old to a supper dance in uptown Middlemarch. I leaned against the door jamb and shuddered most of the night, but I did hear an excellent riposte to a cheeky attempt to get some free medical advice across the supper table. A guest asked what he should do about a troublesome throat. The doctor spooned an extra helping of trifle onto his plate and suggested, 'Pour a kettle of boiling water down it. If that doesn't work, cut it.' Adults, it seemed, played it rough.

If I was awkward, consider: for two and a half years I barely met a soul my own age, let alone any girls, and my annual fortnight's 'holiday' in Dunedin, where I knew no one, was my only chance to rectify this.

But some shearers took pity on me and took me with them to the Macraes Flat pub. I drank a beer and it tasted fine. 'Try one from the top shelf, Snow.' Driving home one said, 'Want us to dig you up a girl, Snow?' I was young, inexperienced, newly inebriated, in the night air and lusty: 'Yeah!'

They pulled up alongside the cemetery, and that about summed up Macraes Flat.

Next morning, after throwing up green bile out the door by the separator, I decided to leave spirits on the shelf.

The worst job at Gladesmuir was mowing the big lawns. I suppose some like mowing lawns but I never have — grass is for animals to eat, not humans to mow. The boss ambled over once and asked, 'How'd you like that job, William?'

'I don't bloody like it.' This was quite mild considering my inner thoughts on the matter. Another 50 mows and I would have become a communist!

'No. But learn to do all these little things properly and you'll end up managing a big sheep station some day.' And he ambled away.

A vision came over me. I was riding a big chestnut with white socks: 'Do this, my man,' and 'Do that, my man.' All about me bowed and paid obeisance.

There was a way out, a better world, a dream to pursue, a worthy role in life and I knew my destiny.

But first there was the bloody lawn to finish.

Got a great reference, apparently. A good solid citizen, Charlie Patterson. He completely understood that I keenly wanted to escape mowing lawns, milking cows and other such mediocre tasks. I'd seen an ad in the *Otago Daily Times* for a real shepherd, not an apprentice shepherd-cum-dogsbody. I had an interview with Wright Stephenson and set sail for Glenlappa Station and The Real Thing.

CHAPTER FOUR

Huntin' 'n' Fishin'

It would be a most advantageous and attractive thing to the Otago Settlement, if some Scotch proprietors would send some red deer to be turned out here. In the course of a few years there is no doubt they would increase largely. The sport of hunting them would be highly attractive, and would conduce to the improvement of the breed of horses, and afford a manly amusement to the young Colonists, fitting them for the more serious occupations of stock-rearing and wool-growing.

William Haywood Wakefield,
Report 17 of the New Zealand Company, *1845*

SOME FERRETS, LIKE PEOPLE, ARE BETTER THAN OTHERS. FLUFFY and Duffy were my two top ferrets in the Millers Flat days and my small luxuries were a direct result of their labours. I used to carry these ferocious rodents about under my shirt to keep them amused and happy, but when they were released down a rabbit burrow they were killers, which isn't the idea for a skin seller who needs the furs intact. A stubborn rabbit, aware that nets, dogs and death awaited it upstairs, often tried to tough it out in a blind alley of its warren but to no avail. Ferrets would eat it from the rump forward. But if they were flushed out and sprang a trap, or were grabbed by me or my terrier for a quick, polite neck-wringing, the skins, particularly those of whitish bucks, were intact and saleable.

City folk and even many rural people don't quite grasp how severe rabbit infestation can be, how a stone set rolling can create a wave of rabbits down the hillside as if the hill itself was rolling. It's still like this today in places, but nothing like it used to be. The enormous hopes farmers pin on the calicivirus is entirely reasonable. When Dick Wardell read reports of the virus's spread in Australia, he reckoned it spread at the rate of a Holden ute in top gear.

Rampant rabbits can drive men to madness and extreme action. A fellow in Ettrick had a great rabbit warren complex he could see from his kitchen window, and nothing he did seemed to curb the growth of Troglodyte City. So he caught a bunny, tied three sticks of geli to it and lit the twisted fuse. He figured it'd bob down a hole and take the citizens out in the quake. But it ducked under his wash-house and hid. He didn't need any kindling cut that winter.

But sex is a powerful rabbit motivator too. It gave me the opportunity to brag about a fine bag: 28 hares shot in one spot, without my moving an inch. In spring, when a hare's mind turns to love, does in season are often seen striding it out pursued by three or four bucks. I saw this one evening near the wall of a dam. I was hiding behind a fence, and gave the thin-lipped whistle that hunters allege sounds like the slipstream of a diving hawk. Whatever, the noise stopped the doe in her tracks, giving me the chance to shoot her. The bucks cleared out with the gunshot, but lust and her scent still fresh in the air brought them back one by one. Others followed.

In my early years my ferrets caught feral rabbits. But if noxious goldfish are a problem, there's nothing like rainbow trout. Bill Elliot of Glenlappa had a lily pond at his front gate. At afternoon tea, when Alan Chalmers and I had our tongues trailing in the dust we were so thirsty, Elliot would forever be stopping at it to admire his goldfish. When the Mataura River flooded we found a big rainbow trout washed up, still alive, and knew just the right place for the hungry carnivore. As we passed by for afternoon tea there was a splash.

'What the hell was that?' Elliot asked, stroking his chin and thinking it through. No one knew. But the next day the rainbow was belly up in the pond. Heart attack brought on by indigestion, probably: the goldfish were gone.

'How the hell would that have got there?' Elliot exercised his chin again.

'Dunno. Might be like eels, crossing wet paddocks at night, do you reckon?'

A lot of city fellows are mad keen to shoot a deer, an ambition that seems to take root in them as boys. Growing up in deer country, I wasn't untouched by this desire either, and shooting deer came to take its place in the whole of high-country life. Mustering didn't pay big money (still doesn't), and deer tails and skins, and later venison, were a useful supplement to a bloke's wages, not to mention a break from eating mutton. Mustering work is on-again off-again, so I, like a lot of contemporaries, would live by the gun in down times, like the off-season when I was at Nokomai.

The trouble was that deer were hard to get there in the winter and I didn't do too well. I would collect lunch from the cookshop and, with my dog Poi, the first gun dog I ever had, climb up on the Garvie Range. Poi hated the gun, but if I sent him up into the bush and he came tearing back with his ears down, you could be pretty sure there was a deer up there. No barking or chasing, but a roughie spotter by gunshot-shy association. One morning he nearly bowled me over running out and flushed out a stag two metres above me. I shot it in the heart and had to step out of the way or it would've rolled over me 'n we were so close. I was back at the cookshop by midday with a big heavy hide that earned £5 15s, more than the £4 a week I might have got digging postholes or cutting wood. But such success was rare. I spent a lot of time walking hills with gun, binoculars and sleeping bag when I might as well have stayed in my bunk and read a book. I stayed in huts — Nokomai's unpredictable weather made sleeping out dangerous anytime, and especially in June or July.

A bloke came up from Invercargill, a blade shearer and freezing worker who was a mate of the Nokomai manager, Con McGrath. I had the deerstalking rights but he was mad keen and for peace I let him come with me. We walked up Fiery Creek and didn't do any good, so I went to a bit of trouble, loaded up my horse with tucker and took him a long way out on the hill to the Estimates Hut. Some mates were going to pick him up. He came back browned off, moaning about how he'd be better off back in Invercargill digging his garden. Off he went.

I went out the next day to where he'd been. Huge icicles hung off the bluff above the track and the odd one would fall as the sun melted its attachment; it was a place where you could've got speared. I clambered over the bluff for safety, taking no special care to be silent. Hadn't he told me there were no deer around? For a moment I thought I was looking at

35

30 jersey bulls lying in a meadow, hey ninny, hey nonny, hey no, but it was the sort of set-up a deerstalker dreams of. Some stags were taking a spell after rutting. It was like a sea of antlers rising when they caught wind of me, Serengeti not Southland.

Most shooters have heard of buck fever, the excitement that results in wide wild shooting and incompetence in the face of prey. It's killed men. Buck fever in shooting companions makes me cantankerous and I'm not above making such comments as 'You could've strangled them if you'd wanted to' or 'Easy as hitting a woolshed door at 20 yards front on' or 'They waited about fer ya.' But I admit it got to me that morning.

Bullets went everywhere and I got seven, but I should've got twice that many. A bloke had lent me his red-hot peppery deer dog but all he did was shudder behind me with his ears on the ground, so I wasn't the only one to lose on reputation.

Books by shooters don't much dwell on the work post-kill. This omission tends to paint an unrealistic gung-ho picture. Staggering down the mountain to the hut under the weight of seven big wet skins left me buggered. And I still wasn't done when the skins were hanging on the fence to dry. The old cook on Nokomai would cadge a smoke or two; but she paid me back — she filled up Edmonds baking powder tins with plum duff for me. I'd eat half in the dark at night and the rest on the hill at midday. But the duff was long gone; I only had a half a cup of oatmeal left.

Still, I decided to rest up in the hut and have my half a cup of porridge that night instead of going back to the station. When I woke next morning the hut was wreathed in silence. There were no windows and no candles, but I knew. Snow, about a foot of it, outside the door. Getting back was a long walk for a hungry man and dog. I considered going back up the gorge for all the venison lying there, but that would have been arduous and dangerous, and even further from safety. I had dark glasses for eye protection but I smeared charcoal from the fire on my face to cut the glare as well. Conundrum. Rock and hard place.

I remembered a patch of bush in a gully close by and intuition took over from sense. I ploughed over there — and startled a hind. She took off into the bush and I thought I'd lost her but she re-emerged. A nice heart shot at 50 metres while she was bolting helped me redeem my reputation somewhat, and of the thousands of times I've pulled a trigger that time was the only time my life hung on it. It was undoubtedly the most important shot of my life. I fed the useless one and took a hindquarter up to the hut for a feed. On the top ridge the fence was covered, top wire under snow and the red-hot pepper got snared in it every time we crossed, which was — of necessity — often, exasperating and wearying me further. On the other side I simply walked down the creek for ease of passage, to hell with wet cold socks and the dog. The station mirror was a shock — I was the colour of blackberries from the sun.

The eight hides stayed on that fence until summer, when we picked them up and put them in a barrel to soften before drying them again.

Tails were earners too. I swapped them for .303 bullets. Bullets were hard to find in those days of postwar rationing but Ah Lee in Dunedin always had some, so he was a good contact. And he paid cash, promptly, every time. He once sent me a letter saying he was always pleased to receive 'tales' but 'please no ferret tales'. It eventually dawned on me he meant fawns' tails, which didn't have the gland required for Chinese medicine.

A fellow musterer and I left Estimates Hut one afternoon to get a leg of venison for the gang and skins for extra cash. We walked a good deal further than we thought we'd have to before we dropped two, one bullet each. Then we had a bit of a snooze in the sun. That sun had been busy on snow and ice upstream too, and on the way back the trickle we passed earlier had become unfordable. A horse! A horse! My kingdom for a horse! We waved our shirts at the hut a long way off on the other side, but the bloke waved back amiably, didn't get the distress of our message. Eventually, too long, we climbed and fired a shot to signal our distress, but by the time he rode up to the opposite bank the torrent had become too fierce even for a horse.

Our fire was pathetic for lack of decent wood and we gave that away. We wrapped ourselves in deerskins, settled in for the night and crossed easily in the morning when the cold night air had locked the supply of water up in the ice on the mountains. Our horses were waiting and we rejoined the muster. I told the story to an old pro shooter. 'Right way to go. Better a night in a stinkin' skin than ending up a carcass in a willow tree downriver somewhere.' The Balclutha police regularly searched the willows at dawn when the river was down, for the bodies of victims of accident and suicide along the Clutha. A lot of people would be alive today if they had waited out a day.

Deer hunters have different attitudes. Guy Morrell at Duncraig was always interesting. Out the window one evening, rifle nearby, I yelled, 'Deer!' Three of them were moving across the open part of the home paddock, easy targets.

'How's the venison, dear?' Guy said mildly. Fine apparently, grumble, hurumpf.

Next time this happened, same question. Bit low apparently. We fixed that.

Morrell must have been living something of a dream for his old mates steeped in Central European *volk* hunting traditions, the mystique of the Black Forest and all that. That's half the reason the Germans are a major venison market, according to the experts. Deer practically knocked on his door. But he never got carried away, just shot for subsistence.

When we came up on a herd in the flax we'd wait for as long as it took before shooting. Eventually, if one was patient, a head would come up or a puff of vapour would be seen. The old watch hind was testing the air. We had to get her first; that would give us time with the others. One cough, a light bark, from her and the herd would be off into the bush and refuge.

I had a rifle that wasn't sighting dead right, I thought. But there was no livestock about and I was going home, so a shot didn't matter. I saw a big spider's nest, very white, in a lonely piece of bush where I could see the dust come up behind if I missed it. I stepped out 550 paces down the hill, lay down and carefully aimed and fired. No dust went up. I climbed back to see if there was a hole in the web. A dead deer lay on the other side of the target. I'd never seen it until that moment! Sheer coincidence, I acknowledge, and also one of my least believed stories.

I love a feed of wild duck. But two trips to Glenavy's lagoons hadn't put a single duck in the larder. A bloke told me the way to fix it was to get a few bits of fishing line with hooks and bread for bait, so I got 28 hooks. But I felt a bit sleepy, so I tied the lines around my middle and dozed off. A whole squadron of ducks must have flown in because suddenly I was airborne, lifted by 28 ducks struggling up and with the help of the nor'wester that was blowing. Pretty soon I was over the sea and a few of the ducks were looking dangerously tired, but luckily an easterly blew up and, as we made our way back over land, I released the tiredest-looking ducks until I was deposited, gently as a top paraglider, outside the Glenavy Hotel. I was pretty shaken and ordered a drink before anything else. Gin Jimmy saw me land out the window, but no one believed him when he told them and he was my only witness.

Guy Morrell taught me the best way to kill a pig, aside from shooting, axing or sticking it with a knife. A hard crack on the forehead with a musterer's stick does it. A pig's skull is of heavy bone, reinforced with more bone, except for that window of opportunity. We killed dozens on Duncraig in this economical way, but left them for the hawks. Full of worms for some reason.

Opportunism during a muster can certainly vary the diet, either on the hill or in the hut or for the larder back home. Wild pork and bred pork taste very different. So when George Innes and I heard the boy say, 'Pig!' we let the dogs go. Two heading dogs soon eyed off a patch of matagouri and we went in. George axed one and I knifed another. Can't shoot with collies about; besides, we had no gun. Then the dogs bailed up a boar. My Big Bess, heavy with pup, didn't hesitate for a second when she arrived. She chomped on the boar's ear and hung on. The boar fought like fury. I asked the boy politely to catch hold of the pig's hind leg to upend it so I could dispatch the beast more easily. His right hand crept forward tentatively and jerked back in fright three or four times. Catching a snarling, frothing, snorting black ball of fur is not a sane thing to do, in truth. 'You're like an old woman feeding hens! Grab it!' I yelled. He did good, too. Shamed into it, he grabbed, twisted and rolled the boar over. Bess, bless her courage, rolled with it and was still fastened to its ear like shit to a blanket until it relaxed in death.

Young Donald Anderson of Ben Ledi — they were a chalky-boned lot — broke his leg playing rugby in Millers Flat, where he was working for Lloyd Smith. 'WV'll be doing nothing. Get him to come and get you,' suggested Smith. So I drove over and fetched all 6 foot 3 inches of Donald home. After Roxburgh Hospital we headed straight to Ben Ledi, his heavy right leg resting on my bony old left one. In the Lindis, Don, who was a polite boy, yelped, 'Pig, Mr Kerr!' It looked a good eating pig, too.

'Get those .303 shells out!' I called, and reached for Big Bertha, for some reason named after my placid-tempered mother.

I didn't do it well; when you are in your sixties, a head shot saves a lot of hauling, but this was a rib shot on the steep slope off the road; the pig kicked and rolled to the base. Groan. I beheaded and gutted it without a drop of blood getting on my sports trousers though, and I had a dog rope for dragging it.

Don stood on his crutches. Easter tourist traffic made the road busy. 'Stop the next car and ask the driver to give me a hand,' I said. But cars whizzed by him, thinking he was a cheerful cripple coming back from a pee behind the ute. But he eventually stopped one and an 18-stone Maori bloke came down, ignored the rope, and lifted the carcass across his shoulders. Even so, the veins on his legs stood out. 'Pretty heavy, boss.'

'You can do it,' I encouraged him, and he did. 'Want a bit?' Didn't all Maori love pork?

'No fridge.' He and a blonde woman were heading for a crib in Naseby.

'Do you know how to cook pork?'

No. So much for the idea Maori are great pork eaters. I cut off a hindquarter and told him to call at the Danseys Pass pub to ask Mrs Mohnihan how to do it.

Don and I headed off with our three-quarters of a pig, Don strangely quiet. 'Mr Kerr, you could've given him the shoulder. He wouldn't have known the difference.' He'd got those Anderson genes that make hard negotiators along with breaky bones. I miss Don; he died a few years later. Fine young man.

Hunting where I have, I should say something about Canada geese. Contrary to a widespread belief, these are imports from Canada who live all year round in the Waitaki Valley (and the big Canterbury valleys) and the only way they'll get back to Canada is with an airline. They destroy plantings, foul paddocks and incur the wrath of farmers everywhere. Shoots are regularly held to keep their numbers in check, with jetboats, aircraft spotting, dogs and a lot of guns, but so wily is this beast that kill numbers are never spectacular. But they love green grass and I have found the best way to shoot them is to throw a lambskin over my back and stalk them with a shotgun.

For years the debate about whether or not the kea, a native mountain parrot, kills sheep went on and off the boil. Farmers expressed their hatred of the kea's habit of sitting on a sheep's rump and pecking into the kidney area. Anyone who's pondered a sheep's dressed carcass in a butcher's shop will see the sense in that — it is the easiest way into the meat and the kea is not stupid. A hawk could probably do it too, but doesn't, probably because it's not bright enough. Night-sight video has decided the debate for ever, filming keas at their grisly work. I've shot them, but found the best way to kill them is a whack over the head with a mustering stick. You can attract them by leaving your shiny watch within striking distance on the end of a bit of nylon line. Curiosity kills the kea. I learned about the line after I lost my watch. Striking a balance between protecting this cute native bird and protecting stock will pose problems for many years I'm certain.

Now I want to get a few things clear about guns, game and the high country. These rules would save a lot of needless aggravation.

Rules for Townie Shooters

1   Seek the owner's or manager's permission, as your gunfire may scare stock into places their innate good sense would keep them out of, if they remained undisturbed.
2   Don't shoot what you can't carry — unless there is a feral pig problem and the owner requests culling.
3   Don't shoot anywhere within coo-ee of dogs.
4   Ensure rabbit poison hasn't been laid out — if it has, the owner will want those rabbits quiet, peaceful and eating, and gunfire puts them off eating.
5   If there is a choice and you are working close to settlement or stock, a shotgun will not scare animals half as much as a rifle.

Peter Clulee, head shepherd at Hookariri Station, took Sam Boynton and me out to a bluff over a big waterhole in the bend of the Pomahaka River. Eagle-eyed Sam said, 'Hell!' but I could see nothing notable. I asked, 'Where were you lookin' in relation to that big patch of weed?' There was a dark patch the size of an average bedroom in the middle of the hole, lazily turning around and around. *That* was the fish — about 200 eight- to 15-pound sea-run brown trout, 50 kilometres upstream.

So we set out next morning and happened across an old bloke called Bob, a fisherman from Christchurch, who promptly let us know he had permission to be on the property. He was camped in a hut and had been coming there for years. We got to the hole in daylight and put a dead mouse, some cockabullies, minnows and bread on the hooks, but no way would they strike. The frustration level was rising: we spent two days trying to catch fish that ignored us from 30 metres away. They don't eat much during spawning, but we'd have served them lobster thermidore if we'd thought it'd do any good.

Meanwhile Bob ambled up and caught two fish in the time it takes to make a Gregg's Instant Pudding, right alongside us. He took Sam under his wing a bit — didn't address me at all, which I thought strange. The only bait they'd take was red garden worm, so Sam went back and dug the garden. Bob promised he'd fillet his fish for us and invited us to come with him next morning to another good hole he knew. He had cousins arriving and was going to leave this hole to them.

The next morning we got to a ford. I had my rod and mustering stick in hand and heard Bob say to Sam, 'Don't know about the old fella.' I was in my late sixties and turned my head to see who he could possibly be talking about. Despite my protests he insisted on holding my hand. How humiliating. He was my age. But he knew his fish.

At the hole I caught one, Sam caught one and then I caught a bigger one. I'd helped Sam net his but neither of them helped the 'old fella'. Still, I landed it. 'It's a good one,' I said. 'Ten or 12 pounds.'

'Aw, wouldn't be that,' said Bob. So as I was laying out the fish and they were casting away, I popped a wee round pebble down the trout's gullet, then another, and another. . . . When we'd caught eight, we stopped and set to having a feed of fish. I put my bigger fish on Bob's scale. 'Eleven pound.'

'Jesus Christ,' said Bob, 'it is, too.' But just as he was peering through his specs at the pointer a stone popped out. Apparently Bob didn't think it was funny; the way he went on you'd have thought I'd crucified the bloke he was swearing about. Sports fishermen can get overly serious, I've found. On the way back he was going to take my hand again at the ford, but I told him I used to own 7000 acres of worse country, and marched past him.

The finest trout I've ever tasted wasn't caught or cooked by me or a sportsman, but by the tough former mountain guide Guy Morrell from Duncraig. My mate and I were mad keen to fish his property while working there, but he had a quota system for venison and we felt he might well have one for fish. Especially fishing with a .303. You could see fish in the black water from the jetty and we couldn't help wondering about the spikes up in the willow there above it. They were obviously steps, but what for? We raised the subject about a dozen times. Eventually he took the bait.

'You like trout?' Does Mae West float? 'Okay, we'll get a couple. We won't get them with a rod.' He clambered up the spikes and along an overhanging branch, threw a few breadcrumbs down and fired. I'll swear he did it quickly so he wouldn't kill too many. That tree was his fresh fish market — he liked them fresh and hated waste.

Three trout bobbed up, swim bladders burst by the bullet's shockwaves. He had to move quickly before they sank. Down the tree, behind the bush and into the dinghy. In seconds he'd speared the sinking fish on a bamboo pole with an ingenious double-spring gaff. Stuffed and wrapped in silver paper, they were the stuff of a gourmet subsistence existence. The Morrells were the perfect environmentalists if you judge by results, not rules hatched in Wellington.

I haven't fished in the sea, and I never will.

When I met my father-in-law, Ed Broad, for the first time, he said, 'By Jesus, Snow, you'll be just the man for the deep end.' Mainly short blokes, the Broads seized on the chance to put this tall new in-law on the deep end of a flounder net. The argument was that I could get the net a bit further out, but if they thought I was going to walk into the sea off a beach up to my armpits in the middle of the night . . .

'No.'

'Why not?'

'Sharks.'

'There's no sharks down here.'

'There's no bloody fence to stop them either.'

'Snow, look . . .'

'No, you look. If there's a blade of grass on a hill, a sheep'll find it. I can't see how a shark'd be any different. No. No. *No*.'

Today, I still nurse a desire for a stag head worthy of my wall — an 18-pointer from Fiordland perhaps. I'm like Barry Crump and many others who have shot hundreds of deer: not one was a decent head. I don't care to shoot anything ordinary again, and I'm content to watch the elegant de-horned red and fallow deer that parade before my deckchair on the patio. But an 18-pointer would cap it off. Preferably from an armchair.

CHAPTER FIVE

Single and Shepherding

Words written on a wall of Blue Lake Hut, Glenaray Station, after a mistake had been made in supplies:

We've mustered around the Southern Alps
And shorn in a union shed
We've climbed Glenaray's roughest heights
And slept on a speargrass bed,
We've tuckered in the roughest joints
And seen the whisky freeze,
But we've never mustered yet,
On half a pound of cheese.

From Colin Wheeler,
Historic Sheep Stations of the South Island, *1973*

S UPPOSE I'D BETTER TELL YOU WHAT MUSTERING IS, BECAUSE there's going to be a fair bit of it. Skip the next couple of paragraphs if you know.

A group of men, a gang of three to eight, depending on the size of the block, will leave the homestead or camp hut to muster a certain number of sheep or cattle off a specified area for dipping, weaning, shearing, sale or whatever. The boss will allocate and point out beats, 400 to 800 metres apart, for the day. Breakfast is timed so the top man — the one with the highest beat — can reach his starting position by daybreak. That can mean as early as 2 a.m. with a two-hour climb out. The others leave at intervals that get them to their starts at dawn too. This avoids the extreme heat and catches sheep just up from their night camp, when they travel better because their bellies are empty. On higher beats there may be no water for thirsty dogs, who dehydrate and die quickly, so prudent musterers carry an emergency bottle of water.

When daylight breaks the top man starts the gang by voice — 'Ho, ho' — and a loud chorus of barking. Each man replies in turn. Contact is essential. So is position. The top man moves off with others slightly behind to stop sheep breaking back behind them. If a man sees a sheep halfway between him and his mate he sends a huntaway (barking dog) to hunt the sheep ahead or down, where his mate takes control and directs it the way that's wanted. If sheep do slip through the line, the nearest man sends out a silent heading dog. That dog runs like hell, casts around for escapees and pulls them back to be hunted ahead.

Around the mountain the gang goes, giving bark-ups at strategic points to keep sheep moving and to maintain contact and position. At the end of the block the mob are put in holding paddocks and the gang retire to the homestead for a big feed and, unless it's a crook place, a beer. This might be midday or later. The gang may take a siesta, then go back to camp to do the other side of the mountain the next morning. Walking country is rough, steep and rocky, not suitable for horses. Easy country you ride. Musterers' adage: 'A quick muster's a good muster.'

My first real dogging job was at Glenlappa Station, from 1943. Grand title, too: permanent shepherd. The word 'permanent' had a nice ring about it for a child of the Depression, just as it does once more today, sadly. The scary thing about the position was that it held a certain degree of responsibility; a high level of unsupervised work was expected and I wondered if I'd be good enough to handle it. I was pretty confident in the main, but of course a young man's doubts surfaced from time to time. I knew there would be a lot to learn and I would have to learn fast.

First, I had to get out of Dunedin, so, insanely even then, at 8 a.m. I rode my new cob with five dogs at foot through scary unquiet traffic to the railway station, where they boxed the livestock. Then I caught the train to Balfour, between Lumsden and Gore, to await the train bearing horse and dogs. I whiled away the time in Balfour's pub, drinking portergaffs — stout and lemonade with a dash of raspberry.

It was a long ride out overland to Glenlappa and soon got dark. In the Ardlussa Valley I was cautious enough to seek directions and advice on crossing the Mataura River, which I knew to be a formidable obstacle and dangerous. By good fortune the first house lights I saw were those of the Keown family. They offered to put me up for the night, but, though tired and hungry, I felt it was important to arrive on the day I said I would, so I pressed on. But I didn't care for the way they talked about the river; I have a healthy fear of rivers. They led me through paddocks to the ford and shone a torch. I rode through without incident, but vowed never to do it in the dark again.

About midnight a scruffy young bloke emerged on the road. Alan Chalmers, Glenlappa shepherd, must have been feeling a bit lonely and decided to greet the new man. He helped me stall the horse, and feed and chain my dogs.

The old housekeeper had been trying to encourage Alan in matters of grooming and to take a bath more often. When I came in to breakfast she said, 'There you are, Alan. I told you.' She'd been harping about how the new boy was neat and tidy, with his hair nicely parted in the middle. I *was* flattered.

We were kept busy there. If we weren't lambing or shepherding there was dog tucker to kill and dress, fences to repair or put in, wood to chop, pebbles by the barrowload to get out from under the woolshed and more.

I was back on Glenlappa six years ago for a field day. I resented the $20 entrance fee — what 30-shilling-a-week ex-employee wouldn't? But some old mates were there, like Chris Cochrane of the Ranch. And I met the guest speaker, Christchurch lawyer Tipene O'Regan, an important Kai Tahu expert on Maori land law. 'Chris, Tip, I lost a pocket-knife here 50 years ago. Can you keep an eye out for it?' It rebounded on me. The PA system crackled into life: 'Will anyone finding a green-handled pocket-knife lost on this ground in 1944 by WV Kerr please hand it in to the announcer's booth. Thank you.' It pays to advertise. Dick and Beth Wardell hadn't known I was there, nor I them, until that announcement.

I needn't have baulked at the entrance fee — the present owner's generosity easily made up for it. Over a few drinks I asked, 'Bill Elliot still live around here?'

'No,' said Dick, 'but he's alive and well, living in Wellington. Pity he wasn't here, though. You two could've had a great yarn.'

'Nawh, wasn't that.' I considered leaving it at that, but continued. Tell the truth and shame the devil, I decided. 'I just wanted to tell him I've worked for a lot of bosses since him in my life, but he still has to be classed as the bloody worst.'

Bill Elliot said we could go to the Gore dog trial and we had a great day. Our opinion of Elliot was as high as it ever got. At the time he was 'not a bad bloke'. So when he called at our hut with a bottle of beer and his town smokes and asked, 'Did you enjoy the day?' we were effusive in our gratitude. But we were not pleased with what came next: 'The cow boy's left. How're you two going to share up the milking?'

I was good with cows. Chalmers was impatient, intolerant and bad tempered around them. It was a con job, and I lost.

Bill Elliot had a huntaway called Lofty, with a long black tail and a white tuft at the end. He wouldn't work properly because he was too busy looking behind him, admiring his tail. We talked Elliot into cutting the white bit off — told him an old shepherd we'd met had advised it. (One really did.) He agreed, but didn't want to do it himself, so Chalmers and I took Lofty off and cut three inches from his tail. The recipe worked: it turned him into a different dog.

One day we were mustering the Mataura river face. Bill Elliot assigned himself the top beat, the easiest one, as usual. There was a whiff of fog about and he instructed us that, if the fog came seriously down, we were to wait it out because it was a heat fog and would clear. Foggy summer mornings often do turn into clear hot days. We started off, then the fog did come down, so we pulled up and waited, each on his beat down the mountain. Bill was in some pinnacles when fog descended a second time, and when it cleared a little local fog persisted around Bill. I will confess I didn't start a bark-up to let him know we were in the clear and moving on, but I covered for his beat, so there was no shepherding problem. We ended up five kilometres away, coming off with the sheep, without the irate boss. He sat two hours in his personal fog.

Jack's missus had to go to hospital. Jack was the cow man at Glenlappa and his wife was the cook. Her daughter came up to take over her mother's role. 'Now, you two behave yourselves,' was the cook's parting shot to us.

A bit of geography is necessary. Jack and his wife generally shared a room in the house, but the daughter took that when she arrived. The house abutted the cookshop, which abutted the single men's quarters. Her dad was in the room nearest the cookshop and his daughter's room, Chalmers was in the next one, and I was on the outside. A bit of yard work was required.

I got a bit dressed up one night, but I knew Chalmers fancied her too. I heard his tread, whipped into bed and pulled the covers right up. But I suppose he was on my wavelength by then, because he didn't hesitate. He pulled the covers off me when I started on about wanting an early night. 'You bugger! You're going up to have a crack at that sheila!'

I appealed to his better nature, but he said, 'I'll make the dogs bark and wake up old Jack.' Well, I got the girl, but the price was giving Chalmers my top-potential huntaway bitch pup. That's how he got the best huntaway he ever had, the bugger.

Bill, Jack and I were in the woolshed next day and saw the indentations in the crutchings bin, two great basins. Bill Elliot asked, 'What'd do that?' and stroked his chin. Any mystery made him stroke his chin. 'Old cats sleeping?' I volunteered.

Alan Chalmers and I kept on–off contact until his death. He worked freezing works yards and shepherded around the traps, then got a bit of dirt of his own, south of Invercargill. The last time I saw him was the first time at his own place. I'd gone on holiday dog trialling with 11 dogs and, on a weekend staying in Invercargill, drove out to see him. We hadn't met for a good long while, but the grapevine led me to his place with ease. I hadn't phoned; shepherds tend not to bother about ringing first. He came around the corner of the house driving a Fergie tractor towing a dead cow as I pulled up. We didn't shake hands or any of that. 'I bloody knew it. The moment I get a bit of decent free dog tucker, Kerr turns up.' But he banged up 33 feeds for me.

Andrew Chalmers, Alan's boy, worked for me. His mother was from Nine Mile and keen for her boy to go to the high country. Ray Hamblin, who suffers boys as badly as I do, was reading when Andrew interrupted him. 'What's that up there?' There was a mousehole in the plasterboard ceiling.

'Jesus Christ, it's a mousehole,' said Ray.

'How'd it get up there?'

'Well-ll-ll, the mouse waited until everyone was out and got a ladder, climbed up and ate the hole,' said Ray through gritted teeth. Andrew believed him! Boys . . .

We'd had a fencer dig some postholes. The eventual aim was to plant some poplars in them to wind-break the house, but we got busy with more pressing matters, and they filled with water and twigs as they do,

Loburn dog trials 1959. Photograph, Otago Daily Times.

Above left: *John Alexander Kerr marries Bertha Ferguson.*

Above right: *Me and Tip, fox terrier, terror to rabbits.*

Left: *Me and Cliff Kerr* (right, no relation), *New Zealand dog trial championship, Taieri, 1948.*

Above: *Pack team on Glenaray Station, 1949. Alan Chalmers and me taking building materials out to repair a mountain hut.*

Below: *On the great King, the outlaw gift, at Nokomai, 19 years old (me, not King).*

Left: *With Ima on honeymoon at my sister Daizie's place in Green Island, Dunedin, 1949.*

Below: *Omarama Station days. Me, John, Ima and Fiona*

Above: *Simon Williamson and I taking wethers over the ford on the Ahuriri.*

Below: *Cattle crossing the headwaters of the Ahuriri River, Birchwood, high in the Alps.*

Left: *With Trix, Lowburn
Collie Dog Club, near Tarras,
when she came third in the
yarding event of the South
Island championship in 1972.*

Below: *Ron and Simon
Williamson watching our
progress at the head of the
Ahuriri Birchwood Station.*

Left: *The swingbridge between Peak Valley and Bog Roy, source of human and ovine aggravation beyond belief. Now drowned beneath Lake Benmore, RIP.*

Below: *Feeding out at Dunstan Peaks Station during a typical winter.*

Above: *Ken, Duncan, Ian and John Anderson — son, father, father, son.*

Below: *Dunc Anderson in his late sixties.*

and the rim of dirt around the surface caked. A pup wandered from the shed one night — a nuisance, but quicker if all hands looked for it. Andrew said, 'But what made these holes anyhow?'

Too much for Ray: 'Oo-ahs.'

'Oo-ahs? Where do they come from?'

'Out of the hills in the dark.'

'Why's the dirt around the outside?'

'Because they go around and around the hole and scoop the dirt up with their little paws.' Andrew never did ask how they got their name, but an old shearer who'd seen oo-ahs — before my time, because they became very rare way back — told me they ate clay and straw, shat bricks and each bowel evacuation was punctuated with the creature's telltale cry, *Oo! Ahhhhh*!

Where Glenlappa might offer a man and dogs five days here and seven there, Nokomai Station had over 200 straight, and little of the mediocre tedious work Glenlappa needed done. I'd been at Glenlappa three years and I wanted out. Bill Elliot was unforgivably lazy, perhaps as a result of being spoon fed and a willingness to rely on family money. He'd not been much of a stock agent, and, while it's no sin, had poor stock sense and precious little patience or tolerance. When I left his employ — which you're entitled to do — I went to the Waikaia pub, hard by the mail coach place. He rang. 'Where are the rabbit traps?' he asked, like they were the family silverware.

With Alan Chalmers, that's where, but Alan'd gone. I couldn't put his weights up. But Bill was full of booze and had to have a parting kick. There was another niggle, so I said: 'You're all right on the phone, Mr Elliot. I'll talk to you tomorrow, face to face, at the mail stop.'

At the mail coach — looking like the OK Corral — he opened with: 'You've got three dogs and think you're a full-blown musterer, eh?'

'You think you're a full-blown runholder, but all you do is hand out Wright Stephenson cheques.' I'd heard the gossip.

'Never set a foot on Glenlappa again,' Elliot spat at me, and turned on his heel. This posed a problem: my swag was at Glenlappa, and he knew it. There's an old law I'd heard about, a good one too. If an employer picks up an employee's personal effects from a train, he's obliged to get them back to him.

'I'm calling the police,' I told the publican.

49

'No.' He shut me up. 'Don't argue. Hughie'll drive over and pick it up tomorrah.' And his son Hugh did.

Two years rolled by. A mate slapped my shoulder in my quarters at Nokomai. 'Guess what! I've got us a week on Glenlappa!' Musterers tend to negotiate on each other's behalf if they know how you're fixed. But this deal fell in a heap.

A few weeks later I happened on Bill Elliot on the street opposite where I'd just stepped out of the Waikaia pub. 'Bill Kerr! Come over here.' Will the mountain go to Mohammed?

'No, here.'

Luckily, there was no traffic and we met in the middle of the road. 'They tell me you won't muster for me?'

'"Never set a foot on Glenlappa, again," remember?'

'Oh! I was wrong there; I've learned a lot since.'

'Me too.' He wasn't going to win the Bigness of Heart Stakes. We called it a day. I agreed I'd muster Glenlappa if asked, but it never came up again.

CHAPTER SIX

The Land God Gave to Cain

Had Cain been Scot, God would have changed his doom
Nor forced him wander, but confined him home.

John Cleveland, 'The Rebel Scot'

NOKOMAI STATION RAN ALONGSIDE THE NOKOMAI CREEK, A sidestream of the Mataura. Nokomai's owners had a reputation for being tight with their pay. This was true enough — they deducted the cost of a set of horseshoes from the wind-up cheque of their faithful old boundary rider, Bill Keenan, after five years there — but everyone forgets that the Cameron family had the place more than 90 risky years, through slumps, wars and killer winters. They were forced to sell good blocks in the 1930s, and when they sold it off entirely, they came away with little but a cleared mortgage. Little wonder they were tight with us; they were tight with themselves. You can't be financially big-handed in any business without revenue and security.

Donald Hay was the first pakeha on Lake Wakatipu, guided by Maori who knew it well. His report encouraged brothers William and Donald Cameron to look south of the lake. They found Nokomai but called it Glenfalloch, Hidden Valley in Gaelic. William took up the Remarkables towering over Queenstown. Brother Don brought 5000 sheep over from Australia to Invercargill and drove them up the Nokomai in 1860. Ten years later Don had 9000 sheep. The Camerons between them had 19 000 sheep, some 14 years old, when Snowy Kerr arrived for the first real high-country mustering job of his life in 1946.

Another musterer on Nokomai, Jack Sadler, a quiet fellow as a rule, took off to Invercargill to have a troublesome tooth pulled in my first year there, and he poured whisky into the hole to his brain all day. When we arrived at the Parawa pub to pick him up he declared famously, 'If New Zealand was a bull, Nokomai'd be izz harsehole.' In some ways I agree, but you'd have to be visually handicapped or dull of soul not to be impressed by the dark ridges of the Garvie Range that form The Nok's south-eastern boundary above you. Or the diamond-sparkling transparent waters of the Nokomai at your feet, one of three rivers, with the Mataura and Nevis, that bound Nokomai in the north-west with over 80 kilometres of riverfront.

But those dark ridges were cold, and lambing was a disaster. The 5000 breeding ewes had only produced 2500 lambs by marking time and 1300 at weaning. They went on a high shady block, and when the hoggets were brought in for shearing only 800 had survived. Shearers would reach over into the pen, pick hoggets up one-handed and snip away 'to whiten them up a bit' before sending them down the chute.

Snow moved in by April or May, and put pressure on musterers to sweep the heights clear or face moving sheep through snow. Casual musterers like me were secure in seven months' 'work' as the employers saw it, 'pay' as we did, from November to June. We got six weeks of down time around February. We could stay and do odd jobs, like splitting wood for the back huts if we wanted, for keep and a few quid; employers were less ruthless in that regard than they are today. But you were free to find other work. I shot deer freelance on The Nok; mustered the Ardlussa, Fiery Creek, Greenvale and Canard; lambed Dacre, Goodgers', Dillon's and Kean's down country; and worked Duncraig during breaks and off-seasons: a wealth of experience and education for a high-country man in five years.

One bloke used to have to spend from June to September in a tin hut at the very top of the Nevis Valley, pushing sheep off cold ridges, away from snow-filled basins, and snow raking if they got trapped in drifts. Snow raking entails finding mobs, sometimes by spotting steam from the exit hole their breath melts in the highest part of a great cavern of snow, and treading a path out for them. He'd take coal out for his coalrange or stove on two old draughthorses, take them around the shady side of an old harness shed and shoot them for dog meat. Then he'd add his own freezable supplies to this natural deep-freeze. Bill Keenan did that hard stint one year I was there and then went to Dunedin for a spring holiday. In three years' boundary riding he never caught a cold, but he caught one in Dunedin and had to take to his bed for a fortnight. Still, he won the beard-growing competition at the town hall. There was a turn-the-handle telephone in the hut that connected to the Nevis pub and Keenan walked 13 kilometres to the pub for bread once a week. No one ever spoke of the uselessness of the phone if Keenan broke his leg away from the hut; the risk was accepted.

The first season at The Nok I had nine dogs and the head shepherd 10, which was just as well because we were short two men and needed the big teams to cover the ridges. I was asked back the next season, but there was a new limit imposed: six dogs. Dog tucker was money. I wasn't an obnoxious youth, but I didn't like being walked over or exploited. 'Full gang?' I asked.

'Yeah. Seven men,' replied the shareholder–manager, Con McGrath. He also used to brag that he mustered all Wakatipu with three dogs, but he didn't usually go out on the hill at The Nok.

'Oh well, that's all right then.'

I came back with eight dogs, the head shepherd nine and we were one man short. Con had to fill in with his famous three. One got chewed up by the other dogs and spent several days of the muster in a saddlebag Con made up.

I was the best-fed man on Nokomai. The Camerons' contribution to social welfare, called 'kindness' then, was to put up a destitute couple work free, rent free in a cottage. Out shooting rabbits one evening I passed the old girl chopping wood, leaned my .22 against the shed and took over. I told her not to chop wood again; I'd do it, and I did. Plum duffs, sponges and all manner of tucker flowed my way thereafter.

Brothers Tom and John Goodgers, returned soldiers, fine Chewings' fescue seed farmers — top lawns for the gentry, tennis courts, bowling greens and cricket pitches, not dog men — worked with me at Dillon's Nine Mile. They were kind enough to invite me — a cocky, irritating boy — to the Waikaia pub to celebrate Japan's surrender. It was a privilege and a profound joy to join men who'd slogged through North Africa and Italy on a day of such moment. I was no seasoned drinker but I acquitted myself well, though we drove a hundred metres or so over railway sleepers, *bang, bang, bang*, when we missed the turn coming off the road–rail bridge getting home. A return performance at a party in Mataura went well too — at first. A gorgeous, captivating girl about my age didn't care for her sherry and didn't want to offend our host, so I gallantly knocked them back for her while drinking beer. Next morning I emerged, somehow, and Tom said, 'Christ, John, look. Snow's found his legs overnight!' Leading up to the door were two sets of firm footprints and drag marks between them in the snow. Never forgave that girl. Never drank sherry again either.

The Goodgers were contracted to buy Nine Mile but the owner's wife died suddenly. They let him off the hook in sympathy. They didn't have to; money had changed hands. So they bought a place at Waimumu, near Gore. They pleaded with me to bring dogs for their lambing and I did whenever Nokomai's brutal calendar allowed.

The Camerons sold Nokomai to Frank Hore for £36 000 and missed the wool boom of the Korean War by a few months, after owning it a few years short of a century. Frank's first wool cheque was £42 000. Frank started up the goldmine again too. He'd wash his hair in the sluice and cover his head with gold dust. There's Jason the Greek's golden fleece and there's Frank's.

Today Nokomai has an airstrip and a Directors of Things and all the rest of it. Back then it was giving me ideas above my station. I didn't have the runs on the board in those days and no one would have listened to my ideas if I'd had any. Quite right too. But years later, at an Omarama stock sale, I did, and Frank Hore bailed me up. Someone had quoted me as saying, 'If ever a place should pre-lamb shear, it's Nokomai.' Omarama didn't shear pre-lamb; it didn't suit the place.

'Why would you say that?' asked Frank. Me and my big mouth . . . Nokomai had only one holding paddock, about 30 acres. All the sheep would be penned there after being dogged hard through cold creeks and over shady hills all day. A lot of Nokomai is the land God gave to Cain when he murdered his brother: austere, beautiful, legendary, loved, but cursed. Shorn sheep would be held on the paddock so the lambs could mother up, but a lot didn't and they died. They had eight blade shearers — too many — and that meant big mobs and multiplied risks of mis-mothering and the like.

I took one of the town smokes I was offered. 'It'd be different nowadays, with you there, but 30 years ago they brought in too big a' cuts of ewes, had too many sheep around the place. It was too much of a rat-race, they got smothers, the wee fellas were away from their mothers for about two days before they got back out and were held in a corner. The whole thing was hopeless. It's harder to find a woman's tits when she's wearing a fur coat. I reckon the risk to shorn adults in lamb is outweighed by t'other.' I quoted the appalling lamb survival statistics.

He grinned and said, 'I'm sorry to tell you, but nothing's changed.' They shore pre-lamb the next year. Of more immediate consequence though, neither of us had bought the sheep we were there to buy. Too much yakkety-yak about Nokomai in the good old days.

There were six huts on Nokomai: Dead Man, Dome, Estimates, Donkey Flat, Lyon's and the Upper Nevis. On neighbouring Glenaray they had four: Dome (shared with Nokomai), Blue Lake, Bush and Jack's Max on the higher country.

Musterers aren't silly enough to think all huts are equal, and those who mustered Glenaray hated Jack's Max. There were no trees or scrub around it, and it had no toilet. You had to squat over a tussock with a southerly blowing up your back passage like Aunt Daisy, then get a shovel or spade and turn the sod over so dogs didn't roll in it. (Town people shitting in the high country should always do this too, or cover their turds with a decent-sized flat rock. Nothing worse than grabbing a dog's collar and getting a handful of human shit. Have you got that?) We cooked and got warm water from peat fires at Jack's. The station's two fencers would routinely cut wet bricks from a bank, stack them on a horse-drawn sled and leave them to dry in a shed for mustering teams. It was fibrous dry and burned with a horrid smell that got into your clothes and blankets — and worse, if the packer didn't have the skill to stack it properly in the fire so ashes could fall free, it filled the hut with ash. Good packers always took the camp oven off the fire to turn meat. Dopey ones tainted the meat doing it on the fire.

I was back there in 1988 and am pleased to report that the peat fire is history. Helicopters fly coal in for a coalrange now. And the packer doesn't have to cart water; there's a gravity-fed hose from a high creek to the hut. The 1988 team also packed a big roll of alkathene hose. Never heard dog men talk so much about plumbing in my life. They rigged up a big cross on the flat below the hut. I thought they were Ku Kluxers for a bit, but they ran the black hose down and rigged up a tap and shower nozzle. Each night the riders' pace would gradually quicken as the men stretched out their horses to get the first shower in the hope the sun would've heated the water lying in the hose. To see Ray Christie, a big man, naked on the flat in a southerly after a cloudy day was particularly hideous. No way you'd catch me doing it. What's 18 days without a shower? There was a wetback on the coalrange. Is it beyond the genius of Southlanders to connect that to a hose? Or is the technology lost to these laptop-tapping buggers? (And you still had to squat over a tussock with a southerly blowing up your back passage like Aunt Daisy.)

Going back in 1988 introduced me to new rites and rituals that didn't exist 40 years before. I record this in the spirit of a pioneer anthropologist. 'You'll join the Inner Circle tonight,' someone said mysteriously. That night in the Blue Lake Hut the head shepherd called, 'Inner Circle.' They rose from their bunks like devotees and gathered around the boss like Incas around the virgin whose heart was to be cut out. They brought exotic potions, each to his preference: lemonade, water or cola. The head priest ceremoniously poured 80 millilitres from a bottle of Inner Circle overproof rum into a glass for each man, and all sat before him and drank it while he gave out the beats each man would cover the next day. Then, 'Good luck.' There was a general draining. One young fella put his arm across his forehead like a pukeko, his face grimacing like he'd bitten a lemon, so distasteful he found his libation. Then 40 mils were poured and drunk. Conversation was desultory for about 10 minutes, then, suddenly, the mobs got bigger, the mountains higher and dogs were so smart in their heading they should've worn mortar-board hats. In an instant it was like a bar after hours. A feed and bed followed shortly after.

For form's sake I took part a couple of times, but the rum tasted like the piss of a stallion fed too many sugar cubes. Pleading that rum made me snakey and got me into fights, I was granted whisky as a substitute. Once, when my supply had run out, Skip Johnson must have run into a station truck with a car-phone because there was a bottle of Black Label for me in the supply drop. Exactly 120 millilitres of it.

Southland people talk a lot of tommyrot about how much friendlier people are the further south you go. I've watched an American woman spend half an afternoon of her precious holiday picking up broken glass from the side of the Lindis Pass road and stuff it down rabbit holes after

I showed her a dog's bleeding paw. Friendly people are everywhere. But Southlanders are a bit special. A neighbour up Nokomai way lent me his grey gelding and jogger — a seat, two wheels and shafts — to travel the 130 kilometres to Dacre where I had duties. At 73 I could still ride it, but wouldn't enjoy it. At 23 I felt like an aristocrat of the road on it. But the wheels packed up on an overland section of the journey. Hungry, I rode bareback to Brown's Hotel, but meals were off at that time of night. Then I knocked up a mechanic from Ground's Garage — could he fix it tomorrow? 'There'll be nothing left of it by morning. We'll go and get it now,' he said. So we got my suitcase and the bunged-up jogger on his truck. Back at his home he asked, 'Get a feed at the pub?' and I told him I'd had wine biscuits and cheese. His wife rustled up bacon and eggs. That 10 o'clock feed kept me going until my jogger was fixed. Kindnesses are remembered and there was a lot of it about down south. Still is.

We are about to leave Nokomai now, and before we do, this story will tell you why it was special. It concerns the Nevis Hotel and the changing of the generations. The Nevis pub was owned by Johnny Williams and his wife — old folk, the last of the mining community. Johnny had a calendar that read:

PUBLICAN, POSTMASTER, GROCER, BUTCHER

Apart from two summertime miners, Johnny and his missus were the only people in the valley. When The Nok gang were working from the upper Nevis hut and had a short day they'd go down to the pub, a journey of about 13 kilometres, and they'd be as interested in bread as they were in beer. But the pub would have to send over to Bannockburn for the bread, which could take some time. What do you do, waiting in a pub?

This is a pub that held a licence to provide spirituous liquors to a population of — what? Two? Six?

Tommy Dunlea was older than me and loved rum. He rode an ex-trotting mare, Trixy, top sort of horse. He climbed on, announced he'd beat us home by miles and left at a good clip. We plodded along on our heavy horses, at peace with the world. Then Dundee Sandy, for such we called Tommy, trotted out of the night, heading back to the pub. We spun around, yelled and gave chase. The old mare Trixy would have beaten us easily but Tommy fell off at a bend and faithful Trixy pulled up. We propped him up in the saddle and, one each side, holding her reins, kept him upright on the way home in his Jamaica fog.

The Williams tried for years to sell the old pub. It was no architectural masterpiece: every wall was made of roofing iron, because of the ease of transport, I suppose. But there's a mug born every minute, and I guess if you look in Auckland there's a high likelihood of finding one quick. The Williams' patience was finally rewarded when a young Englishman, Kenneth St Clair Newman, and his young wife bought it, with plans for swimming pools and tennis courts.

The last time I went there, about 1947 — and I was a good, but rare, customer — they didn't have any beer, just half-bottles of spirits. Then the pub was no more.

CHAPTER SEVEN

Of Horses

A horse is a horse,
Of course, of course,
And no one can talk
To a horse, of course,
Unless, of course,
That is, the horse
Is the famous Mister Ed

Theme song to TV series
'Mister Ed'

I LEARNED RESPECT FOR HORSES IN THE USUAL WAY BOYS DO: INITIAL cockiness followed closely by fear, pain and humiliation. Gladesmuir's boss man, Charles Patterson, had a big grey, Jerry, who was a bit tricky. 'Don't be getting on Jerry, son.' He'd supplied me with a quiet nag, but I had no fear and waited for the opportunity to show Jerry who was boss and who was hoss. It came when I was told to ride out leading Jerry for a drink at the creek. While Jerry was drinking I slipped on him with the object of riding him home in triumph.

It turned out both horses made their way home without me and I followed covered in mud and wringing wet. Only my cheeks were hot because the water was cold. Charles picked it straight off. 'Jerry?' I nodded ruefully. 'Well, you were warned, William.'

I learned respect for horse traders the hard way too. Before I went to Glenlappa I bought a proper team of dogs, five of them — turned out I would have done better at the RSPCA — and needed a horse. My father rustled up a loosebox, where I could tie up my dogs and stable my as-yet unpurchased steed, at Forbury Corner in Dunedin, and I travelled out Green Island way in response to an ad.

The horse for sale looked a cross between a rhinoceros and a brahmin bull, but I mounted. He reared and I cracked my head on his. He had no brains so wasn't hurt, but I did and it hurt like hell. 'I don't think that horse'll suit you,' said the man. Couldn't have agreed more.

'What about that one?' I asked. There was a cob — a horse with its tail cut short, illegal now for some reason — tied to the fence: silky coat, good head, sensible manner.

'Aw, can't sell you her! My sister'd *kill* me.' He explained his sister had promised £20 for the beast. I looked at the bovine rhino again, rubbed my head and took a long look at the cob.

After much argy-bargy this skilful young negotiator was £25 poorer — nearly half a year's wages from Charlie Patterson's — and riding his fine cob into Forbury Corner. The rhino was worth 10 times his weight in oats; after all, he was the best assistant salesman a horse trader could employ.

But the cob was as useful as a pocketful of singlets on the Glenlappa hills: no stamina. I rode a station hack, poorer and a good deal wiser.

It was later, on Nokomai, that I got my first dirty shit of a horse and learned the power of redemption. I was so scared he'd buck me, I stayed on him for hours across the flat, but when I got to the hill I applied a metre of manuka to the beast and broke his spirit. After that, everything was possible. A bloke shod him for me. Top horse.

But I still owned the useless expensive cob. I was riding her down the road to a mate's place in Waikaia to get her shod one morning. I'd left dogs with a neighbour. An old fella came out of a house. 'Lost a dog?' he yelled.

'No, don't think so, but I'd better have a look.'

It wasn't mine, but fellow shepherd Alan Chalmers and I had admired a big black gelding on this place for some time, and while the elderly bloke and I chatted, a big Bulldog tractor came into his yard, *poom-poom-poom*. The sluggard cob pricked up her ears and found a spring in her step. 'Is that mare quiet?' the old chap asked. Quiet? Practically comatose.

'Yeah.'

'Would you sell her?'

'Tell you what. I'll swap her for that gelding.'

'Aw, it's not a good horse. It dumped me and put me in hospital.' An honest man! He rode the cob, felt safe on her.

'Look. I'll take a chance on the black bloke,' I said.

But the good man wouldn't see a straight swap. He gave me the gelding — and £25!

I had the new horse in the lagoon smartly. This is an old trick in mounting problem horses; the water resistance and mud slow their movements down. But not this one. He reared and I cracked my skull on his head — getting to be a habit. I was close to passing out and they laid me on the sofa with a glass of warm milk for a time. But my pigheadedness returned, I mounted and rode off into a brave afternoon.

Bill Collins, a wise old horseman, roped the gelding's leg up and lunged him around a bit for me, and I thought we'd taken the fire out of him.

He got a bit sore on the gravel road, so I took him to an engineering shop that used to do blacksmithing. 'Can you shoe my horse?'

'Is he quiet?'

'Yes.'

The smith shod the front feet, but when he picked up the back leg he ended up prone out the door on the road. 'Get him outa here,' he growled. He didn't charge but I heard him say to his offsider, 'That's the last horse coming through these doors.'

King was eventually shod and I took him to Nokomai, where he became a great hack. I eventually sold him to the Nevis publican for £25.

Old Tom Dillon asked me to stay on a bit after lambing one year and I'm glad I did, because I got to know six draughthorses. They'd pull a plough two abreast, or six leaves of tines — a wide rake — all six of them side by side. People get all sentimental about draughts, and they are truly most wonderful. Their strength is awesome, of course, but they are clever too. Around and around they'd go without pausing until I called a break. Then, when they passed the gate to home (oats and soft hay) at 4.55 p.m. they would halt expectantly. 'Gid up!' I'd yell, and they resembled reluctant schoolchildren sloping off to school. Then, three-quarters of the way around, the pace would quicken as if they had pulled out a fob watch and seen the big hand on 12.

Urine on hay can smell awful. I'd made love to a girl in the stables at Nokomai on clean hay as far from the horses as possible, but the odour took the edge off the pleasure a bit. So when the draughts returned to their stalls I'd be keeping a file on them. 'Not you! You haven't done it yet!' Those great legs would spread and they'd gush on the grass outside every time. After all, a young man never knows when he'll need a nice clean stable.

A good co-worker and mate on Burwood Station, Wokka Cooper — probably Whaka, but we weren't exactly fastidious about Maori names in Southland then — was a bugger for a laugh. The owner's runs were full of recycled thoroughbreds from his stud and racing stables. Wokka and Old Tom Erskine from Mount Hamilton had ex-steeplechasers. One day Tom wasn't looking too flash after last night's booze and Wokka couldn't resist such vulnerability so close to hand. Country people know the score: if you're off the boil, you'll catch a go for a laugh.

As we wound up the day's work, Wokka undid the throat lash on Tom's bridle. Then, as we plodded towards home, he whipped Tom's bridle off and yelled 'They're off!' like the radio racecaller. Instinct and training took over and the two gates were just part of the course. Old Tom went look-mum-no-hands over both, but he was sourer than a bitter lemon after his horse sledged to a stop at the stable door.

Ian Anderson's horses, Long Gully Tom and Big Woman, were the biggest hacks I'd seen and, after Bill Hazlett's thoroughbreds at Burwood and Glenaray's fine hacks, ponderous-looking brutes. Ian was offended when I asked which paddock he wanted us to plough. You could be heading west on his zigzag track, look behind you and see Tom's rear quarters still coming around the corner from the east. Ian was mean when it came to his horses. He'd shout expensive booze without a second thought but worry about the cost of a quarter-bale of hay. I found Keith McAughtrie gathering up some straw on the ground and asked him why he didn't just take from the stack. 'Ian gets shitty when he sees the broken bale.' We snuck whole bales to poor old Smoky, Tom and their mates so the Aberdeen Jew wouldn't see cut strings. Keith and I could have ridden the steppes killing Christians with Genghis Khan on those fuelled-up beasts. Lucerne hay: world's greatest horse tucker.

All Ian's horses had shoes on their front feet but none to the back, something I could not understand. Horses go lame or get footsore on any foot, surely? It couldn't be that all those high-country Anderson legends were a mite afraid of tackling those powerful hind legs? Perish the thought!

When you think you've seen 'em all, a horse will surprise you. In my sixty-third year I met the best I've ridden, Glenaray's Seb, a large trotting draught with French percheron blood, $17^1/2$ hands, 45 centimetres of steel around each hoof, a bit toey, great stamina, brains and an agreeable disposition. Skip Johnson, head shepherd, reckoned Seb was permanently grinning with me on his back; the contrast between my 11 stone and Terry Dennis's 16 the four muster seasons before was his explanation. When all the other horses were floundering up to their guts in peat bogs, Seb's camel feet didn't even break the crust. I dubbed him 'Mister Ed'.

One other horse stands out, Captain, only $14^1/2$ hands. I rode Captain at Otairi. This grey mare, raised in steep tough North Island country, ended up with me on my retirement block, and I floated her around South Island musters. Sam Boynton rode her on El Dorado once and said she was like a Rolls-Royce compared to the other horses down here. I altered the woolshed to accommodate her with a loosebox. A retired man who's looking after himself should do the same for a horse in its retirement.

Fairly obviously, if you want a horse, you have to buy one, get one given to you, breed it or catch a wild bugger. All methods have their problems. A man selling a horse turns into a liar on the spot. I know. I've sold a few. People talk a lot of nonsense about gift horses. If they weren't trouble no bugger would be giving them away. Arranging a foal isn't all peaches and cream either.

We had two beautiful half-draught mares, Daffodil and Blossom. They had done yeoman service snow-raking in the savage winter of 1968 and much else, and I wanted foals from each.

I bought Jupiter, a grey stallion, 16 hands, unbroken but taught to 'lead' — you could lead him around with a halter and a rope. He got Daffodil in foal first season, but he couldn't reach Blossom, who was *big*.

In her second season I put Jupiter in the stock pen and took Blossom up to a water-race going around the slope. I told my young daughter Fiona to go inside the house. The impending union had titanic possibilities, although equine mating looks a lot more savage than it is. With Blossom's back legs in the race I sang out to son John: 'Let him go!' Jupiter came out of his pen like a thoroughbred at Ellerslie, down the lane, missed the open gate, U-turned and came up the slope like a circuit motorcyclist on the lean. I stepped back in terror as he mounted Blossom. Then — a magnesium flashbulb popped. My evil little daughter had disobeyed me! We had a nice roan foal, Apollo, from that.

I'd nursed a desire to own a racehorse for a long time — even tried to breed a pacer but it did no good. Mustering Ben Ledi I read an ad:

FOR SALE — Shares in yearling thoroughbred.
Ring Dunedin 697 0700

I talked Ginger Anderson, manager of Ben Ledi, into coming to see it. A fat lady took us out to her paddock. In our tweed split-tailed sports coats and ties we looked wisely at the tendons of the gelding. Then he and a half-draught mare went for a frolic. He whizzed past at great speed. We paid up our shares. Pakistanian Lad ended up at my place near Oamaru and with TLC he looked a nice horse. When one of the shareholders wanted out, after a bit of persuasion I got our local vet, Alan Pratt, to take a share, putting a stop to the bloody vet's bills from then on. We raced him at Timaru, where I said by way of a banter that I was lucky to be there but had sold some pups for $50 each after finding a stray's litter under the woolshed. Alan said he'd dug into the cats' balls tin to get there. In his practice three vets shared premises and their petty-cash tin was kept topped up by fees for the castration of tomcats.

The Lad didn't run well that day and after that we were advised to blinker him. Sometime later I was mustering up Birchwood when I received a call from the trainer, who asked, 'How many pups have you got ready for sale? Pakistanian Lad's a different horse with the blinkers. Entered him for Riccarton, Saturday.'

'One,' I said, but there was no reply, so I doubled it to $100: 'Two.' Still none. 'Three.'

'That's enough.'

Ian Anderson liked a wee punt, so he came with me and came away $400 better off. I collected $1300 for my $150. We stopped the night at Dunsandel, where, after an earlier race meeting where the Lad had run second-last, I had written on the pool table blackboard:

64

FOR SALE
Lambing Hack
Guaranteed Quiet & Slow

But that night Pakistanian Lad could do no wrong. He won once more, then we retired him and we retired from the racing game.

No gift to a child can hope to match horseflesh. One Christmas morning, while my daughter slept, I took off for Tarras. When I returned I tied a white pony, Gypsy, to a willow tree on the lawn. 'Look at the beautiful day, Fiona.' Sleep evaporated and a smile of unforgettable radiance spread over her face. No movie tie-in doll or video game with white man's magic could do that, be assured for ever and a day.

CHAPTER EIGHT

Burwood

Bbrrrah, bbrrrah

Contented cow's sound

WHILE I WAS WORKING ON AND OFF NOKOMAI A STOCK AGENT phoned. Bill Hazlett badly needed a shepherd for his station at Burwood. It still goes on: runholders tell their agent they're looking for somebody. The agent might place an ad or simply ring someone they know on a hunch. I took some tracking down — I was lambing down Winton at the time — but some of the happiest times in my life followed that call. And I got to know Bill Hazlett.

Big silver tussock on its low land, big shingle faces above, Burwood had a lot of good green downs that have since been turned into runs in their own right, starting with postwar ballot blocks. Hazlett interests included Burwood down Te Anau way, Mavora up Wakatipu way, and Centre Hill near the road to Mossburn and the south, roughly 30 kilometres apart in a great triangle, all running cattle. In the 1940s Hazlett still retained the shores of Lake Mavora, for me one of the most beautiful lakes in the nation, though no one seems to pay it much mind. It used to run 10 000 merino wethers on the back country up the Wakatipu end, as well as 16 000 romneys and up to 2000 Herefords, but the wethers were swept up and sold off when all the labour and management went to war. The head shepherd, Hec McAuley, and Bill's brother Jack never returned. Nor did the sheep to those blocks. Today, even in its reduced state, it may well run 200 000 ewes. It's top-dressed and cultivated wherever possible.

William Edgar Hazlett was an ex-All Black loose forward. He toured Australia in 1926, South Africa in 1928 and played the Lions here in 1930. His brother and nephew were also All Blacks. His family had money from grocery and hotel businesses in Invercargill and he and his brother Jack managed and owned stations here and there through complex family trusts and the like. He had racehorses and stud farms too. His horses won over $900 000 in stake money.

I was drinking with him once, and he accused me of saying he'd never worked a day in his life. I was definitely a cocky young bugger and made a point of never kowtowing to anybody bigger, more important, richer or senior in status to myself. Might've even had a bit of a chip on my shoulder at that stage too.

'Well, have you?' He'd have shares in the Speight's he was sipping, I thought.

'Shore a hundred once. Blades.'

'Go on. Did you?'

'Yes, I bloody did. At Burwood. 1938. Ask Jack Boyd,' and then he grinned. 'What Jack won't tell you — and don't you tell anybody — is that I started at six in the morning and finished just on nine that night.'

You couldn't not like Big Bill Hazlett, and he liked cocky young buggers. Ladies liked him and he liked ladies, lots of them. He played pretty hard in lots of ways. Stories are told of the coach bawling him out under some grandstand in Cape Town or somewhere in South Africa, threatening dire consequences if he didn't pull his head in, but I wouldn't know about that. There were stories that he wasn't above heating up a branding iron on a moonless night, but I've no evidence to support that either. Police raided a place of his once, though. I heard stories of shotguns under his bed in city hotels when irate husbands were stalking him, but I never saw anything.

Hazlett planned things by first deciding what he wanted when. How to do it and who'd do it came in a poor second, if at all. He ordered it be done. Then he worked on things as they went wrong.

High-country leases confuse town people. Most land there is Crown land, which means only that it belongs to the nation, the people. The land is leased to runholders by the real owners in law, and this used to be overseen by the Crown Lands Department under the Minister for Crown lands. Now it's just Land Information New Zealand. The leases do give runholders rights and these vary from place to place: there are 33- and 99-year leases; some have a right of renewal, some don't, and so on.

Word was Hazlett's leases were not going to be renewed, so he sold all his calves — usually he'd have held most back for herd replenishment — to a Gore stock dealer for £4 15s a head, for supply to a Canterbury customer. And he told manager WE (Ted) Stewart to get them to the railhead at Mossburn on Saturday.

There were a few problems with that. One was that Stewart only got four days' notice. Another was that there was no train that Saturday. I hope I've conveyed the big area and considerable distances between the three properties. And that's not all. Extraordinary thing, but calves are not torn from their mother's side without resistance. Mavora, inconveniently, had the only holding paddock worth the name for this sort of exercise, but there were only three dog men to do it.

Ted, a tractor driver, Wokka Cooper and I drove them in and cut out cows in the big Mavora cattleyard from Monday to Thursday. They had no water. Then it snowed. When it came time to drive them off we had trouble on two fronts: calves bolting back to their mothers, and others bolting away from dogs across river terraces to freedom and disaster. My yellow heading bitch averted the latter — just. Ted used a bike's battery lamp in the dark to hold the rear, I rode shotgun along river side, Wokka hill side, and we got them to Centre Hill for the night at 1 a.m. The buyers told us there were 1400; we'd no time to count them. They had negotiated the right to reject one in 10 as too small, and did. The journey by road to Mossburn looked uneventful: they were tired, civil, swinging their tails. But something spooked them and the fences on both sides of the road were flattened. No time to stop and explain.

We got most of them to the waiting train. Hazlett, impatient with Southland's rail boss, had rung the Director of New Zealand Railways in Wellington, who turned on a special train. He had the first electric cattle prod I'd seen and he'd rush in to zap a beast, with the predictable result that the calf behind would turn around and block passage.

Before we rode back to Centre Hill that night Hazlett shouted at the pub. A fisherman there recognised him. 'By gee, Mr Hazlett, that display you put up at the Invercargill Show was the best exhibition of man and dog I've ever seen.'

Hazlett nodded curtly, scowled darkly into his wallet and hailed the barman over. 'Here's 10 bob. Give Snow and Wokka another drink, and shout for that crawling bastard there.' And left.

Hazlett's neighbours were memorable. Mid Dome's owners walked off without a razoo in the 1930s and three tough brothers from Awaka walked on, gaining effective ownership by paying the rent owing, said to have been £400. The Taylor boys did it without capital or assistance, the hard way, surviving by shooting for deerskins, mustering and shearing wild sheep and creating a beef herd without buying heifers, a biological impossibility that would not have escaped neighbour Bill Hazlett's attention. It is also said that they only ever made up one pay. One of the brothers was in agony with a crook tooth and had to go to Lumsden. The chaff-cutting was on, and it was impossible to work the machine without three men so a bloke was got in. They told him 'Thanks' and made up his pay the moment their brother got back from the dentist: two hours' worth. They had a valley of their own, secure from prying eyes, and everyone said that's where they took Burwood cows until they calved.

A Taylor once rode into the Burwood yards at marking time on a young pacer, barely broken, wild dogs everywhere, no socks under his boots. Ted Stewart had instructed us that every calf take the Burwood earmark, for the convenience of the workers; strays and neighbours' cattle were sorted up later. Taylor pointed out one: 'Mid Dome cow.'

'We'll sort it up at weaning,' said Ted, meaning two or more months hence.

'Nah, I'll take it now.' So we all had to give him a hand to cut out 'his' cattlebeasts and watch him ride down the road with Burwood earmarks flapping. The Taylors had a most convenient idea of property. Today Mid Dome is a dream run, with a deer park and farm.

There was one neighbour we'll call Jones who didn't think Hazlett was anything special, riling Hazlett. The old way of doing things right by everybody at marking time was that when you found a neighbour's ewe, you felt her udder and if she had had a lamb you'd mark a lamb, any lamb, not necessarily hers, with the neighbour's eartag. Then at weaning you'd take her and 'her' lamb down to the owner. Hazlett instructed us to mark any black lambs with Jonesy's eartags. Black wool wasn't worth tuppence then. Jonesy got 30 stragglers with 30 black lambs that way. But at the next shearing Jonesy turned up with 30 of Hazlett's hoggets he'd 'accidentally' shorn with their fleeces — all 30 black. He'd pinched the white hoggets from Burwood and returned his black fleeces. It was an elegant tit-for-tat.

I was given a job so sweet I'd have taken it as a holiday. I rode over the three properties, just me, the horse, dogs, some chops and spuds, a three-section fishing rod and a .303, checking for Lonely Hearts Clubs. Any mobs of cows with a bull among them I left alone, but I provided one if they didn't. What a trip for a 20-year-old! The Oreti River sparkled in the December sun. Stayed at the beautiful old homestead on Mavora Lake — now a backpackers' lodge. A chair at the homestead had been made by someone who had seen a shape in a tree that suited a chair's sideframe beautifully, cut and split it, joined the two sides with braces and tacked an old bullock hide to it: everyone who sat in it remarked on its comfort. Trout and venison cooked over wood coals. Starry, starry nights sleeping in the open. Time to think and dream.

Wokka Cooper and I would ride out with the cows or calves, and he'd start singing. People say Maori are great singers; not all of them are, but Wokka had a fine tenor voice, and I would join in badly:

> I drove a herd of cattle down
> From old Nebraska way
> That's how I came to be
> In the State of I-Ow-A . . .

With the lake glistening and the contented cows going *bbrrrah*, *bbrrrah*, and a dog's bark from time to time, peace and harmony reigned. Footrot was unheard of and it was as if the devastating war only two years before had never happened.

All good things must come to an end, but I'd have preferred a different end to my relationship with Burwood. Ted Stewart was a top bloke and a boss I got on well with, and, more to the point, he got on well with Hazlett. Len Jones was the husband in the station's married couple, an essential employment structure in big places like Burwood. We never had Len's position explained to us; I suppose he thought he was being groomed for the manager's job, and he may well have been right about that. Anyway, Ted told me to go to a gate and get a cut of ewes for the shearers, so I got some bread and was passing Len's place about 7 o'clock in the morning. 'What are you doing?' Len asked. I told him.

'Who told you to get those ewes?'

He annoyed my youthful ego, the way he asserted his authority. 'I don't take orders from two bosses. You can go and get stuffed.' The shearers were just leaving the cookhouse and an audience doesn't help peace in the land. We traded blows until we ran out of puff, and I said, 'I think you've had enough.'

'So what's the story now?'

'Aw, it's all right,' I said. 'You stay. I'll go.'

I rang Ted. 'Can I get my cheque when I'm passing?'

'Why's that?'

'Had a row with Jonesy.'

'What's he like?'

'Not too good.'

'Well, I don't know the story, Snow, but you watch the big fella.' Basically Ted backed Len — quite properly — and warned me of repercussions from Hazlett. Reputation is important in the insecure trade of musterer — Hazlett knew everyone from rabbiters to the Minister of Important Things, and was an influential, powerful man. Walking off during a critical time like shearing could rank with getting the boss's daughter up the duff as a cardinal sin in the high country. But I could laugh with Len about our silly fight now. I think.

I went off to the Waikaia pub for the night, and rang Bill Pinckney at Glenaray to see if my professional life had a future. 'Come on up,' he said. 'We'll see about it when the men come off the hill.' He wanted to get me out of the pub in case some other runholder picked me up. But I was feeling a bit sour and didn't relish the thought of going to Glenaray on spec. 'What about me wages?' But I went. On spec.

CHAPTER NINE

An Officer and a Gentleman

''Ten-n-n — shun!'

Parade-ground English

P INCKNEY MET ME AT THE GATE AND ASKED IF I WANTED TO WORK
that day or wait for his head shepherd. 'I'll give you a hand,' I agreed.
I had two great backing dogs, Jim and Duke, ideal for yard work.
Pinckney was summing me up, seeing if I was any good, so I wasn't
surprised when he found a reason to test the other side of the dogging
coin. 'Take this mob up to that gate and put them out on those terraces.'
No problem. I had Lass, a heading bitch keener than a new razor blade
for work, and I knew I had the job. 'Kerr! I'll buy that bitch off you.'

'Nawh. Even if I did sell her to you, you wouldn't be able to work her.'
I was a bit sour still from the morning's stupidity with Jonesy.

'Hurrumpf.'

Bill Pinckney was a sandy-headed bloke with a military moustache, a
legacy from his time at Sandhurst Royal Military Academy in England.
He used an English hunting saddle, possibly a cavalryman's, not the big
stock saddles with leather for the knees we used. After graduating from
Sandhurst he took to Glenaray in the 1920s like Phar Lap to a racetrack,
all 160 000 acres of it. Formal and correct in his manner, he didn't
impress me much at first, but I grew to admire him, and if I learned
anything about handling men, I learned the basics from him. As well as
his boss role, he was an excellent handler of stock and he had 36 000
sheep in his care. I don't think his head shepherd ever got the chance to

learn the complex drafting system the place used because Bill and his wife Kath always used to handle the gates. There was precision in everything he did. Kiwi shepherds tended to take time to roll a smoke when the last sheep's bum exited the drafting race, but Pinckney always knew exactly what he wanted done next — and he got it. Usually. 'Ferguson. That lot there. Number 37.' Ferguson, taken by surprise, asked him to repeat himself.

'I — said, "Ferguson. That — lot — there. Number — 37."'

Stung by the strained look on Pinckney's face and his measured sarcasm, feeling like a dimwit, the poor bugger said, 'I've got a handle to my name.'

'Sid — ney. That — lot — there. Number — 37.'

The task at hand was everything. No one's ego, Pinckney's included, was allowed to interrupt or delay its completion. I felt a bit sorry for Sid then — don't now.

'Kerr —'

'I've got a handle to my name, too.'

'Oh, really?' He muttered something about 'independent colonial bastards'.

Next morning passing the cookshop he greeted us punctiliously, 'Good morning, William. Good morning, Sidney.'

Glenaray had army start — dawn — and nobody worked much after three in the afternoon. Except Pinckney. On the books and correspondence. Once a month we'd be individually called to the office to sign for our pay. Transaction completed, he'd ask, 'Beer?' in a clipped English way. 'Thank you.' And he'd simultaneously tip the contents of two bottles into two pewter tankards. 'Dog's nose?' (nip of gin). 'No thanks.' He would. I'd be halfway through my pint when he'd quaffed his. Then he'd drum his fingers on the arm of his chair. Out of courtesy you had to force the rest down. I used to find myself grinning like a chimpanzee as I passed the next employee going in, but Pinckney seemed as sober to the last man as he'd seemed to the first.

Bill Pinckney didn't run the place for 30 years, he *made* it what it became. The fencers fenced, the paddock men mustered paddocks, the hill men like me mustered hill country, the tractor driver drove, the school teacher taught in the station's school and General Pinckney did a bit of everything while giving orders. Today the place has a landscaped park with managers, accountant, directors and all the smart machines, doing what Pinckney did solo, after real work. His presence filled the place with confidence. He had arrived in 1922 and married Kath in 1926. By 1930 he'd gained shares in Glenaray and was joint manager with his uncle George Pinckney until George died in 1948. Bill died in 1973 and in 1982 a tragic helicopter accident took the lives of his son and daughter-in-law, Peter and Ann Pinckney.

Bill looked marvellous on a horse, upright like a gun-cleaning rod, hands resting on the pommel. He had the pick of the horses and his gleaming oat-filled cob was a bottler. Cutting out cattle in reinforced corners for earmarked culls for the works was where he shone. He'd yell, 'Mine!' and spur in to single out a beast and drive it off to the other side of the big yard, and if you think that's easy, just try it. Alan Chalmers did, when he was still green around cattle. He made the mistake of coming in on Pinckney's inside. It could only have one result: horseflesh collision, bovine escape. Riding home, Pinckney explained in cultured tones, 'Stupid oaf. Never, never try the pincer movement horsedrafting cattle.'

Pinckney made mistakes like anybody else — rarely, but he made them. He was generous hearted when he did, while steadfastly refusing to actually admit his error.

Pinckney, his head shepherd Gibson, Chalmers, others and I were drafting sheep at the terraces yard when Pinckney said, 'Alan,' — we'd educated him on first names by then — 'go and bring down the black cattle.' Alan rode off. By and by the sheep work was cut out, and Pinckney asked, 'Where's Chalmers?' Not many minutes passed before a series of lowing, barking, bellows and roars came clear from the flat below us. Gibson, not the bravest in approaching Pinckney, said, 'I think Alan's got the black cattle instead of the black sheep.' There was no 'think' about it. Chalmers had 120 black cows. The flat was a bad place to yard cattle: there were dozens of getaway places where they could escape through the creek bed and scatter.

We had smoko. Chalmers yarded the cattle and was coming up the road on his old swayback, whistling away. He got off at Pinckney's feet.

'Are you satisfied with the day?' Pinkney asked.

'Aw, yeah.'

'Did you make a good job of yarding those cattle?'

'Yes.'

'Get the lot?'

'Yes.'

'I said black bloody sheep.'

'No. You said black cattle.'

I put my oar in: 'You did say "cattle".'

'Keep out of this.' Turning back to Alan, measuring his words: 'The day I send one man to get cattle into those yards on Glenaray, I'll bend down and you can kick my arse off the property all the way to Gore. Now, for Christ's sake, forget about that nurse you've got in Dunedin and go and have a cup of tea.'

Sometimes, for hard labour such as crutching, he exchanged his usual khaki shirt for a red quilted dressing-gown, in the interests of weight reduction. He had become portly with age and believed he was 'sweating it off'.

There must be something character-building about stuttering. All the stutterers I've met seemed to have gained inner strength from their affliction, at God only knows what cost, but the tally is remarkable. The great Glenaray fall — autumn — muster would begin with the weighing of the swags. So that a horse was balanced, three swags each side, a bit of arithmetic was required. Thenceforth, you always kept your swag with its two companions to preserve that balance. The horses for the fall muster were heavier, and had thicker coats and hairier legs than normal, because they didn't get cut up like thoroughbreds. Many — perhaps most — hadn't been ridden for months, some since last fall. They were brought in and shod, then assigned.

Ray McAuley from the Keys up Te Anau way climbed on his and it dumped him at Pinckney's feet. Pinckney, either from the distorted sense of humour he'd caught here or from the cavalry tradition of the British Army, roared with laughter like he'd burst. Ray got up and pushed his face directly into Pinckney's, an act of considerable personal courage: 'L-laugh, you b-b-big pat puttin' b-bug-ger. I-I-I came here to muster, not break in ya-ya-your puttin' hi-hi-horses. S-s-tick your job.' And Pinckney had to backpedal fast, call in the horsebreaker to take the kinks out of the brute, and mollify Ray. Musterers were hard to get.

Glenaray's musterers were a good diverse bunch as a rule. Jimmy Rodgerson was a top bloke and his Seventh Day Adventist faith, his comical avoidance of swearwords when chastising dogs and clean-living habits attracted only gentle jibes, never malice. He could work a dog and he never shirked his share. A musterer's world can accommodate a lot of saints and sinners, and in Rodgerson's case for a considerable time. He lay on his back in the top bunk one night and exclaimed, 'Blow me down! That's my father's name up there.' A verse had been carved on a rafter:

> There was a Rodgerson from Kiwera
> With a saintly turn of mind.
> He'd rob a blind man of his shirt,
> And leave damned all behind

I was the only bloke Pinckney shouted for when I left Glenaray. His general policy was to ignore employees completely the moment they quit. They'd pack up their furniture and nearly go mad for a month waiting for the truck. 'This over the business of Chalmers?' he asked of my resignation, straight to the point. Alan was my mate and an outspoken cuss. But when he was not invited back that season I had made my feelings known.

'No.' It wasn't an issue in my resigning. 'But I think you were wrong.'

'When you're running a big place, which you might do some day, you'll find out I'm not wrong.'

'Chalmers is a good man.'

'I know *that*.' He was genuinely exasperated with me; this was about *men*, plural, not a man. 'Chalmers didn't click with my head shepherd, you know that, and I've got to back up my senior man. You'll find out.'

I did later, but back then I missed the point: 'I think you've got a few shortcomings, too,' I boldly continued.

'What do you mean by that?'

'Well, riding past me the other day, I could've been an earwig.'

'Huu, huu!' He ejaculated air contemptuously, blowing his moustache out. 'I've had that come back before. What do you expect me to do, William? We've got three haybalers and two of the bloody things'd broken down. The bloody power'd gone off. We're paying eight shearers, with woollies waiting all over the shop. Say "Good afternoon, William"?'

You have to be English aping the English to get the full sarcasm of those last three sweet words. There's no reply.

Nokomai in 1946 was my introduction to South Island high-country station life, although I was born in Central Otago, surrounded by great hills and mountains. I didn't long leave the high country again for 30 years. But in those Nokomai, Burwood and early Glenaray years I often took myself down country during the off-seasons and breaks, driven by the need for sustenance, the requests of good people, and a fear of idleness I've now overcome.

A general account may help explain why I kept away from Southland and South Otago's plush country for the bushy or barren-looking places I came to love.

Dacre had 2000 ewes to lamb and I had 21 years on my clock. The dress code was: longjohns and balaclava if it was likely to get cold, gumboots if it was going to be wet underfoot, and oilskins if rain was likely. Every musterer knows cold must be stopped next to the skin and longjohn wool stops it best. I would carry a sharp knife, some two-metre lengths of binder twine, a bottle of disinfectant and raddle out to the maternity ward in the company of two reliable lambing dogs. Raddle is a powdery chalk in a greasy crayon. Once I used an oilcan of branding paint. The raddle or paint would be used on twins, a number like '40' being written on its near side (its own left side) and a bar to identify it as twin on its far side. If a twin lost its mother, you could find a ewe with a lamb marked '40' and a bar on the other side and reunite the trio.

Lambing for a shepherd is like watching play at Wimbledon. You've got to keep your eyes on the ball, and play continues day and night. A lamb exits its mother front feet and head first. All a shepherd can see is two eyes over two feet, and he or she has to literally catch the ewe, and assist her to drop the lamb. If you don't gently smear the mother's nose with the lamb's wool grease properly, the frightened ewe will career off down the paddock. Then you, poor sod, have to catch her again, tie her up, match her up with her lamb and get it suckling and the mother bond established. None of this is difficult in itself; difficulty lies in the situation and the numbers. As often as not it's dark as top West Coast coal. One drops her lamb here and four drop theirs at the other end of the paddock. Two-tooths must be particularly well watched; it's their first lambing, and every midwife knows the first birth is the riskiest. Keeping track is a worse job than that of the compiler of *Who's Who* — at least he or she can take people's word for their maternity. Breach births. Twinning.

Storms. Pressing orphans on the lambless. Huntaways that slip their chain and wreak havoc in the lambing paddock. As Murphy put it, anything that can go wrong, does.

Lambing at Nine Mile at least held the possibility of making the acquaintance of Thomas Dillon's five beautiful daughters, but they were a bit older than me and Catholic at a time when such things were thought important. (One, Margarita, married and lives at Nine Mile still after her husband bought the property. If I'd played my cards differently maybe I might've ended up owning it, but the elevation isn't high enough and the prospect of years of lambing hangs like a pall.) Greenvale was notable only for the eccentricity of its owner, Barney Butson, the most impressionable man I've ever met. He read murder stories and the lessons of those books weren't lost on him. He took the teapot in his car when he was away from home so his de facto wife couldn't poison him. Then another book alerted him to the subtle cunning of these poisoners: a smear along a breadknife could do you in, so he took the breadknife with him too. His wife looked far from lethal to me. He was intensely suspicious and strange, though he was on the county council and must have seemed perfectly sane to most people. I was stuck for words when he asked me how much it would cost to put a corrugated iron fence right around his entire property like it was a suburban section. Trouble was, he was serious, and it was a bit tricky pointing out the absurdity of the cost and time involved, but he was going to thwart those pesky rustlers he imagined were robbing him blind.

I was conscientious, a good shepherd. Lambing is a job where it is easy enough — and tempting — to slacken concentration and let nature take her course when the cold night wind bites into wet hands and tiredness rises like damp on a plaster wall.

'Couldn't save her, boss. God knows I tried.' I don't know how I had the patience. The best aspect was the territory I covered. I did a fair bit of lambing work around Southland over the years, in the off-seasons from the big high-country places, moving with the spring grass growth, and not simply south. Around Invercargill lambing often began in late August whereas Riversdale lambed in October. I lambed Stan Kane's at Winton, Riversdale, Dillon's Nine Mile and Dacre. I also mustered at Ardlussa, Fiery Creek, Greenvale, Halfway Bay on Lake Wakatipu, and Canard. I didn't exactly hate lambing but I sure don't miss it. High-country sheep either don't lamb at all or lamb themselves. Very sensible of them.

There was six weeks of down time around February at Glenaray, just as there was at Nokomai. Same deal: you could stay and do odd jobs, like splitting wood for the back huts, if you wanted; but you were free to find other work. Harry Barr and I took a job mustering Duncraig, a small run near Manapouri. (Everyone had dropped the 'on' in Duncraigon.) I was there three weeks and got six months' adventure, food for thought, fun by the bale, and an expanded horizon. Guy Morrell came from a well-known Southland family who had owned the Manapouri boarding house, but he'd spent years in Switzerland as a mountain guide for trampers, climbers and skiers. Not for the first or last time I was to learn and love what foreigners and foreign influences bring to New Zealand. Growing up in Central in the 1930s left a legacy: anyone who wasn't a white Anglican or Presbyterian was subject to petty suspicion and prejudice.

Harry and I loaded my Model A with rods, guns and 13 dogs. We stayed at the Mossburn pub for a well-deserved session. Hung over, we got lost in the manuka and stopped for directions. A man came out wearing nothing but a bush singlet, black hairy legs planted, tossle and cods hanging free. Things were obviously done differently hereabouts. 'Why don't you muster here instead?' No, we were booked in, so he let up and told us where to go.

A garage beside the river was the Model A's terminus. A small white cottage on the other side was Morrell's place. It seemed impolite and impolitic to wake him at 2 a.m., so we napped until daylight, then hollered. A pyjama-clad figure waved and rowed across to pick us up.

The Waiau is the wildest river I know, and I grew up beside the mighty Clutha, knew its fearsome toll. I got my 33 yards swimming certificate at school and the moment folk stopped compulsorising me, I never exposed my bare white skinny legs to sun or water willingly again, except once, but you know that. I hadn't seen the sea or big surf at that stage of my life, but when I did, the immensity and power of it awed me in a way coastal folk found endlessly amusing. Years later the Waiau would claim the life of my wife's brother-in-law and his companion. The morning we arrived the Waiau looked black and the surface had the appearance of rippling muscles; currents rose above the general surface in an effort to overtake one another. The bottom was travelling faster than the top: great eddies everywhere. Spectacular rapids lay just downstream but I didn't know that then. Morrell took a peculiar angle across — we could see the sense of it and he expertly brought the rowboat to where we stood — but the route bespoke the river's power and treachery. I wasn't happy.

Dogs, gear and us — there was about two inches of freeboard. I pulled my eyes away from the water midstream and sneaked a look at Guy Morrell rowing one-handed, sweat across his brow and grimacing. He was distinguished looking, grey hair hanging over his shoulders, rare in those days. I dearly wanted to trust his skill. He sensed it. 'Put a .22 bullet through my hand the other day. Had to shoot a pig with a revolver.' I wished he'd waited to explain, but we got over.

The first foreign innovations were breakfast and quarters. The Morrells cooked beautifully, ate well and shared their food and house with employees. To us these were funny but welcome ideas. The hall was octagonal, its wall lined with all manner of fascinating guns — saddle rifles, blunderbusses, muskets, antique military long arms, old-fashioned shotguns and the like, and when he spoke of them, we got a history and technology lesson.

He fed the stove with green manuka he angle-cut on a block one handed: one whack, one wee log, like a Chinese chef's chopper on spring onions, only the manuka was thick as a downpipe. His right arm was thicker than his left. His wool press was a simple wooden box, open at the top. Guy would hook a bale on it, get on top and ram fleeces down the sides with a spade while treading it down. His bales were indistinguishable from mechanically pressed ones.

He often rowed a canoe up to the Manapouri boarding house for what he didn't raise, grow, hunt, fish or gather. He had use of a diesel launch while we were there, and took us on the grocery run. It seemed safe enough but cut out mid-journey. The boat tossed us around, twirled, leaned first to one side, then the other, like a drunken acrobat. Harry turned the crank handle furiously, his fear level akin to mine. He had blisters after. Harry left a few days later, not from blisters or fear, but because he couldn't get his boots on — mossie bites had swelled his feet.

The Waiau wasn't finished with me even then. I once offered to drive the grocery run for a change and Guy said to his wife, 'Would you like to go, dear?' She rowed me over competently enough. But I'd forgotten the car keys, incompetently. Resisting the impulse to quiver, I said, 'I'll row back.'

'Sure you can manage?' she, an older woman, asked a 21-year-old buck boofhead.

'I'll be right.' But I wasn't. I was spun about and drifting downstream, and found out about the rapids for the first time. Co-ordinating two oars proved impossible and I got across with one, Indian style. When Morrell asked me how I'd gone, I hoped he'd offer to row back with his canoe tied behind. No luck. 'Takes a while,' he said gently, and I wasn't going to plead.

He made corker lunches and carried them in his pack — never saw a boss before or since do either.

Following his own theories about hydatids, he didn't have a dog on the place. Unheard of! Duncraig was mustered only once a year. The sheep were shorn and any lambs the pigs hadn't caught and eaten were tagged, castrated and so on. There was only one holding paddock, half of it normal open paddock, as you'd expect, half bush. Yet his sheep were the healthiest I ever saw, and you didn't have to be an Oxford scholar to see why. Survival of the fittest. Adaptation of a new species to an alien environment. Evolution. Darwinism. Any lambs that survived fierce pigs, river, mosquito- and other insect-borne diseases were the quickest of wit and foot, the fastest learners and the toughest of constitution. Few did. They were part merino and God only knows what else, and they retained merinos' instincts. Merinos that escape shearing once or twice eventually die from, basically, having too much wool. Duncraig's big fleecers shed wool like wild sheep. They'd reverted. Guy's woolshed and yards were made of birch bearers, joists and rails, and the sheep ate the moss growing on them, nothing else, for the three days I was away and lost no condition, a long time for grass-eating machines. We saw 17 wild cattlebeasts on Duncraig: 13 bulls, two cows, a heifer and a calf, an upside-down age and sex balance. As the heifers came into season the great bulls would sometimes crush them to death during mounting.

For me thereafter, the conscientious husbandry of lambing was not *the* way, but one way. Pluses and minuses in everything. But in terms of wool economics, Duncraig didn't make a lot of sense.

Mustering wild sheep was more like hunting than shepherding. The dogs would bail the sheep up, perhaps 12 or 20 in a clearing in the manuka. Tally ho! They'd bolt every time. Our heading dogs would go in, doing all the right collie things, but in the end they'd knock them over one by one and we'd rush in and help hold them. Bloody noses and bits of wool all over the place. Guy would make up a rope from flax in an eye's twinkle and we'd tie them to tree trunks. Then we'd go off to stalk another lot.

When we had the last mob of the day we'd try to batter them into submission, tire them out in the heat, march them up to the top of the hill and march them down again like Old King Cole, dog them constantly. We aimed for a nucleus of docile leaders. (Freezing works yarders reward an individual yard sheep, called the Judas sheep, to lead others to the sticking pens. Same principle here.) But each untying session was bedlam, and every clump of brush was cause for renewed bolts. When we got whatever we got to the paddock, perhaps 500 or so, we never saw them unless we were in there cutting a few out; they spent the whole time in the bushy part. We saw deer cross the open ground, but not one sheep.

One day Guy took me to the top of Duncraig, sidling upwards, slow and even; we never raised a sweat. He mentioned he'd taken some 70-year-old woman up there; nothing exceptional about that to him. It was the gentlest climb I'd known.

The problem with this account of the basic muster is that it takes no account of moods. Bosses, men, dogs, horses, sheep, cattle and, as we'll see, weather, wild animals, tourists and vehicles all have them. The one constant is the terrain. Canard was the hardest country I have ever mustered. You had to lie on your back to take a leak or you'd pee on your mate downhill it was so steep.

Whiteouts are eerie. Visibility is measured in two steps forward, and a deathly silence envelops everything in the entire world. I can boast — and do — of an uncanny instinct that alerts me to the arrival of fog. Glenaray's horses shared it. But a whiteout sees musterers holed up under a rock for hours, eight sometimes, waiting for the weather to clear. Some smoke, some talk, some kick tussock. You swear you'll never forget those hours, but like childbirth you do. A musterer at Otematata tried for the hut in one and died. Oddly, he wasn't that far from the road, though he'd not have known it. The rule is simple: find a stream, follow it down and don't stop. Stop and you easily fall asleep and die.

Another went over a cliff at Ohau. He tried to climb down what he should have gone around, a fatal shortcut. Swollen rivers hold up musters for weeks sometimes. We work in light rain but usually shelter if it's going to saturate clothes. I've mustered at 6500 feet and some blokes have done it higher. You can experience glorious weather up there while everyone is fog-bound below, share elevations with cruising hawks, look down on the tops of clouds. A hoar frost, frozen dew that covers everything — not just the dorsal side of branches but the entire tree — is magical, though no friend.

Birdwood would later see me in shingle up to my knees all day, working slightly uphill. I'd swear and curse and call the dump 'a paddock with its back up'. Even a sinful old bugger like me sleeps the sleep of the innocent after a day there.

In such country the merino will live where other breeds die. Let's clear up a townie misunderstanding. Sheep will eat tussock, but only in dire circumstances. Look closely at a tussock and you'll see a wee world down there, with tiny alpine herbs, green grasses, legumes, mosses and the like growing in the base of the big tussock grass clump. Even shingle screes have shoots of dwarf peas and grasses poking through. That's what sheep eat. The merino can live on next to zero, and stand heat and dust and drought just as it can snow and frost. It has the best wool in the world and, crossed with a Border Leicester or a black-faced ram, as good a fat lamb as any in the world. You mightn't get the percentages, but you get vigour. I often wonder if that vigour doesn't come from the primitiveness of merinos: they still skip-jump as they pass by every tree or gate post, a trait I'm convinced is to avoid the Spanish, South African and Australian snakes their ancestors knew.

And God made merinos for New Zealanders and their collie dogs, a self-evident truth no one can deny if they have worked in the South Island high country a full year, winter and summer, have an eye that sees and a brain that works and are not completely dull of soul.

CHAPTER TEN

A Man and His Dogs

Rover would have enjoyed them bones.

Shepherd, forced by starvation to kill and eat his dog, Rover.
Quoted by Jim Henderson, New Zealand Times, 1984

I GOT MY FIRST DOG WHEN I WAS SEVEN AND HE TRAINED ME AS A thief. I loved Rock, a fox terrier pup, but we were too poor to buy him milk. At night, with a honey tin, I'd sneak down the road, milk the neighbour's cow that was tethered on the roadside and feed Rock. I came home from school one day and the dear old neighbour was complaining to Mum; her cow had dried up in one tit. No problem. Took a bit out of all four tits after that.

Tip and other foxies followed. We learned the ways of rabbits and ferrets together. And we made a few bob.

You can't teach an old dog new tricks, but an old dog can teach a young boy a very great deal, as I'm entitled to point out again. It would be tedious to detail just how Charles Patterson's three old brood bitches taught me the ropes, but a young musterer couldn't hope for a gentler introduction to the trade, wiser tutors or greater patience than these, my first collies. I've claimed I learned patience with animals at Gladesmuir; I wonder if collie dogs have patience? I think they would have needed it with me.

I liked dogs from Day One and thought I was red-hot with them. Apparently, because I didn't know it then, this came from my genuine affection for animals. Not in any sooky way, though. I wanted to be

84

master and the dog to do whatever I told it to do. If I outwitted it, we got along. If it outwitted me, I'd shoot it. New Zealand collies are spectacularly beautiful to watch working, like well-oiled gig wheels in Ian Anderson's words, but not because they are born like that. For every one you see, there's four mouldering in their early graves because they couldn't make the grade.

A young bloke rang and brought his dog around one Sunday afternoon recently to see what I, distinguished old dog man, thought of it. I was looking after a thoroughbred heavily in foal at the time and birth was at hand. The dog took off out of the fellow's car and heeled hell out of the horse, around and around the paddock. We finally got control again and he said, 'What you think, Mr Kerr?'

'See that gully over there, boy? It's full of dead dogs, all better than this one.'

My reputation as a dog killer got out of hand once. I walked back from a disastrous North Island trial run with Syd, mumbling that I was going to skin Syd, cut him up, get my wife to make a stew, sit down and eat every bit of him. A radio journalist looking for copy heard about Syd's intended fate and, by the time I got home, so had half the South Island. Well, I couldn't eat him after that, but Syd never knew how close he came.

At Glenlappa I had four dogs when I bought a stumpy, a dog with a cut tail, which according to the bloke who sold it could do everything except cook duck in plum sauce. I figured I'd been conned when an old shepherd told me that if I couldn't do anything else with it, I could always teach it to stand on its front legs and use his arsehole as an eggcup. He pointed out that I could eat the egg without worrying about the tail getting up my nose.

When there's a murder and you can't blame your butler, a dog's handy. Wokka Cooper and I took our thirsty dogs down to Hamilton Burn while moving cattle from Burwood to Centre Hill. Wokka saw a big trout and got him with his mustering stick. 'Got yous fellas!' came from behind us, the ranger's voice. A beardie pup was frolicking in the burn.

'It's not like you think, sir. He went in for a swim and that big trout grabbed him in his mouth. We had to beat the shit out of him to make him let go.' The ranger expressed scepticism, but he let us off.

When a dog man meets another dog man, usually each knows the other by reputation — their strengths and weaknesses, style and skill. But not always. A young fella, Peter Kerr, no relation, came to work for me at Omarama. He knew of me but I didn't know much about him except that he was off Nokomai. And I'd have guessed that. He pulled up and a big team of dogs, about six black-and-tan huntaways and three heading dogs, jumped out. I always like to get a grip of a fella if I can. So at breakfast I asked, 'All those dogs work?'

'Yes.'

'All working dogs?'

'Yep.'

I could see him visualising it: was I going to ask him to take 3000 wethers out the back block on his own? What?

'Well, I'll tell you what you can do. Take this bucket of scraps and go down and feed the ducks.' When 30 or 40 muscovies were pecking away around his feet I said, 'I'd like to get a photo to show the Nokomai boys.' The next day our job was to lay stones and concrete up a culvert, up to our knees in mud. There's a lot to do on a high-country sheep station besides running dogs.

Suppose I'd better give you a bit of background on New Zealand working dogs, sheepdogs. There are two types: heading dogs and huntaways, each baked according to the following recipes. Heading dogs: mix a good dollop of Scottish collie with a cup of bearded collie and a dash of old English sheepdog. Huntaways are classic mongrels based firmly on the Border collie, Old English sheep dog, the Smithfield labrador from London's meat market, and the hound. But years of breeding here could soon cancel out their mongrel origins; the academics reckon the New Zealand huntaway could be our first native breed in its own right.

Musterers often talk of 'a bread-and-butter dog' — this is a qualified compliment meaning he or she might not look much and isn't particularly elegant around a flock or herd, won't win prizes at trials (though they may surprise everyone, owner included, at times) but works and gets the job done. My Tammy and Tord were such dogs. The reason Tammy lived long enough to work at all was because Fiona, my daughter, picked her out from a litter. Tammy's overshot jaw and twisted tail didn't appeal, and black, white and tan markings are not signs of great breeding, but she was a nice working bitch. Some dogs' main value lies in their genes. Bess was a top brood bitch and I advertised her pups as 'not for boys and very few men'. Tyne too.

Short names are preferred for dogs, because dogs get it more easily and quickly, and who the hell wants to be yelling 'Aristotle' or 'Virginia' all day? One syllable's clearly best and there is a surprisingly short list to choose from. Working Quake and Jake together would've been hell. A dog might be 'Super Syd' to the marshal chalking on the Methven Collie Dog Club draw board, to distinguish him from his father Syd in the records, but he's 'Syd' on the hill.

Dogs have industrial accidents, sickies and absenteeism like any other worker. Distemper used to be a killer but inoculation fixed that. Hopefully parvo disease will go the same way if everyone keeps the boosters up. Dogs rarely drown and never get frostbite, but their paws can become red raw on rough ground and hot rock burns them just like barefoot picnickers. They may call it a day and hole up on the hill in distress like this, to await the dew's kindly softening and make their footsore way home. Poisoned rabbits kill them, both the old strychnine and the modern 1080. Pigs, bulls and horses gore, stamp and kick them, often to death. They fall over bluffs. They pull hamstrings faster than an All Black winger, and rip themselves on barbed wire and rock, a vet's bread and butter. Arthritis takes its toll, especially in Southland where they swim cattle in cold streams and Southland dogs seldom get past eight or nine years old. But Waitaki's drier country sees dogs reach 16 years sometimes. A 30-year-old ex-workhorse, unimaginable in Southland, isn't uncommon.

No animal on earth is quite as fascinating as a collie dog in my opinion and experience. Old dog men can talk good sense and not cover much old ground talking about dogs until the candle gutters or the whisky gives out or their golden wedding anniversary takes them by surprise mid-sentence. The real problem is what to leave out. Take their senses.

Their hearing is more than twice as acute as a human's.

Their eyesight isn't great. They see, practically, in only black and white, but it's good at detecting movement.

But dogs have 220 million cells that smell things. Humans have 5 million, but that doesn't make dogs smell things 44 times better than a man, it makes them a million times better. Bet none of my doggie mates knew I knew that. Dogs can smell a dead body 50 metres under water — think about that. That's what it said in a magazine I read at the barber's.

Owning working dogs is definitely a nuisance and a potential embarrassment. They must have good manners, but it takes time to get manners through to a dog. They need heaps of TLC: food and a run around every day, and decent housing, though they aren't fussy tenants. Any animal that's locked up, tied up or fenced in relies on a human being for its welfare. But things still go wrong.

I was a guest of Russell Black and his wife, Komika, while travelling with Chief, a notorious slipper of chains and freelance rounder-up of sheep. At breakfast Russell said, 'Chief was off last night but it's okay because I put him in your car.' I asked if he had any sheep about. No. 'Well, that's all right then.' Komika eventually woke from a sleep-in — she ran a busy restaurant and needed it — and went for a walk in the sun. 'Eeee-ee!' One of her pet lambs turned up with a blood-stained ear. Two more lambs were missing. This coward slipped his vehicle into first and slunk down the road. I wanted out before Komika's dismay turned into Samurai warrior wrath.

City people get very gooey about their dogs. I can understand that: some dogs make me gooey too. But treating dogs like people is insane. With all that brain space given over to smelling and hearing, how much is left for language development and philosophy? We cannot imagine the world they know. But with patience and a clear understanding of who is running things, they can grasp quite complex matters.

I succumbed once to the cult of the useless dog, the pet. Ken White was the rep for a dog-nut company. He gave me a walking stick and plonked a Jack Russell pup on the kitchen table 'for your retirement, WV'. I'd retired — again — from trialling dogs. I wasn't keen but decided on a month's probation. Spot was great company, a good mate. He'd tug my trouser cuff at 4 p.m. to remind me to feed the collies, protect my jacket while I dug the garden, and amuse me. But he developed obnoxious habits, gorging until he threw up and causing fights with a heading dog he hated. He was also getting blind, banging into glass doors. When he bit the heading dog and the wound on its jaw formed an abscess that cost $73 to fix, I was a bit sour on him. I took off my hat and did a stint in the garden. When I put it back on, he'd pissed in it. Bang, and down the guthole with Spot. I hope he found a better world, and learned his error in this one. He was terrific fun at first, but he'd become a sour little fellow with age. It happens, doesn't it?

Dogs' fates, even unto death, surprise. Most working dogs end their days with a bullet, either regretfully applied for humane reasons or as the price of failure. But some have odd ends. Dunstan Peaks Station had a dirt road the dogs used to bolt down the moment you let them off the clip at feeding and runaround time. A bitch, Gyp, went around the corner and hit her head on a trailer she didn't expect to be there. Peter Kerr was working for me then and I gave Gyp to him. He went down south for a while and when we next met I asked how she went. 'Started to work all right,' he said, 'but a hen killed her.'

'You mean she killed a hen.'

'No, hen killed her.' The bitch grilled up a hen and got crook. Peter took her to the vet in Alexandra but she died. The vet's post-mortem revealed a hen's quill through the guts.

Sporting dogs and I have shared good times. A labrador called Prince once delivered me up a goose without so much as a ruffled feather by complete surprise one Father's Day. Hate to think where he got it. A white English setter with black spots, Rip was a great bird dog but he simply vanished one day.

All dogs have personalities. They are far more interesting than machines.

Lord Byron said of his dog Bosun, 'He possessed beauty without vanity, strength without insolence, courage without ferocity and all of the virtues of man with none of his vices.' Very nice, eh? But not something anyone will ever say about Jake, God rest his soul. Jake was an outlaw, sticking sheep in lakes, seizing up on trial grounds and causing mayhem wherever he went. When I left the Upper Waitaki area there was a bit of a send-off for me at the pub. I declined the invitation to give a speech but accepted questions. When someone asked, 'What's the best dog you've ever known?' I said, 'Jake.' The groans could be heard at the far end of the Lindis Pass. Jake had had an influence on that community, even if he was notorious. I never use his name without adding 'God rest his soul' and I'd appreciate it if you were to do likewise.

Jake was a dag, good company. We were mustering Peak Valley's Waitaki Spur on the top beat. I must have let my head fall on my chest while I waited for the others. Perhaps I dozed. Whatever, I awoke to see some sheep crossing a sunny face with a red streak behind them, and someone bossy yelling, 'F'crissake, call that red dog back, Kerr!' It was Fred Panting, a beat below me. Ginger Anderson was below him, and the boss Ken was coming around the mountain. I scrambled up and shouted, 'That'll do' and 'Wayleggo' like a good dog bloke should. Ginger said, 'Jake's down here.' That was all I needed: the astute reader will have picked by now that a dog should be on the same beat as its master; this was potentially most humiliating. 'Shut up, Ginger. Don't let the boss know he's down there!' I covered for that dog's sins a lot.

Jake had got over-enthusiastic and ploughed four sheep into the lake, swimming after them, still barking. But he'd left around 30 in some heavy scrub. Not a problem on the day, but when Ken lamb-marked in ten weeks he couldn't understand why there were so many woollies in his mob. In case you think this is nothing, they had to shear them on a drop sheet near the marking yards with blades. A good bladesman can shear 100 every day; a musterer breaks his back to shear 10. Thank God I wasn't there. Unfortunately, they fell to figuring out why they had so many woollies that year when they'd never had so many before. Someone, drat his eyes, remembered Jake.

Jake won one hunt and got second in the other at the Wakatipu trials, necessitating numerous shouts at the booth's bar. On the way home I had a comfort stop in the fog and shouted the dogs a runaround too. When I put the dogs back in Jake jumped in the cab with me, where we had weighty discussions, me talking and Jake nodding sagely. I was too tired to tie up the dogs that night; they were okay in the back, on straw. Next morning a lorry pulled in to cart hay. I was out of bed and into clothes quick smart: can't let folk think one lies abed late. 'Been waiting on you chaps, but you're a bit late. Have a cup of tea.' At that moment Jake's head poked out the front passenger window. 'Morning, Jake. How far'd you drive last night?' So I guess I asked for it when I called in at the lorry drivers' favourite watering hole and one asked, 'Who's driving tonight, WV? You or Jake?' Jake, God rest his soul.

Jake was never popular, but he was the best company of any dog I ever had. Oh, so you don't like Jake either? Try Plug.

Plug's personality underwent profound change after I lent him to Sam Boynton to give a good keen dog a bit of work on Lloyd Smith's Pomahaka River block down near Millers Flat. It was no fault of Sam's, but from then on, if a lorry rattled the nearby bridge or aircraft flew over, a spooked Plug would seek out an overhang and lie low. When he and I were out with the rest of the team and took a sitdown, he'd find an overhang to see the time out, not hang around me. He was deadly to possums and hens, and would sneak into the henhouse to steal eggs. He'd lick the dew from the grass every morning, an odd habit for a collie.

Everyone likes a lost-dog story. This is Plug's tale.

Sam rang me on 13 April 1989. 'Bad news. Plug went over a bluff. Hurt pretty bad. I tried to get him up to a fenceline and tie him up but lost him in snow tussock.' I pondered going down, but Sam assured me they'd had a good look and if Sam Boynton looked, that was that. He and I presumed Plug dead.

He rang again in October; he'd heard my house had burned down and was ringing to commiserate. 'But I've got some good news. Plug's turned up.' After 60 years around dogs this still surprised me — six months solo and hurt.

In September Lloyd Smith's neighbour had been trying to get some sheep to cross a creek without success when a great bark from behind him powered them through. He took the big brindle huntaway under his wing, called him Boy and worked him for five weeks with his team. Best dog he'd ever had. When Lloyd mustered next, the neighbour rang, asking if Lloyd or his team had lost a dog. 'No,' Lloyd said, 'but we did lose one in April.'

John Chittock, one of Lloyd's musterers, promised to detour by there and said he'd ring Smith back if it was Plug. 'But I won't be ringing, Lloyd; you know that.'

But it was Plug and he rang. Sam brought him back to me. He nearly knocked me over with his enthusiasm and, for once, I let him go. He more or less evicted the new dog in his old kennel.

What happened in the six months out there? I think he sought out an overhang and settled in for the slow business of recuperation, licking dew for moisture to conserve his energy. Then he foraged for birds' eggs, birds, rabbits, possums and carrion deserted by hawks. He'd evaded men who sought to kill him, for wandering dogs are — must be, I have no quarrel with this — shot on sight in the high country.

CHAPTER ELEVEN

Married and Managing

Friday night too tired, Saturday night too drunk, Sunday too far away.

Traditional shearer's wife's lament

I WAS RIDING BACK FROM BUSH HUT ON GLENARAY, SPANKING ALONG in the dying of the sun. Cath Patterson, wife of the packer Gordon Patterson, Glenaray's married couple, and her friend were out in the garden. The friend was a stunner, a beautiful brunette, a prize. I rode up and was introduced. Ima Collins noticed the holes in my old English worsted jersey: 'Bring it down later and I'll darn it for you.' It was with her that evening. We had a yarn and I invited her to a party in the Model A the next night.

Over 50 years later she's still darning my jerseys.

But the first date didn't turn out too good. She wasn't used to drink and when I got her back to the packer's house I ended our evening holding her over the packer's tomatoes while she threw up for ages. She and I ended up in bed — me in mine, she in hers — but the packer had a bumper tomato crop.

Ima's husband of less than two years, Mick Collins, had been killed in a deershooting accident and Gordon had been Mick's mate. He invited Ima and her 12-month-old son up from Invercargill. I'd been knocking about with Gwenda Thompson, who I'd met at Nokomai. I spent a week off with her, sunning ourselves on the deck of the ss *Earnslaw* on Wakatipu, a boat big enough and a lake placid enough for me, and visited her in Invercargill a couple of times. Excellent woman, Gwenda, but she'd

92

always be a city girl and best left in Nelson, where she'd moved, for both our sakes; Ima, on the other hand, looked adaptable.

A chance conversation on a grassy knoll sealed the poor woman's fate. I said to head shepherd Colin Gibson I wouldn't mind the married couple position coming up on Glenaray. 'Snow, you want to give it a go, the job'll be yours. But you'll need a long-haired partner.'

I jumped in the Model A, drove to Invercargill, parked outside Ima's and caught her outside. 'Will you marry me?' She hadn't any reason to be expecting me, but I had taken her to a picture and a football match before that, so she knew me pretty well.

Stunned silence.

'Well?'

Back at Glenaray, Colin had heard whispers about Gwenda. 'Tell you what, Snow. You'd better be getting up to Nelson if you want that job.'

Couple of days later I told him I'd take it.

'What about your long-haired partner?'

'Yeah, got that.'

At the wedding the man who had accidentally shot Ima's first husband was best man. Rex had told me the story of that fatal day and it was clear he was entirely blameless and the incident was freakish, no one's fault. Ima was aware of that, but he was taking it hard. I hoped being invited to be best man would help him feel better.

When I went down for the wedding I had drawn wages in advance, but by the time we took off for our honeymoon I had calculated a budget that meant petrol was strictly rationed — and not because of the postwar austerity programme or ration cards. We tootled to Tapanui and Dunedin, staying with hospitable and generous relatives, and rolled into Glenaray with half a gallon to spare. Colin Gibson had met Ima but he wasn't expecting her back in this role.

I'd bought the Model A at Nokomai for £225, borrowing £100 from brother John and still owed him. The pay I'd been advanced meant a pay skipped when I got back from the honeymoon. Ima couldn't understand how I resented paying the pastor £2. In fact, the real difficulty I had over these debts was explaining them; I wasn't as good at subterfuge then as I became.

Life up until then had not been an A-grade preparation for marriage. I'd left home around puberty, spent my time overwhelmingly with males, lived in bunkhouses and single men's quarters, eaten at cookhouses and grown comfortable with my own company. I'd enjoyed opportunistic romantic encounters and had had a few affairs of the heart that lasted a few months but these were always characterised by long absences.

Ima was a warm-hearted woman and gregarious. She had four female friends from town who were engaged in our first year together and she'd invite them or they'd ask to stay with us. Holidaying couples cavorting or lazing around while I slogged, eating our tucker while I shot for deerskins to supplement our adequate but hardly regal wages, and consigning me to the sofa whenever our bunks overflowed, made me scratchy. I'd grumble, 'The bugger who said, "Two can live as cheaply as one" ought to be taken out and shot for tucker.'

Ima grew up on the outskirts of Invercargill, among small holdings, so knew milk came from the end that doesn't moo. She'd worked for Thomsen & Beattie in Tay Street, sewing soft furnishings and the like, for six years. The days alone in the sewing room there were probably her best preparation for life as a musterer's wife. Glenaray was her first experience of station life and a tough transition. The journalist who asked the high-country wife what she did when she wasn't working got the truth: 'I go to the toilet.' Nevertheless, the wives of married couples at Glenaray had a cake-walk existence compared with what was to come in Ima's life. Glenaray was a well-run village. Toddler Billy could watch the horsebreaker ride, and going up to the cow boy's for a billycan of milk was an enjoyable walk for Ima and a daily adventure for Billy. Glenaray had a school for the future. She got on well with the 10 or 11 married couples, and was even impressed at the maturity and politeness of the horde of 18- to 22-year-old boys. Ima adapted.

Marriage was the best contract I ever made. I doubt Ima can say the same thing, but we muddled through those difficult early days, and beyond.

A couple of years after we married I saw a job ad for manager at Otamatapaio Station. 'Wouldn't mind that,' I said. Ima said, 'You couldn't do it anyway.' She always claims that she worked reverse psychology on me. It's nonsense, of course, but her comment really got my back up, so I wrote a letter of interest that night. Months passed without a reply.

On the eve of the fall muster, two sweeps, each of three weeks' duration, the reply came. HJ (Harry) Wardell apologised for the delay; he'd been in London on Wool Board business as the board's chairman. Could we meet? I explained the critical timing on Glenaray and how, if anything befell the head shepherd, I was the deputy sheriff. His next letter explained his 'complete understanding' of my 'position' and could I come to Dunedin in June?

He took me to a tearooms. He had been busy, checking with the Goodger brothers from Winton who'd told him I was a dedicated sheep boy who spent his evenings training his dogs in the woolshed and had sold dogs to farmers. 'Still do that?' he asked, psuedo-absentmindedly sipping tea.

'I sold a few dogs then. I was saving up to get married, but now I'm permanent, no.' Of course I didn't save up to get married, I went into considerable hock, difficult to explain to Ima. I still traded in dogs, sure, but I got his drift.

'Pleased to hear that. My country's very cold. Hard. Don't want the sheep knocked about. It's all walking country. Think you'll stand up to it?'

This laughable worry was not an unfair perception. Since puberty I've been a constant 11 stone 3 pounds, but dropped a stone after long hard yakka like the fall muster. 'Nokomai? Canard? Glenaray?' I said and laughed. But it's a hard one to counter for a skinny bugger. If he'd lifted my trouser cuff I'd have been a goner.

He looked thoughtful. 'Had a holiday?' Negative. 'Okay. Take a fortnight on pay, start 15 August. Drop your dogs off at Otamatapaio. Blair'll see they're looked after.' The resident manager's time was drawing to a pointed close.

Ima and I ended our holiday with a night at Anne Meike's modestly famous Oamaru guesthouse, and drove up the Waitaki Valley to start work. Ima had never seen the area before that hot June day. Her eye was trained in Southland, a land of abundant rain and suffused by a flattering light that highlights greens, makes them unearthly, especially in the early morning and evenings. Two things gnawed at her: a foreign dryness and the absence of sheep — where were they? And what on earth did they eat? By Kurow she admitted she 'didn't know what to make of this place'.

Our world contracted thus: there was just Graham Wardell, back from overseas, aged 21 (and later, his wife Rosemary), Blair Gardener, his wife Eleanor — a Wardell, and us. Blair had sustained a back injury and was on light duties while recuperating. They left shortly after.

Ima changed up a gear. She liked the cottage, enjoyed the vege garden and was soon in demand for dressmaking, a skill not widespread there. On the other hand she had to drive Billy to the school bus and make tobacco runs to Omarama, then a store, hotel and garage. She tried to get out of it, pleading that she couldn't drive and had no licence, but she soon learned, even got a licence after 20 years. She'd never cooked for crowds before, and got no sleep the night before her debut as she went over and over the timetable for the breakfast for the musterers, then the shearers, the packed lunches, the smokos, shed lunch and dinners staggered over the next day.

Nowadays grandchildren come around to my place and watch old 'Looney Toons', with Bugs Bunny and Elmer Fudd. I'm on Elmer's side. Ima was turning the bacon when she looked out the window and saw dat pesky wabbit that'd been eating all the young shoots of our garden plants. She got the shotty, rammed two shells home, went out, lined up on the rabbit, closed her eyes, pulled the trigger and blew Bugs into history — disintegrated the bugger. The shearing gang were just walking around the corner when the peace of their country holiday morning was shattered by the loud report. (A shotgun seems to make a hell of a row to humans, but a rifle, any rifle, .22 or .303 or whatever, seems to affect stock and dogs more — have you got that, townies?) 'Good morning,' Ima said. What do you say to a woman holding a gun smoking from both barrels? From there on politeness was Super-Dooper: every man jack of them carried his plate out to the kitchen, there was no backchat, and even I brushed up my ideas a bit.

The spirit of the people around this part of the high country was to really grow on me. Many years after Ima and I had left I was coming back from a dog trial in Central and called in to say gidday to Tim and Jeeva Innes. They had a cracking bitch called Jane who had come into heat, and my crack heading dog Chief was in the back. Tim said to stay the night, it being cold and dark then, and the company warm, and we decided to leave the mating to the morning. Jeeva said sensibly, 'Have you locked her up, Tim?' Tim contradicted himself. 'Yeah, I'll do it in a minute.' Then scotch fog descended.

Jeeva was up and about early as always and Tim and I were sitting at the kitchen table drinking our morning coffee when a neighbour, Jane Thomas, arrived in her usual hasty skid to drop in a bundle of clothes for the kids, and just as quickly, left to visit Tim's sister in the nearby A-frame. She arrived there with another skid, then passed away at speed. Before the reverberations had died away there was a shriek from Jeeva, who'd gone out to milk the cow.

'What's wrong with 'er now?' Tim grumbled as he launched his large frame from the table.

'Oh, Tim, you're too late! You're too, too late! Jane's been f——d.'

A mechanic working under Tim's Land Rover, yards from the skidding and shrieking, just able to glimpse Jane, came out from under so fast he cracked and cut his head. He thought there was a rapist preying on women in the valley.

Ima was once reading me out some advice in a magazine to women alone in New York apartments: 'Don't yell rape, yell fire.' High-country men take a bit of flak about being patriarchal, traditional, overly chivalrous and generally unliberated about their womenfolk. So would you, man or woman, rather live in New York? That mechanic was *concerned*. What had happened? The old labrador had escaped from his dog motel.

At Otamatapaio I made the transition from taking orders to giving them and being the on-the-spot boss pretty well, I think. HJ's son Graham Wardell was under me — a top bloke and I took to him straight off. My most memorable achievement was the surge in lambing percentages; Waitaki men weren't good lambing farmers then and all that wading over Southland paddocks finally paid off. I thought HJ Wardell was happy too, but confirmation came in two roundabout ways.

HJ wanted a cattlestop to replace the gate on the station's only entrance–exit. I expressed misgivings about the safety of cattlestops on sheep places, but if he wanted a cattlestop, a cattlestop he'd have. Graham and I concreted in the railway tracks, very sturdy and tradesmanlike it was. Then Graham came to my breakfast table one morning, disconcerted and distressed. Jerry, the packhorse, had both front feet firmly stuck between the rails. Graham's wife Rosemary had her dad down from his North Island farm. Mr Andrews was a Big Chief of the Meat Board and had stayed overnight in order to attend a Very Important Meeting — aren't they all? — in Alexandra early that morning. He couldn't get out the gate. I took one look at Jerry's skinned legs and saw that he was in pain. The poor old horse was done for. In those days before angle grinder tools there was only one humane solution. 'Graham, get the tractor and a chain.' I went to the house for the shotgun and a butcher's knife, blew Jerry's head off, cut through the joints in Jerry's legs, the hocks fell away, and we hooked up the corpse and towed it out of the road. I gave Andrews a low bow and flourished him through. He said, 'I heard you were a very efficient manager, but I wouldn't want to get my foot stuck in a cattlestop round here.' That bloke would have been on 'Harry' terms with HJ. Interesting choice of word, 'efficient'.

Later, I was helping out at Bog Roy when Bill Hazlett turned up. 'What have you got that bloody mug working for you for?' he scowled to Ian Anderson, who replied, 'There's only one mug around here, Bill, and that's you for letting a top man like that one go.' I'd heard of Ian Anderson, a dog trial man with a good team, down in Southland. I had a good team too. Not better, but as good. Now, at Otamatapaio, he was my neighbour, across the Waitaki on Ben Omar. I met him on a muster, a lean stick of medium height. He became my friend. I only heard that story much later; Ian was no flatterer or telltale. But I soon got — coincidentally or not, I don't know — a typically tentative offer from Hazlett to manage Burwood Station. I talked to HJ about leaving and he said something sensible as usual: 'I'm building up your pay, but I was going to do that anyway. But know this: if you're not happy, I won't buy you to keep you on.' Burwood was a bigger place, probably more money, and a definite step up; on the other hand, I was warming to the Upper Waitaki and its people and Ima had adjusted well.

Fate took a hand in the form of a ballot. The manager of Omarama Station, Ian McKechnie, was a returned soldier and he drew a bit of dirt down Middlemarch. His departure created a vacancy for trustee HJ to fill on the bigger place. In 1953 he offered me the job, and, significantly, the chequebook. Faith, like trust, was growing. I thought Graham was a shoe-in for my old job, competent and a relative, but HJ continued to keep the reins from him, appointing a manager over him. No disrespect for the manager, but I never understood that. HJ's executive search was lengthy; for a while I managed both places. I loved Omarama Station, but I still didn't have my own land.

A bit of geography here. Skip it if you know the area. The Waitaki is a great big braided river with shingly channels, ox-bows or billabongs depending on whether you fancy American or Australian usage, and runs strongest in the spring melt. It meets the sea north of Oamaru. It drains the Mackenzie Basin's three big lakes, from north to south Tekapo, Pukaki and Ohau. But it drains a lakeless area south of that too, through a tributary, the Ahuriri River, which rises up near Haast, forms the northern part of the Lindis Pass through to Tarras and Central Otago, and drains into the Waitaki at Benmore, where the Ministry of Works built a great dam and formed a lake in 1965. Omarama, the township and today's station, lies in this southern drainage area; Otamatapaio Station, Otematata and Kurow are all progressively downstream from it, Kurow township lying firmly in the main Waitaki Valley. Canterbury is north and Otago south of the river. The Hakataramea River flows in on the Canterbury side.

Otamatapaio and Omarama stations were and still are big as stations go, but they are mere remnants of the first holdings there. In the 1850s Alexander McMurdo and Hugh Fraser arrived in search of new country. Both decided they desired the warm tussock land between the Ahuriri and Ohau rivers, and, rather than race each other to the Christchurch land claim office for the Crown lease, they raced to a designated matagouri bush. Alex's horse proved the better, and Hugh had to be content with Ben Ohau.

Alex's Benmore was 300 000 acres, rose to over 6000 feet and got 20 inches of rain in one corner and eight in another: ideal sheep country. Robert Campbell and his son took over at some point. Between them they were said to have leased or owned one million acres in Otago, Southland and the North Island. The story goes that one man, directed by their manager to get off the place and never to be seen there or anywhere the manager might happen to be, replied, 'Do I have to leave New Zealand, Mr Sutherland?' During the First World War 21 runs, 240 000 acres, were created from Benmore for ex-soldiers, though amalgamation later reduced this number. Ian Anderson's Ben Omar and his father John's Peak Valley were two such.

Omarama Station was vast too, once boasting 32 kilometres of river frontage, but it too peeled off blocks that became stations in their own right, 13 of them. George Innes's Dunstan Downs was one, John Anderson's Bog Roy another. The original Omarama Station had a massive 22-stand woolshed of Baltic pine, imported and assembled in the 1870s, which has stood the test of time. Though it is internally much altered, the basic structure has never needed a day's attention since. The station's English shareholders heard in an annual report of a poor muster tally because of 'fog and snow'. One old dear sent a bale of sheep's bells to help out. The station became Cecil and Wilfred Wardell's in 1920. These grocery entrepreneurs of Dunedin, whose shop was the scene of looting and riot in the 1930s, have, one way or another, kept it a family concern to this day. HJ Wardell ran a trust that administered Omarama and Otamatapaio stations when I arrived. He had once lived on the former and managed the place.

Otematata Station, just down the Waitaki, had a similar size and history. When the rep for an Australian shearing gang at once suggested a bit of lettuce and tomato should supplement the spud and mutton, Walter Cameron, one of the last original landholders, is said to have wheeled about: 'Tomatoes? You buggers live on snake and goanna at home, and you want bloody tomatoes here?' (They got them.) Walter first mustered on old Benmore in 1899.

I was eager to prove myself a good manager and when HJ asked me if I could shoot a horse, I modestly said I'd done a bit of it. In fact I'd shot hundreds of horses, but no one who's done it brags about it. It's no fun and I understand people, like HJ, who can't bring themselves to do it. On Glenaray I always seemed to be the horse executioner and for some unfathomable reason my services always seemed to be called upon around dusk. The stock agents bought up a lot of horses there for dog tucker when tractorisation, as the wireless in the 1950s put it, arrived. There'd be up to 50 turned out on the river at times. The musterers would herd them into a corner and I'd shoot one in the cross between its ears and eyes. Below that it's all cavities. Shooting two was tougher — after the first one dropped, the other would explode and the musterers couldn't hold it. When the dog-tucker herd got down to two or three, these intelligent animals knew the odds, and it was particularly difficult and unpleasant work. Botching a shot meant a galloping target, a heart shot, and I dropped one in these circumstances that turned tail over head at

Colin Gibson's horse's feet as he went to head it off. Colin had the most exaggerated Southland burr I've heard, painful to listen to after he'd had a fright. 'Birr Christrr, Snowrr boyrr, thatar wasar bitrr closerr forr comfort.' But in general I was good at it, and would rather shoot them myself than watch some poor bleeding-hearted fool bugger it up. My philosophy is that once an old horse begins to suffer, shoot it. There's too many Old Dobbins, who've perhaps given their sooky owners 10 or 13 years of service, out in swamps in winter, uncovered, with crook teeth, digestive problems or cancerous tumours on their lips.

As arranged with HJ I drove from Otamatapaio to Omarama and waited opposite a fenceline. It was a hot day. I fell asleep cradling the rifle. The outgoing manager of Omarama, Ian McKechnie, and his man later said it was a relief to see me jerk awake — they thought I'd done myself in when they came tearing up. But HJ's new Otamatapaio manager was simply embarrassed about being caught sleeping on the job. I plugged one horse and sighted on the second, wondering what all the yelling was about. 'Look out for Longview! Look out for Longview!' Nice heart shot. But Longview was a house, not a horse, directly in my line of fire. A .303 bullet doesn't travel far after entering a big animal like a horse, but it does if you miss . . .

I've told you my skinny white legs never saw the sun after my Gladesmuir days, but there was the exception of My Day on the Rugby Field. The Otamatapaio cow boy, Bob Williams, 16, was a keen footballer. When I watched him play I was never backward with my armchair criticism: 'Why didn't you pass to A?', 'You should've gone for a drop goal!', and 'How come you let B run all over you?' It must have annoyed him, because when I took him to his game in Omarama, and the local team was two players short, he saw his chance to call my bluff. 'The boss'll play; he's really good too.'

Someone once gave me this advice: 'If a bloke offers you a whisky, you might as well make it a big one. If he likes you, he won't care; and if he doesn't, it'll be your last anyway.' The way I figured it, if you were doing the rugby team a favour, you should be able to pick your position. As fullback, if the team was winning, there wouldn't be much to do and little danger; and if they were losing, they wouldn't care. But Jimmy Hemera, the other ring-in, stood firm and wasn't about to give up his favourite position. I was on the wing. My opposite number was a contract fencer.

The post driver was still a thing of the future and he was a 15-stone ball of muscle. Think Jonah Lomu. He got the ball and I went in for The Tackle. When I stopped bouncing I just had time to see him dot the ball down between the goalposts. As he passed me coming back, he said, 'Sorry, old chap, hope I didn't hurt you.' Whenever he got the ball after that, I found something to do elsewhere, and I had to be helped over fences for two days afterwards. I still wasn't right on the third day. I officially retired from rugby after that. But it was a rare triumph, worthy of recording somewhere in the annals of the game: in 40 minutes each end, in a high-scoring game, I only got one knee dirty.

CHAPTER TWELVE

HJ's Man in the Waitaki

The inquest was held on Sunday on the body of the late Mr Thomas Middleton, late manager of Benmore and Station Peak stations, who was drowned while crossing the Waitaki River, when a verdict was returned that the deceased had met his death by the kick from a horse, there being evidence to show that although found in the river, death ensued from a blow to the head. The river was low at the time. He was leading one horse and riding another when the accident occurred.

> North Otago Times, 8 July 1900. *This was the most unlikely official explanation for a death many maintained for years was foul play. Lake Middleton was so named after this man rode across it when the lake was frozen.*

IN MY FIRST DAYS ON OMARAMA STATION I WAS FILLING IN THE DROP dunny for the shearers' hut and cutting a new one, thinking of old Charles Patterson's words at Gladesmuir about being the manager of a big place and my own splendid vision. Where was the bloody chestnut with the white socks and the men to do this and do that? A parson visited me in the middle of these thoughts. 'Do you want to go to church, son?'

'Aw, no, I don't think so.'

'You'll find, Bill, if you get to know the Lord, he'll point you to new things in life.'

'Well, if he points me away from this bloody business, I might be only too pleased to meet him.'

That was the end of our pastoral association.

Let me show you around Omarama. The manager's house was on a hillock overlooking the road to the entrance, easy walking to the township, school, pub and general store, and if you think that's average, you've never lived in the high country. The house was old, warm, cosy and comfortable, about the best house in the district.

There were a Dutch couple there, the Molders, Johann (dubbed John) and his wife, and a single bloke, Keith McAughtrie. Keith was a top man, a dedicated shepherd you could trust, and we worked as mates for 10 years until he got a job managing Rostriever down Otematata way, where he remained even after his retirement. One attractive aspect of station employment was that accommodation and a high proportion of food was supplied: you were, in high-country speak, 'found'.

The Molders didn't like the new management — which they were entitled to do. They had no car and John asked for a £400 advance to get one. I told them I had no authority, would have to put it to HJ and that it could be a bit delicate if they and I should have a row. I thought they had no show. Keith McAughtrie's request for an advance of £1000 to on-lend to a mate to set up a beekeeping operation had been turned down flat. And McAughtrie had mustered Otamatapaio every year for little more than points on his scoreboard at the Pearly Gates, so had more call on HJ than the Molders.

HJ often turned up on the odd weekend at Omarama to discuss things. We called these visits 'Special Sundays'. At one such he surprised me by agreeing to John's request. John paid it off, went for a holiday, called in to see HJ in Dunedin, quit, and said he'd lined up another Dutch couple for his and his wife's old job. HJ saw the new couple's three years of marriage without issue as a distinct advantage: no changes were likely to be required in existing accommodation. When HJ put it to me as an almost done deal without my involvement, I was sour. I fizzed, and blew into him.

'Well, you've got to be the boss. I understand you have meals with the men?' he said. I didn't want to leave my main point for this new one.

'Yeah, and I don't want to do it differently. Look, if you interview them and send them up, I'm just the pannikan boss, not the one who controls the storeroom.'

Graham Wardell, who was travelling with HJ, said, 'Bill's right, Dad.'

'Keep out of this, Graham. All right. You come to Dunedin and interview them. Come to my flat. I'll be there.'

'You're doing it again, Dad. Why should you be there?'

'All right. At the store.'

RB Dennison's ex-delivery boy felt a wee bit grand sitting in HJ's leather chair behind the desk in the big glass office on the raised dais of Wardells Grocers, cleared of typists and watched with acute interest by 40 counter-jumpers wrapping parcels and bustling about. Only there was no ashtray. A fair Dutch couple entered and I forgot about Dutch plots against the sovereign state of New Zealand. Fred Hondelink's recent history included timber felling and Cadbury Fry Hudson's factory. He'd never milked a cow and Liedavei had not really cooked, but what the hell? They could learn. We gave it a go.

The Molders had a baby and another on the way. When the furniture truck disgorged one load and ate another, we learned Lied was pregnant. She was to have four in time. I mentioned the forthcoming arrival to HJ on a Special Sunday. 'Omigod! Sorry, Bill. I'm really sorry. Man'll need a periscope for interviews next.' Fred had endured a hell of a time in a slave camp in the war. He must have liked Omarama because when he retired, he stayed there.

It is a fascinating place. The first Paheka in the Waitaki (which means Noisy Water in Maori) found hapu or subtribes living from the coast to Omarama (Place of the Moon or Light) and the lakes, but many fewer apparently than there had been in the past. Warfare with North Island raiding parties and among themselves, and measles brought by sealers from Sydney, had taken a fearsome toll. The Araiteuru canoe wrecked at Shag Point was said to be their New Zealand landfall and there's evidence of occupation (sharks' teeth, moa skulls, flake tools of foreign rock, dog bones) by moa hunters back to the ninth century as far inland as Ohau. Rock paintings under overhangs of limestone and clay still exist. Nor were they the only moa hunters about: the Haast eagle, the world's largest bird of prey with talons the size of a tiger's claws and an attack weight equal to a dropped concrete building block, flew out of those mountains then. There was a greenstone trade route to the West Coast through Haast via the Ahuriri River and Lindis Pass.

It has generally been held in the district that the Maori were evicted because their dogs were 'worrying' — killing — sheep, but a powerful chief and tohunga, Te Maiharoa from around Temuka, always maintained that he and only he could sign over land to the Crown, and he had not done so. The government's collection of signatures were, he claimed, worthless. But Paheka settlers had been there 20 years by then, the government had granted Maori land near Wanaka, and mounted police settled it. Drays, wagons and spring carts took away 140 people, including the ailing Te Maiharoa, along with 100 horses and 100 dogs. £300 000 since paid to the Kai Tahu Trust Board has settled the matter.

Bush rangers, including a Kelly-type gang, roamed there during the goldrush era, holding up hotels for liquor and shepherding gangs for purses for a short period. Some were hanged for worse crimes.

People say of Omarama: 'Nothing but merinos, matagouri and Munros.' The Waitaki Munros are descendants of Mrs WG Munro, who owned the Otematata Hotel, and received an award from the Church of England for her assistance to the Omarama Maori. Walter and May Cameron, the Aubrey family and the Andersons contributed to the gene pool early in the district's paheka history, and those names litter the phone books and land office files today.

Graham Wardell and I visited Todhunter's up the Rakaia in Canterbury to look at rams one blizzardy day in 1956. Afterwards I coughed dryly just before the Methven pub. Graham, sharp bloke, said: 'You've got a cold coming on. We'll stop for a drink.' We had quite a few whiskies, then plugged away home. I went to sleep against the car-window jamb.

Next morning I rolled a cigarette but didn't get to light up. It fell from my mouth the instant it went in. I felt crook, and blamed Scotland. But a rabbiter called that evening and said, 'What's happened to you?'

'I'm not too good.'

'You've got Bell's palsy.'

It is amazing what you don't see in a mirror if you're not looking for it. On close inspection I saw one side of my face had dropped. I had a lazy left eye, which proved permanent.

Heat treatment helped a lot, but it's no fun seeing a moth at a yard and being unable to close your slack jaw. I tried a hook in the corner of my mouth that hung from my ear like specs, but it was no advance at all. Lost my whistle, disconcerting my dogs. While I should've taken to bed as ordered, it came back a lot of the way after a couple of months. The bloke called Pirate in childhood finally looked the part.

'What's wrong with your eye, Mr Kerr?' kids would ask.

'Well, I shot so many deer over the years, my left eye got permanently half-closed from shutting it to look down the sights.'

I was to find advantage in negotiation, investigation and interrogation in that left eye. It'd close off a bit and if I wanted to clinch a point, check if someone was telling the truth or increase the pressure in my quest for answers, I'd fix my left eye on the subject. Flicking it wide open with a forefinger helped too. It was my 'steely blue'.

Life went on. Tussock burns well — too well sometimes. Donald Ross, local runholder, was helping with some burning out Ohau way when he got trapped in a tussock fire. Four dogs died that day and he was badly burned about the hands, ears and nose, needing surgery. You wouldn't pick it today, though: great grafting. If he'd been wearing a nylon shirt or socks, or wearing shorts, he'd have been dead, but his woollen shirt and longs saved him.

I got a taste of how he must have felt when I was burning Glen Creek over Cuthbert. I tried to catch my personal horse, Mickey, but he was playing hard to get, so I saddled up Dick, a big dumb white-faced half-draught. I didn't obey the laws as I'd intended; the idea was to ride to the headwaters and drop matches peacefully as I rode back. A side gully, heavily overgrown with a lot of ground matagouri, which burns like a witch, annoyed me, so I dropped a few matches in there first and went back to the plan. Fire noise made me look up and a wall of flame was ahead of me — the fire had consumed the side gully and snuck around in front of me. I looked about. There was fire on three sides and if I'd had Mickey I might have had a show of making it up the basin, into a saddle and out. One look at Dick and I knew that was hopeless. But Dick had a big long tail, so I tied that in a love knot. The fire was roaring up to a patch of silver tussock, which doesn't burn as high as snow tussock. I took a collar off a dog, climbed on Dick and larrapped him downhill into it, commanding the dogs to follow. Not many horses would've gone through that, but dumb Dick did. The blood in my temples throbbed like hell as I rode on a last gasp of air through the oxygen-free zone. On the burnt ground on the other side the dogs flattened themselves and put their paws over their eyes like huskies in snow. Dick coughed and tears literally streamed from his eyes. It'd been seconds, but that burnt ground and blue sky looked good, the air sweet. I sat on a rock and rolled a smoke, apologising to Dick for ever calling him dumb.

Harry Wardell had a sense of perspective and was a gentle, tolerant, patient man, despite his foibles and miserly attitude to the addition of small children to his 'found' bill and building costs. Never saw him do his block. He was up from Dunedin and we'd been mustering wethers off the Range all day. Rain clouds threatened. He always kept a couple of dogs at Omarama, Romp and Tweed. 'I'll keep an eye on the sheep and the shed,' he said. 'You go put your feet up.' For a kid, there's a bit of glamour to the muster, and it had touched my four-year-old Billy. When a few spits heralded the downpour to come, HJ looked around for Tweed but couldn't find him. You need a barking dog to yard sheep and you can't shear them wet — an emergency loomed. Then Billy went by with Tweed on a string, ready to rope 'em, tie 'em, brand 'em, yippee-yii-yoo, cowboy.

'Where are you going, Billy?'

'Out the Range. Mustering.'

'Aw, Billy, I don't like the look of the weather. I think you'd better do it tomorrow. Better lend me that dog.' That 'lend' said a lot about Harry Wardell.

If I needed confirmation by contrast it came in Dunedin in the mid-1950s when I was invited into Wright Stephenson's boardroom, along with other growers, for drinks during a wool boom. Bill Elliot from Glenlappa walked in with his head shepherd, and he and I talked about dog men. He was talking of a shepherd he knew: 'He'll be good, gentle bloke, won't knock your sheep about at gates and that . . .' Suddenly Elliot cut in: 'A bloody sight better'n you were,' nodding at me.

War had been declared.

'And do you pay him 30 shillings a week too, Bill?'

The stock agency manager must have known more than I did because he had a hell of a time hiding his mirth from Elliot.

HJ's consideration extended to adults. Des Polson was our shearing contractor on Omarama Station. I heard he'd lost his cook before he was due there and had employed a nubile young stunner. Mrs HJ heard too and, worried about a young woman around shearers' quarters, communicated her concerns to HJ, who duly passed them on to me. Meanwhile, everything was proceeding as planned for the Otamatapaio shearing and Des said he'd be on Omarama after Christmas. 'Full gang?' The local grapevine had been twitching with gossip.

'Yes.'

'Cook?' I'd heard the cook was pregnant.

'Yes.'

'Sure she'll be back?'

'Guarantee it. I'm the father. Actually, I'll need to slip off to Kurow for a day. We're getting married.'

The account of the following conversation comes from Eric Boyle, who was bending over a ram on the board at Otamatapaio at the time. Des started the ball rolling: 'Oh, HJ, a word. Could I get a day off on 7 January?'

'Heavens, Des! The sheep have been hanging around long enough as it is. Do you have to?' Des off the board a day meant at least 100 more unshorn, later cut out perhaps, greater risk to the stock and more cost.

'Well, I'm getting married.'

'Then we'll have to let you go!'

'Can Tom have the day off too?' Potential delay odds doubled.

'Is that necessary?'

'Best man.'

'Oh, I see. Certainly.'

'And the cook?'

'Oh, goodness . . .'

'She's the bride.' Harry agreed and left the shed, then returned.

'Des, you've taken us by storm. You'll need a double bed in the cookhouse.'

'Aw, it's a bit late for that now, HJ.'

Ima lent her wedding ring for the ceremonials, the show went off well, and a top high-country marriage resulted.

Foibles make for better stories than sound management, and I'd better put the record straight on HJ. He had a knack of keeping the pressure on managers to perform, and he brought town business practices to the back country. The latter was in some ways unfortunate, but it was probably inevitable. I crossed some Hereford cows with an Aberdeen bull and produced about 100 black calves with creamy faces during a tough time for prices. I thought we'd get £20 for them, but Harry was sceptical. A local, Ted Williamson, agreed to a forward sale at £20 and his agent was to turn up with a sale note regarding price, numbers, delivery and so on. But HJ said Ted was 'only a dealer' and the calves would 'lose their identity'. I focused on the price and security, felt Harry and Ted must've fallen out over Wool Board politics somehow. We eventually sent them to the Studholme sale in South Canterbury and topped it with £16. We lost £400 but Omarama cattle got a source identity. In running a business, sometimes cash is king, sometimes building a future. I know that now.

I didn't get much R&R on Omarama, but I did shoot up the Ahuriri to get a feed of trout from time to time, precious time. One Saturday afternoon I dug up four clay worms, rare as the sooty stilt up there, and passed a car and caravan on the way to the riverbank, and again on the way back. The driver stopped alongside me, our windows both down, and asked, 'Been fishing?' I said I had, and he asked, 'How'd you go?' I jerked my head to two nice wet shiny bright-eyed rainbows, a four- and a six-pounder, alongside me. 'You mean to tell me you caught those in the half hour or so since I passed you?' I admitted this was true. 'What'd ya use?' I'd prudently taken the bare hook off the line and replaced it with a black minnow with white spots; the Ahuriri is an artificial bait stream — lures, minnows, store and workshop flies only.

On Tuesday I called into Collins' general store. Gunner's son Arthur asked: 'Been fishin' lately?' I said I had. 'Had a tourist in here. He bought all the minnows with white spots on them. Said a local had caught two fish in half an hour. Good sale.' High-country folk pull together, even inadvertently.

But you've got to do formal community things too. Which brings us to the weighty matter of education. In the 1960s I was on the school committee. Omarama Primary School needed only one teacher, but he or she wasn't always easy to find. The Education Department found us one once in a hurry and they couldn't have got it more right if they'd advertised nationally and conducted extensive interviews. Ima and I put Miss Govan up at the station homestead. She'd come out of retirement with her white-haired bun and firm ideas intact. Me, I had none, but Miss Govan put me right. 'Oh, no, Mr Kerr, I will need to be introduced to the parents and children. Good night.'

Well, I was up early and very tidy and a bit at sea. I drove her down to the school, and Percy Kelland, another committee member, was dropping his kids off and looked like getting away scot-free. There were kids screaming, running, acting up everywhere — bedlam. 'Hold on,

Percy. You've got to give me a hand with this. Miss Govan, Percy Kelland, committee member.'

'Hello, pleased to meet you. Well, I suppose we'd better get going. Where's the bell?'

'The bell? Percy, where's the bell?'

'Bell, ah, hmmm . . .' He didn't know either. Dorothy Kinder, one of the older kids, was passing by in a jet-stream. I grabbed her.

'Dorothy, where's the bell?'

'We haven't got a bell,' she said and went off to create chaos. The energy levels were too much for me: it was the worst lamb break I'd seen.

'No matter,' said Miss Govan, 'I'll get Old Faithful.' She produced a polished old cow horn and gave a blast. I'd only seen them used to imitate stags in the roar and provoke dopey sex-crazed stags to their doom. But Miss Govan's blast was as good for pulling up kids as any stock whistle was for a heading dog. 'Let's fall in, children.' Those high-country kids hurtled off to their classrooms; they'd never 'fallen in' in their lives. For Percy and me it was like another lamb break, but we mustered the little buggers. I did the introductions in the usual manner, not helped by a cheeky snotty-nosed Peter Menzies poking his tongue out and doing the devil's wiggle fingers, thumbs in his ears, little bugger. Then Miss Govan started talking to them, quietly at first and expecting more as she went along. The kids were spellbound; started standing up straighter when she said standing up straight was a good thing. She was the educational equivalent of Pinckney. I'm glad she never took up dog trialling; she'd have been a world beater. She coached the boys in rugby like it was the most normal thing in the world, and she had strong ideas about a halfback's role. But she was old and only helping out, and the Ed Department sent us a younger woman as an assistant, Wilma Blair.

Ima met Miss Blair as she stepped off the bus at Kurow. Wilma was a creature of the 1960s in the makeup of the moment, white-faced and full eyed, wearing a mini-skirt. Quite the antithesis of Miss Govan. Ima and I looked forward to hearing Miss Govan's view of Miss Blair when Wilma excused herself early, pleading a tiring day on the road, and went off to bed. We needn't have worried: 'Aren't the children going to be thrilled? She's *lovely*!' said Miss Govan, and meant every word of it.

Another assistant teacher arrived at a later date and called to see Ima. Omarama Station's electricity was generated on site and was DC. DC isn't as dangerous as AC but if it shorts, it's more spectacular. Ima brought the new teacher, Janet Wilkins, inside and introduced her to the figuring-it-out-as-he-went-along electrician, and they passed through to the lounge. I had a bit of a glance over my shoulder at her ankles. I must have touched something while distracted because there was a blue flash and a large number of volts went through my body. The end of my screwdriver melted. Janet's ankles were easily the hottest I've ever seen. In my life.

But work on the farm went on. The hardest day's work of my life wasn't on a hill, it was in a plane. Each time a new rabbit board pilot appeared I would fly with him to show him the boundaries and I had faith in all six in my time in the district. Scotty Fraser, rabbiter, came around one day and said something was killing my wethers in such-and-such a paddock. Turned out six of them had been trampled to death in a smother getting at a salt lick meant for a few rams. We had turned 1500 sheep out there, overlooking the salt factor and learning a lesson: land salt on ridges not valleys. When we had six tonne in 25-kilogram bags — to salt Mount St Cuthbert, a plane sure looked the easy option when packhorses were the alternative. Trouble is that when the plane is tilting down it's a titanic struggle to get a bag off the floor and when it tilts up the bag leaps near into your face. It's to do with gs, and they are buggers, whatever they are. I'm not a big sweater, but I was soaked that day. As to precision dropping, the one intended for a specific ridge along Old Man Gully bloody near hit the shearers' quarters over three kilometres from its target by the time I got it out the door.

In 1960 I got a phone call from Hector Munro who said he wanted to see me. Hector was an ex-rabbiter, ex-blade shearer who'd got two properties, Birdwood and a farm down on the flat. Hec was getting older, his son had a crook chest and Hec didn't want the boy getting crooker on Birdwood. He wanted to sell. Hard work was all Hec knew. He hadn't got off the place much. For example, he got on like a house on fire with one of Ima's Southland rellies, Will Hoffman, who fixed his old grandfather clock and they talked mysterious mechanical stuff. They both liked the gee-gees, the kind you put money on, and when Hoffman rang Hec about some nag, Hec told me, 'By Jesus, Bill, you wouldn't believe it. It was like I was talking to you.' It took me 15 seconds before I realised he'd never had a phone call from as far afield as Invercargill before. But he was far from stupid and he had a good point about selling Birdwood when he did.

He offered me the place. I've no doubt he'd have got more for it on the open market, but Hector wasn't like that. He wanted to give a bloke a go. What he asked me for the stock was fair and market value, but he sweetened the deal on the lease by leaving money in the place at a low interest rate. I gave him all the money I had, and it was a humbling experience. I paid him back in four years but was never in doubt about who was indebted to whom. Nor do I think he ever regretted his generosity.

CHAPTER THIRTEEN

Owner and Employee

The go-between wears out a thousand sandals.

Japanese saying

BIRDWOOD WAS 7000 ACRES, A DRY (NO BREEDING) LEASE WITH A limit of 1320 wethers on it. All shingle scree where the sun explodes the rock to bits, snow tussock on the dark sides. The Ahuriri River made the boundary for 12 kilometres and the top ridge made another. Casual musterers used to say the place was 'a paddock with its back up', but six hours out there and they changed their minds.

If the Birdwood run was to work well, HJ had to agree to keep me on at Omarama. The alternative was living at Birdwood in a house designed to accommodate workers who visited, not families who lived there, and take on casual mustering, dressmaking and knitting. It would have been a style of life not far removed from the nightmare days of the 1930s: a roof of sorts over our heads, itinerant work and taking what was going. We'd become accustomed to the big house, boarding schools and cash in our pockets.

I stayed at my mother's at Forbury Corner in Dunedin for the meeting with HJ at one of his flats.

'. . . so I propose to eye-clip Birdwood at Labour Weekend, shear after Christmas — when Omarama's cut out — during my fortnight holiday, and fall muster at Easter.'

Harry closed his eyes and leaned back. 'Sounds a viable proposition.'

'It's up to you,' I ventured.

He straightened up immediately. 'That's where you are entirely wrong,' fixing my eye. 'It's not up to me. As trustee, my job is to make sure you're earning the salary the trust pays you. *You* think you can do justice to Omarama Station. It's entirely up to you.'

Silence. 'In theory, I can do all that. In practice, if we find differently, I'll go.'

Then we had two whiskies, the only ones we ever shared. His daughter joined us and my new venture was explained. 'If you really want to make money up there,' she said, 'buy the hotel. Omarama's the crossroads of the tourism industry. It'll make a fortune some day.' Time proved her right. The breadth of vision she had imbibed with her mother's milk in that clever Quaker family and the talk from the town's hard Scots grandees had given her a formidable business brain. Groceries, wool, tourists: she could cover them all.

Back at Forbury Corner, Mum asked me bluntly, 'Did you win?'

The answer wasn't so easy. 'I got what I wanted, but I don't think I won.'

'There's an old saying, Bill: you can't serve two masters.' In one day two women had made spot-on predictions.

Meanwhile, I was on probation at Omarama.

Woolclasser Mick Griffin loved women. And he loved a drink. The more he drank, the more amorous he became, and if he didn't score, there'd be some other kind of trouble. After hearing of an incident where he was alleged to have had an inopportune ill-timed crack at the sister of a shepherd on another place, I decided it was prudent to have the wool-classer stay in the Omarama Station homestead. He could be fun. My policy while boss anywhere was simple: no booze on the board and anyone showing up for work under the influence or badly hung over was out; otherwise free time was free.

The shed cut out without incident and I suggested to Mick he stay with us over Christmas. He was okay and I wanted to keep him that way for the Birdwood wool table. But he couldn't. He was committed in Oamaru. His two lawn-proud sisters, hairdressers I think, needed some mowing done. That's what he said.

The night before the start, the shearers and rousies were all gathered. Paddy Mathias, in his sixties and not to be through with the blades for a good few years even then, would beautifully shear a steady 100 sheep a day regardless of his state of comfort or the heat of the day, and wrote 'woolfeller' on his IR5 tax form. Alec, from Timaru, would grin and tell of his continued bull virgin status when asked, as usual. Billy would work the press. A young townie relative would learn to pick up, starting on the morrow. But would Mick turn up?

A vehicle pulled up at 4 a.m., there were voices, and it departed. Mick walked in, blue with the booze. He'd been to the races and caroused in Oamaru that night, and travelled over 100 kilometres by taxi to the end of a dirt track the driver must have thought was still the land of the moa hunter.

'Thought you weren't coming.'

'Hell, Bill. Would I let you down?' He was aghast I'd even raised the subject.

'Get your sisters' lawns cut?'

'Get off my back. Christ, you're as bad as them. On and bloody on . . . Bloody lawns.' Took a while, but I got the story. He was gonna mow them, and gonna mow them, but his social life over Christmas was pressing. One night he came home from the pub, they niggled, and he pulled up the blind in a grand flourish.

'They're getting mowed now. *See?*'

A billy goat was tethered on their verdant suburban swathe. Mick had paid a bloke a quid for the loan of it.

When we settled up, I asked how much the taxi had cost. £5. He was off to Australia the next day, so I slung him an extra £5. If I had known he was to leave Omarama in a private chartered plane for Oamaru I might have thought twice, but he probably didn't know then either. Not a planner, but a likeable rogue.

In Oamaru later I visited my cousin Hec Kerr at Knight Motors. At the races I discovered Mick had said he was skint and had to get up to 'your cousin's for the shearing', so Hec had lent him £5 for the fare. And Mick paid it back on his return from Australia.

Ian Anderson's portly but physically powerful brother Duncan had a terrific sense of humor, but he had a short fuse, especially when working and things went wrong on the job.

Duncan had two places, Bog Roy and Peak Valley, with the Ahuriri

River between them. A swingbridge crossed the river, about 4 metres above the normal surface flow. The bridge had on- and off-ramps, a pulley system to pull the bridge up during the spring melt or when the nor'wester made it swing about, forcing pens like a funnel on the Peak Valley side, holding pens on the Bog Roy side, and just enough shoulder room for one sheep to pass at a time. A nervy sheep could block the passage of bold ones, but Peak Valley's ewes were used to it; stragglers, however, thought it worse than the Luna Park Ghost Train when they smelled water under them.

To calm the nervy, a decoy would be tied up on the Bog Roy side, and a shepherd called 'the catcher' would run up, slip a lead over her and pull her across, or step over her, kick her bum and go *maa–maa*. Other shepherds on the shingle riverbanks below poked their 'crooks' through the slats, but over water the catcher was on his own. Ian was tops at it.

But Ian was off chasing a racehorse one hot muster, and Dunc was catcher. Pretty soon he'd stripped to his singlet and jockeys, and was irritable. A nor'wester swayed the slack bridge and there were stragglers, perhaps 200 or 300 of them, peppered throughout the mob. Sheepish nervousness was sending Dunc into a huge rage. He was driven to a simple solution: check the eartags and if they weren't Peak ewes, up and over with them. The two blokes below were astonished when the first ones hit the drink. Until he exhausted himself, it fair rained sheep.

His new wife, Dinah, a former receptionist and PR woman from a big city hotel, arrived with a picnic lunch just as Duncan was reaching Richter scale readings with the ramp mechanism, which wouldn't budge. She kindly offered to go and get three fishermen she'd spotted to give him a hand.

The shortest of the fishermen patiently explained to Duncan how the pulley–ramp system worked and what he should do. 'That's what I've been trying to do, you know-it-all little man, for the last bloody half-hour!' thundered Duncan. Dinah cancelled lunch and retired from the scene. We cried with laughter and for want of a camera.

The humour of it all wasn't lost on Duncan, either. When he relaxed at the end of that day he was in stitches as the gang relived highlights from their various vantage points. 'What was going through your mind, Dunc?' 'Jasus, Dunc, I thought you were going to clock that bloke . . .' Duncan was a big man in more ways than one.

When the MOW dammed Benmore in 1965, drowning the bridge forever, the lake cut access from the Bog Roy side. Dunc was compensated with an old house and woolshed and some acres at the Ohau end of Peak Valley. Sheep now needed to be mustered north, not south. Dunc organised eight men and 48 dogs to do it in a day, instead of the old two-day routine. After a 1 a.m. breakfast we launched off from a spot near the dam, me drawing the short straw with the lakeside beat. The lake had drowned the sandy flats where sheep used to travel with ease, and the sheep hadn't had time to stamp out sheep tracks. It was a long difficult muster made worse by a lot of woolblind sheep. I carried dagging shears and must have clipped 100 lambs that day. Dunc didn't go on the hill; his job was to drive a circuitous route through Omarama and meet us on the Ohau branch of the new lake.

'Well done, lads, come to camp and I'll shout,' he said when he got there. He pulled a two-dozen crate from his vehicle and immediately started swearing. An old Scotsman on his place had a bugger of a habit of replacing crown tops on empties. So much for a beer. He had a feed of tongue and bread for us, he'd thought, but he'd opened the tins before he came out to greet us and his dogs had helped themselves to a rare delicacy. But we tuckered and boozed at Bog Roy and I got back home 24 hours after I'd left, to wake up hung over when Duncan phoned. How could he improve the operation? 'Give it back to the Maori, if they'll have it. Failing that, set up a grindstone on the hill so we can sharpen our bloody shears.' And hung up.

On 17 May 1978 at a sunny spot where he often pulled over to read, halfway between his mailbox and his house, Duncan died peacefully, newspaper spread over the steering wheel of his Land Rover, well past his three score and ten. There was a service in Kurow. Duncan would have loved his funeral. Rick and Ben from up the Lindis were running late, so called on Dave, the helicopter pilot, for a lift. On the way over the pass the old deer hunter, Dave, hugged the valleys of Mount St Cuthbert, flushed out two deer and shot them. He gutted and beheaded them. 'Where can I leave these in the shade for a few hours?' he asked the mourners. Ben, a dry boy, said, 'What about in that woolshed down there? It won't be used today.' Dunc's woolshed most certainly wouldn't be.

No churchgoer, Duncan had not made the acquaintance of the local Dutch minister, so newly arrived he'd only buried one local bloke, a roadworker, before. He spent time with Dunc's son Bruce to get a handle on the man. He told the mourners '. . . Duncan loved his dogs and his dogs loved him . . .' at one stage. 'He was no saint . . . he loved his whisky, his gambles and his . . .' and then he ran out of material. We cringed, everyone remembering Dunc's alkathene hose and temper tantrums with 'stupid sheep!' The poor parson went on to say Duncan had died the way he would've wanted it, 'with his boots on'.

Arguable. Ten years before, brother Ian had coerced Duncan and me into mustering a small block on Ben Omar. Afterwards, at the house, Dunc took his boots off his poor tortured feet, threw them in the back of the car, and said, 'There, you shits, I'll never wear you again.' And he didn't.

After his body was piped from the church there was a private cremation in Timaru, so we moved to the Kurow Hotel to farewell him the way he would have wished.

Men who breakfast at 3 a.m. and the women who live with them look idiosyncratic foibles square in the eye. They have to. City folk pick their friends from a big box, can arrange themselves to show their best sides. High-country folk see each other in the round, working and playing together with a smaller cast on, in some ways, a more restricted stage. In the case of the Andersons, Scottish Presbyterianism, however far from ideal in practice, was not a flinching code. Humour is vital, tough-minded and generous up there.

A pallbearer recalled the preacher's words on Dunc's love of dogs: 'Christ, remember the time Dunc's Jack sat down at Haka?' *Everyone* remembered that. It was a legend, a community possession, after it travelled down phone lines, across tables at the Omarama pub, drifted from one bed to another in a dark hut, was heard for the tenth time — with pleasure — in a booth at a dog trial. A lot of people thought they'd seen it, forgetting they weren't there after a bit. Of course I saw it.

Inexplicably, unimaginably, heartbreakingly, Jack had sat down yards from the top set at the end of an undoubtedly top run at the dog trials, with his tongue out and his head to one side like the His Master's Voice dog on old records, snatching defeat from the jaws of victory.

Dunc rumbled. All the berserk fury of an earthquake was rising, but there was little he could do on the grounds. He tumbled Jack and his wife Dinah in his car, drove home rumbling, stopped in his garage, dispatched

Dinah to the house and closed the doors. Then he gave Jack a round or two with a metre of alkathene hose.

Ian called in a bit later and Dinah said mildly over a drink, 'If you are going to behave like that again, Duncan, I won't go to any more dog trials with you.' Dunc's eyes glazed over. Ian reported later: 'I thought Dinah was going to be going around the kitchen table with three foot of alkathene after her.'

Back at the trials next day Dunc's Jack came second. The story was related at the wake, again. Laughter, even amid grief.

'Gidday, WV, how are you, old chap?' Dave, the pilot, a big man in a bushshirt, came over with a triple-header. 'I got you a drink.' Dave was a venison hunter, one of the oldest, boldest and best in New Zealand. Dave's research office was the Anywhere Public House. He'd find a landholder, say he'd flown over the man's property, and say how the bloke's sheep were the biggest and best in the district. He would ply the victim with triple-headers from a big roll of notes in his old bushshirt pocket, then casually ask, 'Any animals around?' Victim's tongue, loosened by whisky and flattery, would wag: 'Saw six in Dead Man's Gully.' Dave would have the six deer on hooks before the victim was out of his warm bed to greet his hangover. That was his living. On the day of the wake Dave asked how I was settling in, down country. 'All right, but I miss a feed of venison. Can you get me one?'

'Hell, WV, animals are hard to get now.'

True, too. Deer are now rarely seen in the Upper Waitaki. 'How much for your copter, deerwise?'

'One for you, two for me.'

'Could you,' I said quietly so we'd not be overheard by my fellow funeral-goers, 'get three out of 18? I saw a mob while I was mustering this week.' A telepathic message must have gone out, because Dave's shooter, Tim, was at my side within seconds, and I didn't see Dave blink.

'WV's got 18 lined up. He wants one of them. We'll go now.'

'Go to hell, Dave. You've been boozing.' Did he fizz! He angrily told me deer were his living. Easily convinced, I slipped out of the pub with them. At the copter Tim pulled overalls over his suit and we lifted off over the gully where I'd seen the deer. I thought I'd enjoy the shoot as a spectator in the middle seat, but Dave flew to a knob clear of snow and said, 'Get out, WV.' Seconds later they were off, and I was in a suit lighting a cigarette with their fuel cans for company, 10 or 12 nips of whisky circulating through my body at 4000 feet above sea level. I sat on a dry rock in the warm sunshine. This was hunting as it should be. Four reports and Dave dropped a fat young stag at my feet. My deer. Then he flew back for the other three. 'What about a bit of wild pig?' I said.

'Where?'

I pointed out some country, but said we wouldn't be able to hang around as the landholder was touchy. They flew off again, struck fog, went down to inspect some pig rootings and nine deer turned up. Tim shot the lot, head shots, and started dressing the carcasses. Dave flew back to pick me up. 'Got a job for you. We'll put the deer in that wool-shed. You hook 'em up to the strops.' I thought he was going to squash me and I dropped the strop and ran — the whisky and courage had worn off, and you try being calm with half a tonne of metal hovering a metre or so above you. But the second attempt was successful.

'I'm too old for this, Dave,' I opined. He agreed, but our commiserations were brought to an end when 10 deer showed up on the saddle we were flying through. 'Look, Dave!' The machine spun around back to Tim, Dave dropped me off, and set off with Tim on the skids. A barrage of shots and they had the lot. By the time the dressing was done, fog was rolling in and light was fading, so we left the deer to be picked up at first light. We had to follow the road to get back to Kurow, and my thoughts were of the pylons thereabouts. Tim washed up in a water-race.

We walked into a hotel still full of liquored-up mourners; nobody had noticed we'd gone. It wasn't a good funeral, it was a great one. Dave and Tim shot two more deer on the way out next day: 25, their best daily tally ever; mine too. I got home well reinforced, courtesy of Dave's roll of notes, and bragged endlessly to Ima about how I hadn't lost my old hunter's instincts, but that was my last hunting trip.

My deer duly arrived and was beautiful eating. There was only one thing wrong with it: I couldn't share it with Duncan Anderson.

CHAPTER FOURTEEN

Squire of Dunstan Peaks

paddock: *n.* **1.** A small field or enclosure; esp. one for horses adjoining a house or stable . . .

Shorter Oxford English Dictionary

paddock: *n.* **1.** A piece of land of any size marked off by a fence or natural boundary; a field large or small . . .

Oxford Dictionary of New Zealand English,
ed. H. W. Orsman, 1997

O UR PURCHASE OF DUNSTAN PEAKS PROCEEDED THROUGH THE financial hoops in 1964 okay but Aunt Nell went through a wrench before Arthur put his foot down and insisted she pack and go. The Kerr family holed up at Birdwood, which I retained, for six weeks while the squire and his consort sorted out their departure. Nell wasn't the only one with misgivings. Our young Johnny had urged a compromise: we should continue to live at Omarama Station, close to his mates around the township, MOW employees' kids and others, and 'just own' Dunstan Peaks. He had never bussed to school before, rare for high-country farmers' kids.

When changeover day came, Nell whispered to us in her — our — driveway: 'Look in the linen cupboard.' When only their dust on the road was visible we raced to the linen cupboard. A map of a goldmine Arthur had secretly worked? What? It was a bottle of Famous Grouse whisky with a note: 'For the new squire of Dunstan Peaks.' It tasted fine and a number of toasts were drunk that very night. I was just on 40, with a big patch of high country, 13 000 acres — 21 000 with Birdwood — all my own (if you didn't count rapacious banks and suspicious stock firms).

I'd dreamed of this and had laid my plans. I'd improve or replace a lot of the buildings, and in a year or so make good my oft-quoted principle that a high-country station should supply itself from what grew or grazed on it. This meant painting and papering the house in the first year, building its big equipment sheds, henhouses, dog motels — my first experiment with fresh running water constantly available and pens on a clean concrete surface with untied dogs, hay barns, fences and water-races.

Arthur's cowbail was a bugger of a thing down on the freezing flats and his cows had warty tits, so I sold the cows, bought one new one and built a new high dry bail. The new cow calved in the paddock; the time had come to get her used to life as a house-milk producer. This happened during the five o'clock rush — a little management technique of mine, long practised. The idea is that as the working day closes, you and everyone around you put on a last spurt and achieve something extra for the day. Billy and I decided — well, I decided — we'd milk the cow before we went in. First we had to get her into the bail. I twisted her tail while Billy grunted on a rope tied around her neck, but the fiddle-faced big sheila wouldn't budge. I got sick of it, called for the old Ferguson tractor, threaded the rope through the bail and hooked her up. She spread her legs in the soft soil and wet grass — we'd just irrigated the paddock — and baulked. The Fergie's wheels spun uselessly for a while, but the tail twisting eventually got her in.

I was unshaven and wearing an old beekeeper's sunhat next day when a shiny car with 'Norwood' on it pulled up and discharged a shiny bloke who started on about fuel capacity, compressions and horsepower. Don't care much for machines, never have. Bores me stupid, and I knew I must be looking the part of the local yokel that day. 'Never mind horsepower, son. What's its cowpower?' He must have thought he had a right rural idiot. I explained that the old Fergie wasn't even one cowpower. A carpenter on the roof had seen all and knew what I meant. I bought nothing from Norwoods, but two second-hand Fordsons from Southland proved necessary in time.

Tractorpower wasn't all we lacked. Derek Wootton was gathering opinions about the gold bracelet he had bought for his wife on their twenty-fifth wedding anniversary, and asked what I'd got Ima for ours. I told him: a new cowbail with a nice concrete slab floor, easterly door for sunlight, brand spanking new bucket and a nice stool she could sit on. He seemed perplexed and asked how she had liked it. 'Good,' I said. 'So would you if you'd been milking in that cold old draughty bugger of a thing she used to have.' I have to put up with a lot of stupid questions, don't know why.

I had a new set of neighbours and Brian Waldron was one of them. He was always busy when I was mustering and didn't come out, and I was always busy when he was and did. One muster I borrowed a mare from him for Ken Anderson to ride, not a top horse but a plodder. Ken and I set off along the boundary fence near Brian's house with 1500 wethers; the rest of the gang had gone home. Ken reckoned a visit to Brian was in order and we'd get a beer. Brian had whisky and gin, but no beer. Ken, a long fellow, loved a long beer. After Brian had disappeared from sight we were joined by a two-year-old stallion squealing on the other side of the fence. He'd been born with a twisted front leg and should have been put down. Brian's mare was in season. High-country musterers are always looking for something to brighten their day so when we'd put the sheep through the gate onto the road, the tightest, best provisioned paddock on any station, Ken suggested Brian might like a foal, seeing he didn't have a beer. Ken whipped the saddle off the mare and the stallion mounted in seconds. A foal was cooking. When her state was obvious, I generously lent Brian my top horse to take her place in the fall muster, but that part was easy.

Brian found the mare on her side with her newborn standing beside her one morning and put through a panic call to the vet in Oamaru, 140 kilometres away. The old girl was clearly unwell. Equestrian George Innes, who owned and rode the Horse of the Year at one time, was the local authority on everything, so he was called over in the meantime, but the mare died. They took an old trotting hack, Berry, to decoy the foal to the yards and tied it up. The vet when he arrived suspected poisoning and wanted a sample for a possible compensation claim. As he walked past Berry, a horse that'd never kicked in its life, he tripped and fell at Berry's heels with a clatter of instruments. Berry kicked him on the jaw and knocked him out. George and Brian carried his limp frame to the house and called the doctor in Kurow, 60 kilometres down the road. The vet came to, minus two teeth, and the doctor was about to leave when

Innes said to Brian's heavily pregnant wife, Odell, 'Honey, you might as well drop your bundle while the doctor's here and the day'll be complete.' The mare had died from 1080 poison dropped accidentally from an aircraft flying to a neighbouring place. Brian was duly compensated, but our humour had fallen flat. The foal was taken in by some horse-lovers.

At the Hakataramea — 'Haka' locally   dog trials, I got a visit from Graham Wardell and his shepherd, Russell Black. They'd been fencing up the Haka Valley and called to ask me to hook up Russell's trailer. Russell wanted to stay and get a run at the trial; Graham to get away home to Otamatapaio. After the trial a very hungry Russell and I called on the publican: 'Meals on?'

'No.'

'Pie?'

'No.'

'Sandwich?'

'No.'

'Food?'

Russell was clearly exasperated. A young couple camping nearby overheard this and the wife offered to cook a feed, but was short of food. Russell tried the publican again: 'Sausages — raw's fine.' He even offered to pay double but the publican wasn't having a bar of it. 'I've got a new cook. The scrap bin used to be that high, now it's only a quarter that. She's too valuable to lose. I'm not buggerising her kitchen around.'

I'd had enough, and said to the guy beside me, 'Put out your hand,' and played at reading his palm and fate. Sure enough, the publican came up like a rainbow trout to a fly. 'Do you read palms?' I became shy about it, but admitted a little success. 'Read mine,' and his mitt came across like a jag-hooked one. I nudged Russell, who slid away from his seat, and I fell into a deep reverie over the publican's palm. 'Mmmm, very serious. Don't think we'll carry on with this.'

'Why not?'

'Are you married?' He was. 'Got children?' He had. 'Have you got insurance? Cos if you haven't you should get some.' I hinted someone was coming to a bad end, and he leaned over further. When Russell got back empty-handed, disappointing me somewhat as I'd thought he was goer, I pulled the plug on the charade.

Russell and I tumbled into the ute at closing time. He had to shift my kea gun getting in and said, 'Licensed Pommie bugger. We should put one in his roof before we go.' Kea guns make a hideous amount of noise, so the publican wouldn't have been the only one to jump. I know I did. I took off! Heavy — very heavy — scotch fog about. 'Take it easy, WV,' said Russell.

'We'll be right. I'll just put one wheel each side of the white line and we'll do about 20 miles per hour. Fair go, though, if we could have had some food.' We crawled over the Haka Bridge.

'Fancy a bit of Tegel chicken?' A drumstick appeared in front of me. 'All right?'

'Good,' I said.

'Like some cheese?' Sure enough. 'Sweets?' We had a pottle of fresh strawberries, no cream though. 'We'll wash it down with a bottle of Bavarian beer.'

Morals crept in after a while. 'WV, don't get me wrong. I'm not a thief, but that publican, he had to have it the hard way, he wouldn't have the easy way, the honest way.' Then he smiled like a cherub. 'Imagine him now, counting all them notes, saying to his barmen how it was the best day they'd had in a long time. "C'mon, me lads, we'll have a snack in the kitchen. I've got a nice chicken out there." But, he had to have it the hard way.' We wove on.

A fencer's car was parked by the side of the road on the Otematata saddle. 'Stop, WV. That's Dennis's car. He might've broken down or something.' We both went up, concerned about road safety, but Dennis was quite safe in the arms of his girlfriend in the back seat. On the nest, in fact, and less than keen on visitors. 'Are you all right, Dennis?' Dennis got a hell of a fright.

'Yeah, yeah.'

'You've got a big job on there, Dennis. Have a bit of chicken.' But Dennis didn't want any so we crept off into the night.

The responsible owner of Dunstan Peaks Station woke up next morning with four things on his mind: breaking and entering, discharging a firearm in a built-up area, receiving stolen goods and drunk in charge of a motor vehicle, to wit a green Mainline ute, very distinctive.

But it wasn't all beer and skittles. In the high country where the people are few and the tasks many, you've got to do your community bit. In addition to the committee of the primary school my kids attended I chose soil conservation.

I've changed my mind about a lot of things over the years, and I now regret cutting down the lilac tree in the garden at Omarama Station. It was in the road a bit but we could've lived with the tiny detour. It was the kids saying, 'Look, that's where the lilac tree used to be' that brought home the fact that the place had lost something loved and beautiful. To the kids. And to me. From then on I have resisted the temptation to cut down trees and bush wherever it could be avoided.

This new nature-loving consciousness does not extend to tussock, which I believe should be routinely burned and should be burned over big rather than small areas. The trend to containing tussock fires to small areas is self-defeating if minimising erosion is the name of the game. When the fresh sweet green shoots fed by the tussock-ash nutrients spring up, the sheep go for them. If the burn-off area is small their hooves and teeth hammer soil and plant, but if the area is large enough sheep spread over it more thinly.

Ken Anderson was turned down for a permit to burn on Peak Valley and his case came up for arbitration. The soil conservation authority of the day, dubbed Soil Con, appointed former runholder and Wanaka community leader Arthur Scaife as its representive, and Ken appointed me as his. Our first job was to appoint a chairman satisfactory to both Arthur and me. Bill Hazlett heard about matters and said, 'I'll be your bloody chairman.'

Hazlett had got a permit to burn Burwood in his usual direct manner, saying, 'Please your bloody selves, but if you don't give me a permit I'll put it in the newspapers how you built that fence over there and killed 500 cows.' I put Hazlett's qualifications to Arthur: experienced high-country farmer, not from the district, well respected and so on. I did not deem it relevant to mention that Hazlett and Ian Anderson had gone to Waitaki Boys' High School together and were mates. Arthur had reservations but eventually decided Bill was just the man; besides, we both knew Hazlett would hound us to the grave if we didn't appoint him. The whole shebang was shaping up well, I thought.

Then we talked to Oamaru lawyer Jim Farrell, and he injected the thing with hitherto unimagined solemnity and importance. 'You blokes' judgements are all-powerful. This is a tribunal, with all the force of The

Law. Everybody who gives evidence will have to swear an oath. Who's your lawyer? Have you done your homework?' We hadn't imagined ourselves needing a lawyer. What homework? But neglecting such things made contests between Joe Runholder and Soil Con a bit one-sided. I was learning lots, and fast: attention to detail was the name of the game, one false step and you were down the ravine.

I went into Soil Con in Kurow to 'discover' — amazing how fast one picks up the legal lingo — some documents and they didn't have them. 'Well, that's not good enough,' I said. 'Our judgements are all-powerful. This is a tribunal, with all the force of The Law. Everybody who gives evidence will have to swear an oath. Who's your lawyer? Have you done your homework?' We eventually got them and I was beginning to take a renewed interest in courtroom dramas on TV and court reports in the newspapers.

Our day in court was in fact in the Omarama Town Hall. Feeling in town ran high: a lot of locals felt burning permits were being unreasonably withheld, and some fewer people thought the applications unwarranted. But first I had to ensure Big Bill knew what he was doing. 'Have you got a Bible?'

'What do I want a Bible for?'

'Everyone giving evidence has to swear an oath on the bloody thing.'

'They can put their hands on their arses as far as I'm concerned.'

But eventually he came to see the job was a big one. We hired a Waimate lawyer and I schooled him up on the documents and background during an overnight stay at Dunstan Peaks.

On the day, John Anderson filled two cars with runholders and it seemed everyone in the district was in the hall. One annoying thing about the case was that I really respected our opponent, Ross Maxwell, Soil Conservator, who turned up with a stack of books a metre high. Hazlett sat smoking his pipe between Scaife and me. Arthur was also a big man, and when someone asked who the small bloke was, someone said I was Bob Skelton, one of Hazlett's jockeys.

I gave Big Bill a nudge, 'Oath, oath!' Ross Maxwell was sworn in and launched into a scientific argument. Another Soil Con guy testified that it was indeed difficult to move sheep through the heavy snow tussock on the dark side of the hill. Sheep would not go into it and they ate out the sweet short stuff on the sunny side. He himself had looked over the area being argued about with his pet hound dog. 'Did you have permission to have that dog on the property?' I asked. No. 'Is it dosed for hydatids?' Yes. I was beginning to enjoy myself.

Eventually we retired to consider the verdict. Things were clearly going against Soil Con and I recommended they oversow and topdress the area at their expense after burning. Scaife pulled up at that, so we reduced our claim to a simple permit to burn. We got it.

After that we formed a committee of five to take the pressure off the soil conservator. It wasn't fair to make him Dr No. The members were three runholders (I was one), the conservator and a Lands Department fellow. We agreed to inspect any area of controversy regarding the rights and wrongs of burning.

We went to Mike Thomas's hideous matagouri patch — a plain case for burning — and someone asked why and how Mike intended to burn it. 'Look, if we're going to argue this one, this committee's had it,' I interjected. 'It's obvious to any sheep man like yourself, Mike wants to clear way for his sheep. He'll put a match to it.' The committee worked well and we didn't rubber-stamp every application either.

The high country, like any place in any time, is no stranger to despair, tragedy, horror and sadness. Or suicide. The reactions of folk there are like anywhere else too, though we have long tended to take a heavier dose of one antidote than, say, our urban countrymen do today: humour.

A neighbour went missing from his home. As he had a .303 with him and had been heard threatening to kill himself where he'd never be found, the usual explanations were overshadowed by one theory. The police found his truck at the top of Danseys Pass and asked John Anderson to check the remote huts on his property. He, being a fine practitioner of the art of self-preservation, roped his dad and me into the search. I was sent to check one hut, while John and Ian checked the other. As they were walking downhill, John got thinking. Perhaps the man was deranged? Didn't care who he took with him? Did he like John anyway? And he was armed. Would a .303 barrel coming out the door be the last thing John saw? 'Father,' John said, 'let's have a conference. I really love you, but you've lived longer than me and had more fun. How about you take the lead?' Ian couldn't argue with that, but John said later he never realised his dad was so thin and narrow.

On the missing man's property 18 months later a musterer chased a double-fleecer under a rock that hung over a stream. He nearly knocked himself out when he spotted a skeletal hand around a rifle butt in the sand. The antidote of humour didn't work so good for the discoverer.

The Lindis Pass joins three playgrounds of the summertime gatherers (and wintertime ones, but they seldom get out of their warm cars with ski racks): Central Otago and the southern lakes, the Mackenzie Country and Mount Cook, and their natural habitat of coasts, airports, parking meters and coffee bars. I've moved sheep down the Lindis since the 1950s, surveying the buggers. My attitude has mellowed, but the observations stand.

Of couples made up of a beautiful woman and an ugly man, I reckon the dough's with the latter. One such pulled up and a German goddess got out. 'Mindt if I valk vith you?' Well, how interesting do you think sheep's arses are after 50 years of looking at them? *Ja, jawhol.* She took photos, petted dogs, asked questions and enjoyed a slow amble for a mile. Herr Driver moved along in first gear, yawning. I don't think she was kidding when she said that walk was the best experience she'd had in New Zealand. My Errol Flynn chord had been plucked. 'Staying in Omarama tonight?'

'Mount Cook.'

'Pity. We could have had a drink.'

'I *vould* haf loved *dat*.'

'Pity, yeah.' She *would* have loved that, too. With this baggy-arsed old shepherd! The thought of distraction animated her.

'Mount Cook, ve're booked.' She rolled her eyes with meaning at the yawner.

Encounters like this suggest my theory has substance.

I was behind Innes's sheep one day, alone, when a car went into the back of the mob at speed, banging sheep up underneath it, killing one and breaking legs on three. Three thirty-ish Scandinavian women in the car were distraught. The driver offered to pay reparations, and I was tempted to pocket a few notes — just to make her feel better, of course; it had nothing to do with Innes's never paying shepherds a cent over the award wage. 'Nawh, you've learned your lesson. Just keep alert for stock.' But Tim Innes was incensed: 'You should have taken a motsa off the old bitch.' Anyone who deprives Tim of a dollar is by definition old, ugly, vile, immoral and unpleasant. I let it go. Why tell him they were young, nubile, humane, impressionable and open to reason? God knows what he'd have wanted.

Tim's father George Innes had been around the world a bit and loved tourists, was always beckoning them over for a yarn. A big fat Yank in sunglasses with two boys around 10 or 12 pulled up in the middle of shearing and George called them over to the woolshed, exactly what no one needs at shearing time. (If you call at a station to find them shearing, if you can't help, go — have you got that?) I was acting the part of an anchor. Tim was dressing the mutton under his block-and-tackle on the branch of a willow. It can hold a bullock but they've never got around to putting sprags — things like yachts have to secure ropes — on it. Usually he used the bumper of his Toyota, but it was off somewhere and muggins, at near 70 years, had the rope over his shoulder while Big Tim punched off the hide. The two boys came over, pop-eyed. Tim is not particularly sartorially elegant: split gumboots, split shorts with a blue-veined thing and a knife-sharpening stone sticking out most of the time. 'Ever seen a sheep killed before?'

'No. How did he kill it?'

My finger crossed my throat, with sound effects. 'Why did he kill it?'

'You know what a cock is?' They did, astonishingly.

'Well, one of those shearers cut its cock clean off.' Its pizzle had been reported cut, hence the cull. Then their father came up to take more photos. 'Aw f'crissake,' I said, 'don't show them this in your New York lounge room. Not all New Zealanders are as primitive as him.'

'I get this old fella up to hold the rope for me now and then,' said Tim like a philanthropist.

We all chatted and I found they were heading for a Wanaka motel. About that time the sheep's guts spilled to the ground.

'Tim, give this man a liver and a heart to take to his motel.'

Tim advanced on his weightlifter's legs with a bloody knife, heart and liver in his outstretched hand. 'Here, mate, take it. Put it in a f——g frying pan with half an inch of f——g fat. Beautiful, best f——g food you'll eat.' The Yank retreated fast.

Omarama boasted a tourist attraction that beat the Ohakune Big Carrot into a cocked hat. Sadly no more, it was the highlight of the Lindis road for a time. Roadmakers' Euclids had left borrow pits — gouges they had dug for fill for the cambered road — alongside the road and as the tourists chucked everything in them, locals decided roadside cleanliness was a lost cause, so they dumped stuff there too. One bloke dumping sheep carcasses forgot to remove eartags — how dopey can you get? Another tossed his or her piano. Mr and Mrs Anonymous set up a huge merino ram skeleton on the stool and took some pains to set it in the playing position, its great horned head and fleshless toothy grin, cloven fingers over the keys, a mad pianist in from hell in rhapsody. Where's the class in the Big Carrot? It's just big. So what?

Town holds few attractions for me, but I have enjoyed a day's shopping there — once. It was after the first shearing on Dunstan Peaks Station.

The shearing contractor had a cook, so I magnanimously told Ima she could take a spell after 13 years' straight cooking for gangs. She and our daughter Fiona headed to Invercargill and her relatives. The cook, Myrtle, near the end of the shearing, gave me a nudge: 'You'll have to cut the lawns before Mrs Kerr gets back.' Lawns! Would I ever escape them! Remembering Mick Griffin I mumbled something about needing a goat. 'I'll give you two goats,' Myrtle said. 'Someone left them with me and never came back. Think she was goatsick.'

I should have inquired about this strange disease, but all I saw then was an end to mowing.

On Sunday morning, cleaned up, I told Billy and a forty-second cousin and shedhand boy, both 16 years old and not licensed to drive, to tidy themselves up a bit: we were going shopping in Timaru.

My good bitch Tammy had injured her leg on the hill, so a visit to the vet in Waimate was required. I thought she'd have to stay with him, but he encased her crook leg in plaster and she returned with us.

We called at Myrtle's home in Timaru and put the two nanny goats and a muscovy drake in the back of the Mainline. I had a dozen muscovy ducks on Dunstan Peaks but their late harem-master had had a collision with a dog's teeth.

Tammy and the drake, with his legs tied, were put in the dicky seat in the cab behind the bench seat we three sat on.

All went well until, in the middle of Timaru's main street, the dog must have moved. The drake took off. Although universally called ducks, muscovies are in fact geese, and have a wing span of over a metre. I couldn't see. Cars tooted. There was nowhere to pull over. The boys eventually got control and one boy sat in the dicky seat between the two animals.

More shopping. Next stop we bought two weaner pigs, each in a bag with a hole for their snouts.

Born to shop by then, we called at a poultry dealer and bought 18 white leghorn pullets in banana boxes.

Homeward bound again, we stopped briefly at stock agent Bill Murrison's place in Kurow. We'd had a puncture and had to get the spare out of the back. It was a hot day and the animals in the back baked while we changed the wheels over. Bill caught a glimpse — and got a whiff — of the Noah's Ark in there. 'Hell's bells! It's like Wirth's Circus!'

Back at Dunstan Peaks the pigs were dispatched to their spacious new quarters, the goats were tied up, the drake introduced to his new harem and Tammy was bedded down on an old mattress on the verandah. It was getting dark by then. These shopping trips took longer than I thought.

My distant cousin and I took the chooks to the old henhouse and tipped them out of their boxes. They squawked, as, being hens, they were entitled to do. We'd forgotten one thing: my turkeys roosted on top of the hen run. When a turkey takes off in fright, it shits copiously and with great velocity: I can vouch for the truth of that statement — we were showered. Big birds, turkeys.

But the results were *generally* good.

The drake did his duty and then some. The pigs fattened, the hens laid and Peg-leg Tammy recovered.

But the nannies — Speedyscythe and Morrison — were a disaster. They ate anything before grass. All the rose blooms, blackcurrant bushes, ornamental willow trees went first. If they got loose — and goats, I found, were Houdinis — they would camp the night on our wooden veranda. They seemed to spend all night tap-dancing and this fancy cloven footwork was not conducive to sleep. Nor were they fastidious about their nightly toilet trips. Goats will do anything — slip any collar, tether or walls, to avoid getting wet.

Two charges of incompatibility were laid. They were on probation. But they continued in their delinquent ways. The court's patience was strained and a verdict of death by bullet at dawn looked near. But they had their charms too, and I stalled. A young bachelor neighbour visited and when he threw his cigarette butt down, Morrison gobbled it up — goats love tobacco nearly as much as roses — and nudged him for more. He was fascinated and patted her. Opportunity struck. 'I'm going to kill them,' I said as brutally as I could.

'I'll take them,' he said. Within minutes they were delivered to his place. First reports suggested he was rapt, but the second report was negative: they were homesick and he was goatsick. He'd been absent for three days and one or both had had problems with loose bowels, the result three centimetres of skitter baking on his verandah. The geranium bed had been annihilated. But worst of all, the apple tree his mother had nursed with TLC for years from a cutting had been ring-barked. His retired parents were due from Christchurch that weekend and he was going to tell them a plague of possums had attacked it, a pretty insupportable explanation with guilty-looking goats hanging about. He wanted help in goat removal.

Billy was dispatched and Speedyscythe and Morrison went to Goat Heaven, passing through the Great Digester first: the dog team loved them. I should've retired from goat work then, but I was to try once more much later.

CHAPTER FIFTEEN

'Enter My Dog in Huntaway'

There were 300 people in the booth and there would not be one who
wouldn't buy you a beer or give you a bed or a feed.

Alan Nimmo, returning from the
South Island Dog Trial Championships

IF YOU KNOW THE BASICS OF DOG TRIALLING, SKIP THE NEXT FEW
paragraphs. People who don't might like to know about the working
origins of each of the four trial categories, for they are not as artificial as
they look on television or to the untutored eye.

Dogs, like their ancestor the wolf, are pack meat hunters, a fact built
into the sheep's wiring. Heading dogs (also called eye dogs) work by
stalking, the threat of ambush and going in for the kill. Huntaways or
barking dogs work with noise: chasing, blocking and pushing to herd
sheep into position. Either way, fear's the key. Breeders of these collie dogs
from the Scottish Borders have just accentuated these basic traits and the
principle of pack labour.

There are two sporting categories for each type, the villains in these
dramas always being three sheep.

The Long Pull, Hold and Ring event derives from the job of the
shepherd on a boundary who sees sheep and needs to look at them closely
to know if they are his or a neighbour's. The dog *heads* them off and
pulls — pushes actually, for the dog remains behind the sheep — the
sheep to the shepherd so he or she can identify them from local
knowledge, brands, earmarks or whatever, and decide what to do with
them. Shepherding is a far older practice than fencing, but even today,

in real farm work, the long pull is needed from time to time.

Folk keep sheep for milk, wool, skins or food. Whatever, you've got to catch your sheep first, in a corner of a cliff or thicket or an enclosure. Dogs will *head* the sheep into one and keep it still for you. Hence the category of Yarding.

Sheep — it is in their nature to be inconvenient — are invariably over or down or up there, and shepherds want them somewhere else. They must be *hunted* to that place, in dog trials off the flat and up the hill in the Straight Hunt.

Between where they are and where they are wanted, obstacles such as groves of trees or big rocks or groups of Japanese tourists may be encountered. The Zigzag uses three sets of two poles to represent such obstacles and the dog must *hunt* the sheep left, then right, then left through them. Such dogs are called huntaways, as opposed to heading dogs. Huntaways have inspired me to outclass Sir Walter Scott:

> They held the dog trials once a year,
> There was a hut for food, a booth for beer,
> The huntaway judge was getting dour:
> The work that day'd been pretty poor.
> Then there walked onto the dog trial ground
> A man that no-one knew.
> His face was gnarled and wrinkled
> But one eye was clear deep blue.
> 'Enter my dog in huntaway!' he said
> In a voice that carried no guile.
> 'I've never run him in a trial
> So I don't know about his style,
> But he's hunted down merinos
> When the snows were coming fast
> And punched big mobs of romneys
> In the summer days gone past.'
> The locals gathered around,
> One or two they gave a snigger:
> They thought they'd have some fun
> At the expense of this old jigger.
> Out jumped those romneys
> Bold and free for all to see.
> The leader turned around
> And stamped his big black feet
> Upon that dog trial ground.

That old Jake, he summed them up,
He'd seen their kind before.
He opened up his great big jowls,
Out came a tremendous roar.
It blew the judge out of his car
And split the poles asunder,
It rattled around the rugged tops
You'd think it had been thunder.
And when the dust had settled
And the judge had picked himself up,
Those sheep were going out over top,
Old Jake was trundling in their rear,
Giving that awful bark.
It was reported later
It was heard all over the national park
So when they scattered to their homes —
Some from far away —
Everyone was satisfied
They'd seen a huntaway

Competitors draw a number that determines when their dog will get his or her run. The judge starts the competitor with 100 points. Each dog fault has a pretty rigid value, which is deducted. If the thing is hopeless, competitor or judge can declare the run a blow-out. The judge has the power to give competitors another run if the sheep are ornery to the point that the competitor is unfairly disadvantaged. It isn't a race: competitors are allowed a (usually) generous 12 minutes before time is called.

Besides the sheep and two types of dogs, the rest of the cast of the drama are competitors (who spend most of their day as spectators), other spectators, judges, cooks, booth attendants, club officials, a president, marshalls, announcers and the club secretary. The local newspaper reporter, a radio or television crew, dog breeders and a busload of tourists may turn up; everyone's welcome. Trials have a low-key carnival atmosphere. It's a sporting occasion, an outing, a community gathering, and a chance to meet or renew acquaintance with people from beyond one's own local district.

But it *is* competitive. Shepherds and musterers could hardly be in their trade for money — it's the life, comradeship, the hope of land of their own some day, a manager's job or the dream of getting that silver tray that says they won first prize in the Zigzag at Opotiki in 2008.

It is egalitarian. The shepherd with a sheen on the seat of his pants —
which might also carry his last $5 and a dismissal notice for sneaking off
to work dogs when he was told to thin turnips — is the equal of the
station owner whose station flops into Nelson, Marlborough and Canterbury. Winners I've known include a hydatids inspector, a journalist, two
pig farmers and a few shearers.

As spectacle it can get boring, so luckily the carpark, booth, hut and
the nearby willows provide alternative amusement. But if a glamour dog's
run is called, it will pull anyone in the know to the stage, at least until
enough deducts come off and interest wanes.

In the end, it's not the dogs you run, it's the people you meet. If you
take trialling too seriously you'll end up with ulcers or blowing your
brains out. Like golf or billiards, it has the potential to turn you sour or
bitter. Obsessive types should be warned off.

I've seen some stunning runs and can modestly claim one myself. The
1980 Wanaka trial produced a high standard of Zigzag huntaway runs,
and I didn't feel too confident but Super Syd and I struck three good
sheep, Syd listened for once, and he had his best run ever, scoring $99^{1}/_{2}$.
Someone asked the judge where Syd had dropped the half point.

'He didn't. I took the half off WV, the old bugger, for showing no
pleasure when he walked back.'

Quake won on the same course two years later with 99, judge Allen
May saying it was the best he'd ever judged. Chief won the Long Pull one
year and Yarding the next at Lowburn.

Quake and Chief were good dogs. I had semi-retired from trials but a
newfound friend, Alan Nimmo, a great and generous guy, must have liked
me. 'Take those two back with you to the South Island. Both have small
faults, but with your psychology and a smaller workload, you could
correct those and have a bit of fun with them.' Quake and Chief went on
to win some 28 open events and became known throughout the South
Island. But there have been thousands — I've counted them — of runs of
no note in my career. Those would fill another (dull) book. I always had
too many dogs with youthful potential before the older ones were fine-
tuned to be true champions, but I love dogs and the comradeship and
fellowship of trials.

Big Bill Hazlett died in the ring in 1978 — middle of a winning run, too. He lived life with all the drama he could've wished for. One thing might have marred it, but we'll never know. He hated long hair and beards, and could become embarrassing and rude around some perfectly innocent youth: 'Why don't you get a haircut and shave your face?' He was on pills but felt okay, he said. When he collapsed, Ken White — who had resuscitated someone previously — rushed to the ring to try mouth-to-mouth, to no avail. The funeral was a subdued affair.

A few months later Ken White came into a dog trial booth, teeth smiling through his beard. I turned my back on him and said to my companions, 'Don't talk to *him*. He killed a good mate of mine. He's a murderer.' Strong words, and White's eyes popped: he wanted an explanation. 'Way I heard it, you came on Big Bill like a fox terrier wanting to get on top of a great dane. He opened his eyes, saw your bearded dial bearing down on him and called it quits.'

A lot of the joys of trialling are to do with bullshit. At Tuapeka West I travelled with Don Anderson and stayed with Lloyd Smith at Millers Flat, 30 kilometres from the ground. I tied my dogs up to a fence and ran Clyde, then Boss, then went off to the huntaway ground for further runs. Boss got first and Clyde third and I got shickered. That night at Lloyd's Don was cutting up tucker and I said, 'Quake, Syd, Boss, Clyde, go and have a drink,' but Boss and Clyde weren't about. I'd left them tied up at Tuapeka West. So at the Waitahuna trials, when young Ian Anderson, all primed up by the bush telegraph, said, 'Hear you got a first and a third yesterday' and 'Feed your dogs last night?' and 'All of them?' I was ready. Feel a bit guilty about it, though.

'Ian, that's the oldest trick in the book. Boss and Clyde were getting trial happy. Just leave dogs tied up a night in strange country. It makes them think.'

Blokes were leaving dogs tied up all night all over the place for a couple of months. How was I to know my pathetic excuse would go down as doggie wisdom?

Whatever works — and a lot that doesn't — travels. After a while the administrators deem things illegal. No sportsman can hope for more than to be so good, administrators are forced to change the rules to get around him. Kerrs don't care much for rules if they can avoid them, and suffer from a strong inclination to test them. I have taken this clan burden to many trials. For example, the rules state that a competitor must not advance beyond the gate he's holding but may use his stick — oh, well, crook, if you must — as a barrier. I invented the banana split, which the judge can't see from his vantage point, to extend that barrier slightly. Ken White, a dog trial man and sheep-nut rep, gave me a proper metal stick when I retired from trialling, but it broke. When I got it repaired, at considerable trouble and some expense, someone had put a couple of ball bearings in it for some unfathomable reason. Nevertheless, this accidental addition, inaudible to the judge, sounded like a snake, which could spook the sheep as they were coming around and help turn them into the yard, giving a slight advantage.

There are two types of competitors at dog trials: cheats and blokes who haven't got the imagination. I went to an AGM of the Otago branch of the organisation that thinks it runs dog trials. Bill Scorgie read the riot act about folk cheating and how they should be banned from the sport. He was chairman, not that I cared about that, but he was also a top dog man, had won lots of trials, which I did care about, and was a sportsman in his demeanour. PL Anderson heard Bill out and said, 'What about WV? We'd lose him.' And Bill, to give him credit, said, 'Oh no, not him. He's different.' Fair enough.

But it is true that my reputation for pushing the rules has preceded me. I came out of retirement — again — at the Toko trials near Milton in 1997. I was going out for a run when I overheard this: 'That's that old WV prick back again. Oughta put the old shit through a metal detector.' Queen won the Maiden, Intermediate and Open events. There were 120 entries and Queen won with 98½ points. Eat my shorts, younger generation.

Chris Cochrane is a nosy bugger, always patting a bloke's dogs. He patted Syd at Haka once, ran his finger under the mutt's collar to find two carpet tacks and said scurrilous things about 'feigned electrodes', whatever that means. I may take legal action.

Ian McRae of Ben Doo asked my advice about a dog that had been getting over-excited and playing up in the yard. I suggested clicking a couple of 50-cent coins in his pocket to make them sound like the bolt of a rifle. It was good for getting a dog to concentrate when rattled. Later that day Gordon and I were having a quiet beer when Ian rushed up the steps of the booth, threw over a $1 note, asked for two 50-cent coins and was away. Gordon said, 'He'll tell his sons about that trick, and next they'll have to call Ben Doo Click Station.'

At Lumsden I was in the Southland provincial champs and disappeared over the ridge for a bit of pre-match training. At provincials and
higher contests, the casual stuff is off. There's a close-off point for entries,
you get a draw and the marshall is responsible for pulling you out of
wherever you are, usually the booth, and getting you to the ring. The
grapevine's off and you have to wear a number on your back so folk can
follow their programmes. An old trial bloke I won't name because he's
still competing told me in confidence about his feelings: 'Yes, once you
put that number on your back, hopes rise and the adrenaline surges
through your veins.' At Lumsden the marshall of the day, Bill Jolly, held
the fence down for me. As I got over a .410 kea gun dropped from the
pocket of my greatcoat, and a stock whip around my waist was visible
for a brief moment. You wouldn't believe what the bugger did! He
announced over the PA to all and sundry that WV Kerr couldn't be
located, but 'a guerrilla fella looks like he wants a run with his red dog'.
That's on my legal action list too.

I suppose you want to know how I got into the dog trial business. The
boss at Gladbrook, Charles N Patterson, and breeder Alec Matheson got
me interested in collie dog trials; before that foxies and rabbiting dogs
were of more immediate interest. I first ran dogs at Gore, on a rare day
off I was granted. I can't have done any good or I would recall it, but I
enjoyed it. Lack of transport curtailed me for years, but I went to local
events. When the transport problem resolved itself I was too busy a lot
of the time and the Wardells weren't keen on their sheep being used for
training. But on Dunstan Peaks, my own man, I revived my interest. I ran
dogs in all categories, but the huntaway events are my favourites. A
comment I once made keeps coming back at me, but it was said only half
in jest: 'I only keep heading dogs while I'm waiting for my huntaways to
grow up.'

The things that make a dog good, on the hill or at the trial, are
keenness, speed, ability and touch with stock. A heading dog is either
born with that touch or isn't. Huntaways are different: they require more
training. Some blokes are heading-dog men and some are huntaway men
and some go both ways, like me and I suppose most trial blokes. Ginger
Anderson is a top heading-dog trainer and triallist, and Lloyd Smith his
equivalent with huntaways.

I had a placing at Hakataramea that was memorable not so much for itself, but because of the timing and what it showed me people thought about me in my presumed dotage. Super Syd was a red-hot mustering dog who proved to be a trial idiot, but he managed to qualify, and was playing up again on Paul McCarthy's training ground the day before the trial. I was a bit crook, despondent about Syd's stupidity and looking a bit forlorn, sitting on Paul's water trough. George Innes came up to me. 'How's your dog goin'?'

'Well, I'm not running him at Haka.'

'What? He's no good?'

'He's a stupid moa. I told Nimmo he could have the fool after this.'

'Don McPherson's here. He's got a hot collar. Tickle Syd up.' Electric dog collars are efficient humane training tools. There may be a saint somewhere who can keep his or her dog keen and obedient all the time using only reward, but the other 99.9 per cent of us sinners need the other side of the coin too. Kicking or beating a dog is an alternative but, while I've been moved to do a fair bit of it with dogs old enough to know right (and left) from wrong, I cannot see how it is a preferred option.

Whips, guns and hot collars are barred from all dog trial grounds, but I had a collar with me anyhow. Before Syd's run I took it out of its box and put it under my jacket, leaving the box on the seat of my vehicle. Syd and I, with my left arm bent hiding the collar, headed for some willow trees. I passed some North Island mates and their wives taking refreshments. I hadn't seen them for a year: greetings all round and an invitation to join them, someone pulling up a chair for me. I thanked them but declined, saying my run was coming up and I was off to the willows for a nervous pee. And I did. I gave Syd a quick tweak and headed back to the vehicle, by a detour that avoided them, to replace the collar. But the box was on the dashboard, courtesy of Alf Boynton's warped sense of humour, along with a sign:

FOR SALE
ELECTRIC DOG COLLAR
APPLY WV KERR

Naturally, I removed this slander. I may still sue. And I went for my run. Syd was doomed from the start: one sheep was particularly flighty and bolted before Syd got close. But Syd compounded bad luck with sin, something he never did on the hill. He got between them. I recalled him and passed in my number, pretty philosophical about it, and hoping Quake might do something good 10 runs down the card.

The marshall caught me before I left. 'C'mon, WV, you've got another run.'

'I know that, dear boy, with Quake, 10 runs away, in two hours.'

'No. Now. The judge decided Syd didn't get a fair go.'

Back in the ring Syd hunted like, in Ian Anderson's memorable phrase, the well oiled wheel of a gig, scored 98 and got his name on the board as a contender. Alan Nimmo grinned. 'That offer of Syd still stand?' The North Island mate who had earlier pulled the chair out for me said, 'Congratulations. Sorry we didn't offer you a whisky, WV, you old bugger, but we didn't know you had an electric collar under your coat. Matter of fact, we thought you'd had a stroke from the way you were walking.'

Three days later Syd's name was still on the leader board seven. He was third in the South Island championship, with a chance in the run-off for the national.

I drew fifth run. The first dog completed a steady, solid run for Lloyd Smith. The second blew out. The third dog missed the poles, big deductions. When the fourth dog blew out, the Big Silver Tray looked a distinct possibility. Toey? Like a kangaroo . . .

Syd started badly, then committed the heinous sin of heading the sheep. I nearly called him off but only one bloke had had a good run and there were only two runs after mine. On the hill, though, it wasn't looking good. Syd rallied and painstakingly hunted them. I was going to run out of my 12 minutes, but Syd got them home with seconds to spare. It was a superb patch-up job, recognised too. There was only one person seated during the standing ovation, and he was in a wheelchair.

The sixth competitor blew out. The seventh and last, Don McPherson, an old campaigner, took his run very steadily. Lloyd won, Don was second and I was third. Syd has a unique place in dog trial history: no other huntaway has ranked after heading sheep!

I arrived on the night of the first day of the Wanaka trials and stayed with Gordon Lucas, who said, 'I had the top run today.'

'You mean you are in the top five?' The top five runs are published each night, but not the points, which the judge can juggle the next day in the event of ties.

'No. Top dog. I quizzed the judge.' You're not meant to do that, but well . . . He was as pleased as punch about his run, a personal best in his estimation.

Next morning I was going down to his open wall-less shed, where I'd tied up my dogs. I said I'd better get some training in, and fired a .303 bullet under the roof, then gave a piercing stock whistle. There'd have been a hell of a report and echoes in the shed. Gordon said, 'Is that your training?'

'Yeah.' Later, on the track to the Straight Hunt, no one on the road, I said, 'Stop a minute. I want to let Quake out. When I do, just slide the bolt of that rifle.'

'I can't do that. I'm an executive of the club.'

'Do as you're told.' He was a bit grumpy about it, but agreed.

As we neared the trial ground I said, 'Now, when I go to run Quake, you just follow me out a wee bit. A wee soft "*G-rrr* Quake" wouldn't go astray either.' Gordon did that, and Quake put up one of his best runs ever. Gordon and I were repairing to the booth that evening when the judge came up with his papers. 'Which of you two fellas do you think won it?'

I, noted for my modesty, said: 'Me.'

'Well, yes, you did. Beautiful balanced run,' he said, and departed.

'You bloody old shit!' Gordon grumbled. 'You weren't here yesterday, you didn't see my run.'

As I got more and more involved in dog trials in the 1980s I developed new tastes and habits. Took to an after-dinner Tia Maria, for example. After I'd returned from a trial and Ima came out from the laundry holding a condom, she probably put two and two together to make five. 'Those? Aw, I just use those to protect the dogs' feet on stony ground.' Lied, of course; habit of a lifetime. But if I ever find the 'wag' who slipped it in my shirt pocket, he'll pay.

You don't even have to be there to create mischief. I once twitched the grapevine with the help of Michael Lucas, an ex-shepherd and part-devil from Otairi, up in the Rangitikei, and, to my amazement, it bore apricots.

Ian Anderson in the autumn of his life.

Above: *Me at 6000 feet, top of the Lindis, 1985.*

Below: *Pakistanian Lad, my venture into racing.*

With Super Syd, New Zealand placegetter, Windsor 1990.
I focused his mind at Kurow cemetery.

As sail gave way to steam to diesel . . . Boots and a mustering stick, to horse to 4 x 4 truck to helicopter. Fat Man's Lodge, over 1000 metres above sea level, Dunstan Downs, 1985.
From left: *Tim and George Innes, Marcus Williams, me and Bob Kerr.*
Photograph, Andris Apse.

Inside Fat Man's Lodge, same year.
From left: *Bob Kerr, Marcus Williams, me and Tim Innes. No cut flowers, no mini-bar, no chocolates on the pillows. If George would put in one of those nuclear power plants, it'd at least keep the place warm.*
Photograph, Andris Apse.

Above: *Me with Tarzan, the hayburner, Tord, Jim, Syd, Chief, Clyde and Quake, meateaters, on Dunstan Downs, 1985. Those things in front are merinos, aka God's own sheep – have you got that?* Photograph, Andris Apse.

Below: *'Now listen boy and you will win someday.'* Mackenzie William Kerr, grandson – the last pup.

From left: *Me, Rick Aubrey, Tim Innes, John Blue and Simon Williamson in Fat Man's Lodge, Dunstan Downs, 1985. Scotch mist has killed more musterers than avalanche or blizzard, but there's no picture theatre at Fat Man's and it's a long ride to church.* Photograph, Andris Apse.

Left: *Out with my pals in the Kahanui Range, Ben Ledi.*

Below: *Me and Ima in recent times.*

He called in on the way to the Wanaka Expo, a competition outside the mainstream. 'Any messages for gullible youths, WV?'

'Tell them you called in here, but I wasn't home. And on the way out the gate you saw Ima on the Honda 90 coming down the road towing a dead hare with 10 dogs striding out behind her. Say you think you've found out how I exercise my dogs.' When I got to Wanaka the tale had grown and someone asked me about the hare business. 'The hare? Yeah, I gave Ima a rip-up about that. She towed it for three days on one side and bloody near wore it out. It took me 10 kilometres on the Red Flat to run it over in the first place.'

By about Thursday night of a championship trial, everyone has had their runs, is sick of dogs and someone says, 'Tell us about Gumdigger Jim, WV.' It's usually Derek Haines or his missus, Pam. Pam will check her watch for the time and I'll tell — essentially — this tale:

After they decided to build the Chunnel between England and France they called for tenders to get it done. Utah Mining and Atlas CopCo and all put theirs in, and so did Gumdigger Jim from Northland. He said he could do it for £100, easily the lowest tender. Intrigued, they flew him over and asked, 'How do you hope to dig a tunnel here for that money?' Gumdigger Jim said, 'Well, I'll start digging in France and my boy'll start digging in England.' A besuited person asked, 'How do you hope to meet in the middle?' Gumdigger Jim said, 'By Jasus, you're a fussy bunch of buggers, hard to please. You'll get two tunnels for your hundred quid.'

It's a weak story, but the reader must understand the role of alcohol and repetition. Whisky coursing through my veins, I'd say 'Glumdigger' and Derek would ask, 'Is it Glumdigger or Gumdigger?' I'd add stuff about the gumdigger's boy, and on it went. So far it's been a success. Every time I've told the story, Pam's watch has proved me a winner: the story had got longer. Derek yells, 'WV, you old bugger, you've done it again.' Such simple folk we are at dog trials. But the story's getting harder to spin out.

A question triallists ask other triallists — constantly — is how pups are selected for talent. A young bloke sidled up to me after a big trial down Te Anau. 'You own a lot of dogs, Mr Kerr. How do you select them?'

'Aw, I don't like to say too much . . . Mightn't work for you . . . All right, I'll tell you. It's an IQ test. Listen carefully, son; it's a bit technical.

I keep the whole litter and rear them until they're four months old and racing all over the place, making fools of themselves. When I'm raking hay, I take them all out. Might have eight pups and pretty soon the wheels will have run over two. At baling time I take them all out again, and pretty soon I've four. (But I must warn you: they do stink something awful in the bales when you're feeding out in winter.) Take them out when you're mowing oats. Now, it's a bit ruthless, but you know how all the rabbits shelter in the middle of the oatfield? And pups love chasing rabbits? Well, if there is one left with four legs when those big cutters scythe that last row and all the oats are cut, keep it.'

After I had had a bit of success, young triallists were forever asking me how I trained my dogs. Fairly obviously I did what most others do, added ideas of my own, adjusted training for what individual dogs do, rejected what didn't work and did more of what did. But this answers no one. I had to get more specific.

Out mustering, Lloyd Sanson asked how I was settling in to my 'retirement' down country, and this led to telling him about the big grapevine at my new place. 'Should get a dead sheep to put under it.' I parroted received wisdom. Lloyd had heard that was the go too, and when one of the big ram lambs on Ben Ledi we castrated late with the knife died on the hill, Lloyd yelled, 'Got a dead sheep here for your grapevine!' So when we finished up we stood over it. 'How're we going to get it back to the homestead?' I asked. Silly question. Lloyd, two pick handles across the shoulders, carried it. Two miles later I asked, 'How we going to keep it for three days?' Another silly question. He just tipped it in the freezer.

I had dogs to transport home, so had to tie the carcass on the roof of the ute. It looked a bit comical with its legs frozen out, and as I turned in my driveway I remembered the fun the parcel-on-the-road trick had afforded the urchins of Millers Flat 40 years before. So I set up the iced-up deadie on the white line of the road and waited out of sight. Sunday drivers came past with loads of wood or a bevy of kids on board. Decent folk, they stopped or crawled around it, beeped and carried on. Children *maa-maa-maa*-ed out windows. No one got out, but their reactions — no one's quite the same — afforded more stifled amusement than the parcel trick ever did. After six or seven cars had passed, the sheep's legs started to buckle in the sun so I put it in my freezer.

But I'd had an idea. Every dog triallist in New Zealand has trouble keeping three sheep together in the middle of a paddock out of the hook, the open enclosure that holds them for trialling. Sheep get in corners while training and trial dogs learn bad habits. After two of my sheep died and were in the freezer with Lloyd's one I was ready to start with a training edge no one could match.

First frosty morning I woke, yelled 'Ima!' and nudged her in the ribs. Pretty soon she had the wheelbarrow out and was heading up the hill with the three of them. She stood them upright and got out of the way. I got in an hour and a half's training before their legs started to buckle. 'Ima!' Back in the deep freeze again. Had my heading dog training sorted out.

But a huntaway poses different problems for triallists, the key one being teaching it to walk sheep at a reasonable distance in front of it.

A caster had broken off the sofa and as I was going to town for a haircut, Ima asked me to pick one up. I had another idea. I asked the hardware bloke for 13 casters. I screwed 12 of them into the dead sheep's hooves and was so pleased with my idea, I even screwed the last one into the sofa without being asked.

Next frosty morning, 'Ima!' Out in the paddock I tied the sheep together and threw a rope over Ima's shoulder. 'Get walking, woman!' I had nearly two hours' good training time before the sun came out. Then back in the freezer again.

So when I hear 'How do you train your dogs, Mr Kerr?' now, I reveal my unique system. An older more experienced man should encourage these young fellows.

In 1998, at a North Island championship, an old friend of mine, Wattie Ross, famous in the dog trials, now passed on but still a famous legend, a few others and myself were sitting around. Wattie was expounding his views when a big black-and-tan dog walked up and urinated on Wattie's back. His nice white shirt went yellow.

He chased that dog right out the gate of the grounds but luckily (for the dog) didn't catch it. When he passed us heading to his motel for a shower and clean clothes, he was livid.

'Find out who owns that dog and I'll do him too,' he said over his shoulder. Naturally nobody knew whose it was. It was amusing to us who knew Wattie's fiery temper.

A few years later at El Dorado on a really hot day, we came into base, and took our dogs and pups and three pig dogs to the river for a splash in the shade, while we had a beer.

Mac, a great ugly bully cross dog, shook itself over me.

I said to Stuart Eason, 'What do you keep a horrible dog like that for?'

Stuart said, 'Don't talk about Mac like that or he won't like you.'

'I don't want him to like me.'

A minute or so later I felt something hot on my back, then there were roars of laughter. Mac had emptied his bladder on my shirt. Yuck!

I returned to the huts for a shower and clean clothes.

Wattie's episode didn't seem so funny after all.

One year later Mac was killed by a boar.

'Good on you pig,' I said.

CHAPTER SIXTEEN

Snow, Sweat and Slog

Robert Kennedy on the election trail at a Chicago steelworks:

Kennedy: Any questions?
Steelworker: Have you ever worked a day in your life?
Kennedy: If you mean paid work, no, I guess I haven't.
Steelworker: Let me tell you, you haven't missed a thing.

O N 28 JUNE 1968, IN OUR FOURTH YEAR ON DUNSTAN PEAKS, WE had 17 inches — 43 centimetres — of snow, the biggest fall I've known. We didn't see the bottom wire of the fence for seven weeks. July and August were cold but beautiful months of sunny blue skies. Great weather for stock and pleasant for us. If it had rained instead of snowed it would have been our best winter there.

Everything froze except the snow itself.

Powder snow doesn't freeze, bind and crust like wet snow does. Sheep can walk on the surface of wet snow and get clear to warm sunny hillsides and safety. This snow trapped them.

High up, unbeknown to me, 100 merino wethers were having a hard time of it. A pilot told me about them. We found them in a trampled-down circle with a dung floor, within a wall of snow 600 centimetres high. They hadn't taken a morsel for seven weeks, but they'd survived. Of the 3500 merinos that endured the worst of that country in 1968 only 100 perished, a tribute to their toughness and instinct. Cattle very soon dehydrate and die, but merinos eat snow.

Dunstan's muscovy ducks lost the points of their webbed feet, their 'toenails'. They don't roost, so left their nails embedded in the morning ice. The calves on Birchwood, at the headwaters of the Ahuriri, provided a sight I'd not seen before or since: their feet froze, hooves cracked and the shells of the hooves fell off.

The high country has a low population spread over a great deal of land, but its grapevine works excellently well, particularly if there is a laugh at someone's silliness or discomfort involved.

Ian and Ken Anderson, Ron Williamson and I had had a day at the Geraldine dog trials. Jake got a second and the others all got placings. We celebrated in the booth, then shopped in town. My feet were cold and wet, so I headed for a menswear shop while the rest went to the pub. I bought socks and a pair of green slippers in a bit of haste. The salesman came into the pub a while after, and when I told him the slippers were a bit tight he looked a bit exasperated: 'I told you. Come on, come with me.' Next thing we were back in the store and I exchanged the slippers for a size larger. Then I saw a Donegal tweed suit I'd not seen before. We haggled for a bit, and settled on £60. He altered it on the spot, I kept it on, and he told me to get back to the boys in the pub. 'Where's the tie?' I said.

'What tie?'

'There's always a tie in the deal when you buy a new suit.' A fellow with a torch came in, asking what was going on.

'What the hell is it to you?' I replied. 'This gentleman and I are talking.'

'I own the shop and want to know what it is doing open at this hour, that's what.'

'I simply want a tie. I've bought socks, a pair of slippers and a suit.'

'Just give him what he wants and get him out of here.' He wrapped my old sports coat and trousers to speed my exit.

The car back to Omarama was leaving as I got back and the rest of them had bought fish and chips for tea. After a stop at a creek where Ian 'knew' there was good water for the dogs but which was drier than the Sahara, I took advantage of the roomy back seat for a kip. As my head laid itself down the smell of chips assaulted my senses and I turfed the packet out the window.

There was a squaring-up for food and drink and fees at the Ben Omar gates. I reached for my old sports coat in the parcel of clothes, and got a parcel of cold chips. Ken reckoned it was the world record for sobering up.

Ron Williamson had heard about it by morning, and rang saying he knew a woman who lived by that creek on the Tekapo road.

I pulled the door to, something I seldom do, so Ima, a soul to whom honesty is second nature, couldn't hear, and rang the woman, explaining I'd been to the dog trials 'in the company of a youth who'd drunk too much and fired his clothes out of the window in error'. Ima snuck up on me, called me a 'gutless bugger'. What wifely treachery! I was still on the phone!

The Tekapo woman had no luck at the creek and I fell into a wee depression — I was fond of that jacket — but she was a thinking, persevering sort. She tried another creek, found it and consigned the parcel to Omarama on the Mount Cook bus. Des Polson, local storekeeper, knew all about the saga and wrote across the thing: 'Bill, a bird left this for you. You'll know who.' Treachery's everywhere. Ian Anderson was updated on this last act at the races in Timaru. A week later I was taking tea in a Southland trial booth when a bloke said, 'Don't lose your clothes tonight, Bill.'

We always kept a few pigs for bacon. The two we had at the time of the visit of Mr Hogg, Oamaru manager of Wright Stephenson, were a real pain, always getting out of their — for pigs — substantial premises and outwitting us one way and another. Mr Hogg was there to grill me about my account. He settled down at the end of the kitchen table with some nice scones, and started his grill plate going. I had my back to the living room and rest of the house. The scone was midway to his lip when I heard *ghuh–huhf–ghuh*. A pig came out of the living room and passed him on its way to the open door out of the kitchen. He'd just started the scone back into motion when his eyes froze on something over my shoulder. The second pig snuffled by. The scone went back on the plate. It was too good to miss. 'Ima, I thought I told you to keep the pigs out of the house when we've got visitors.'

I felt the water-race was going to defeat me, but it became one of those you-can't-let-it-beat-you achievements. The problem was a rocky point of tough schist. We had to bring water across it to get enough height to irrigate the lucerne. A ditch-digger and a D8 bulldozer gnawed away at it. Both gave up, collected fees and said the rock was too hard. I bought an old HD5 bulldozer for $1000 from a Kurow friend, but it barely scratched the surface. Ray Hamblin and I eventually realised that gelignite and only gelignite would crack it. That lucerne was going to climb as high as an elephant's eye, look like it was climbing clear up to the sky.

The government electricity body hired us a compressor, jack-hammer and drill, and I suggested Ray take instruction from the expert. 'Christ, Ray, you're better at it than him,' I said, amazed.

'Yeah, well, I dug up half the streets of Sydney with one of these.'

Nothing was left to chance. We'd tuck the sticks well in. We'd put in plenty — 230 charges. And we'd blow it in one go, for maximum rock-splitting effect.

Ima and Fiona were set up with the camera at a safe distance — we thought. Naturally, I too left nothing to chance in the personal safety stakes and was sitting shielded from the blast in my ute.

It was beautiful, like a chain of small nuclear bombs. I love the smell of geli in the afternoon. Rocks rained down on the roof and tray of my ute, something I hadn't bargained on, but the beauty of it meant they might as well have been peanuts. The neighbours' two boys, in a lounge room 800 metres away, responded, one with a nose bleed, and the other with the comment, 'Has Mr Kerr fallen off his tractor?' The electricity department guy who came to pick up the compressor said it was a good thing we blew at 1400 hours and not 0500 or 0600, when the air was heavy and still, or we might have blown the lads' eardrums. Which gives you pause, doesn't it? But not my pulsating sinewy shepherd Hamblin: he was in the HD5 smashing out a race, shifting shattered rock. Two days later water flowed.

I was fishing in the Mataura River once when I saw a deer ford a tributary. I raced to the car and was fumbling about with the rifle and shells when I felt a nudge in the back. It was the deer, a pet obviously, but it chased me and self-protection was paramount. Such a shame, though.

On Dunstan Peaks my dogs spotted a deer, so I alerted Ray Hamblin. He got his rifle and lay down for a long shot. There were pups gambolling about, licking his face; he tried to chase them away, but it was too hard.

He got a shot away just as the deer went around a brow out of sight. It hardly seemed worth the walk to check, but Ray was delighted to find he'd clean-shot it. Delighted, that is, until he noticed the yellow collar around its neck, suggesting it belonged to a Michael Thomas of neighbouring Killermont Station. The history of this tragedy hinges on a rabbiter. The deer had taken a shine to the guy's horse, near drove him mad hanging around, springing his traps. When he'd lit out for my neighbour's place, the deer must have tried to follow his playmate. We dressed the top yearling in the woolshed. Waste not, want not. And, over a beer, discussed the right thing to do. We'd ring and 'fess up.

'Mrs Thomas?'

'How are you, Bill?'

'We *were* all right, Jane, but, actually, we're a wee bit upset and a bit sad.'

'Oh. What's happened?'

'Well, I'll tell the truth. We've shot Bambi. Ray shot her. He's taking it hard, thought it was a wild deer.'

'No, you tell Ray it's Michael's fault. Bambi should have had a harness on or something.'

'Or one of those red flashing blinker lights like the aircraft have.'

'Exactly! That's a good idea.'

'We dug a big hole. Planted a willow. Ray's a bit white faced . . .'

'You tell Ray it's not his fault, it's Michael's.'

Ray enjoyed his beer more, the logs burned better, the yarns got funnier. Nothing like making clean breast of error. The phone rang. Mike Thomas: 'Where's my half of that venison, you thieving buggers?'

'Mike, do you mean to tell me you'd sit at your table and put forkfuls of wee Bambi in your mouth in front of the kids? No way. We dug a hole and . . .'

But we transferred the deer to another bloke's deep freeze just in case. Mick Thomas wouldn't be above stealing a bloke's venison, you know.

The so-called squire of Dunstan Peaks never stopped working, early mornings mustering somewhere, early mornings haymaking. There was no lucerne on the place in 1964 and 12 years later there was 150 acres. Our mailbox was 580 metres above sea level and I had been reliably informed the stuff wouldn't grow at those heights. An expensive error in seeding meant we double-sowed and had to buy more seed to complete the job, yet the result was a real eye-opener. I swear every seed sprouted, and that was before we irrigated. I negotiated water rights and drew water from the Omarama Creek. Haymaking is hard, start-stop work: you've got to let lucerne dry out a bit before you cut it, but bail it with a bit of dew on it. Too dry and you lose leaf as dust; too wet and it rots. Wet, it can even spontaneously combust.

Irrigation is no picnic either. I bought a motorbike and it was another revelation. It clocked up 18 on its imperial odometer in three days, just running around water-races. I'd been walking that in gumboots! In the year of purchase the odometer hit 2000 miles and that's where it's stayed for the last 28 useful years. But it brought home to me, in one small way, just how hard I was working and how I'd begun to think of daily hard work as normal, natural and the way of things.

I got to wondering what in the blue blazes I was working for exactly. Stepson Bill had gone to Twizel with the MOW and, being a social animal, was enjoying the larger society there and roundabouts. Johnny was big enough for the more respectable tag 'John', and had signalled he didn't want to be a farmer by studying accountancy at the University of Otago. Fiona was nearing the end of her high-school years at Waitaki Girls'. For 21 years we'd paid boarding-school fees, stepfather and sire carefully planning his progeny at seven-year intervals to match his financial programme of never paying two sets in a year.

In our tenth year at Dunstan Peaks Ima was diagnosed as diabetic and faced adjusting her lifestyle to accommodate an insulin regime, eating at set times with great regularity, and a similar waking and sleeping pattern. She was safer nearer hospitals and specialists.

A lot of problems can be fixed by throwing money at them, I don't care what anyone says. The 'squire' was never expecting to get rich quick, but he did expect a good annual rake-off and a slow but steady capital appreciation. I'd wrought tremendous improvement on Dunstan Peaks Station with money and sweat, raised productivity and quality, but it was a struggle more times than I care to recall to make mortgage payments by due date. Wool prices slumped in the mid-1960s and didn't recover until 1972. By the mid-1970s, at the age of 50, my point was: what's the point?

CHAPTER SEVENTEEN

Exit the High Country

Tho'
We are not that strength that in old days
Moved earth and heaven; that which we are,
One equal temper of heroic hearts
Made weak by time and fate, but strong in will
To strive, to seek, to find, and not to yield.

Tennyson, Ulysses

I SETTLED INTO MY 50-ACRE BIT OF RETIREMENT DIRT DOWN country in Windsor near Oamaru with very definite aims in mind, none of which quite worked.

Two things I wasn't going to do any more. One: I'd dug enough postholes for eight lifetimes — no more fencing. Two: there'd been a great deal too much hay in my life. Dunstan Peaks had begun to revolve around hay — not just sowing and growing it, but cutting and carting it, breaking in more land for it, irrigating more and more of it. Never would I pick up another hay bale. Dunstan Peaks, as time went by, could be mustered in two or three days, Birdwood in one, not the life for a dog man.

We sold Dunstan Peaks in 1976. Wool prices boomed in 1978, and the value of high-country stations soared in their wake. Any farmer or ex-farmer would drool over the incentive loans of Think Big, which followed the wool and land boom. I used to think about these factors from time to time, mention them if it was relevant, but not much. Certainly, I didn't become bitter or twisted about the timing of my high-country exit — some blokes grow bitter about their luck — because I became too busy and had, at 50, learned what people mean when they say they've 'begun to feel the cold'. The spot we chose would, I thought, be particularly sheltered, down a good way from the ridge, in the lee of southerlies and off the valley floor. I was right about that and a lot of sour weather misses us entirely. It took me six months to stop hunching my shoulders against the southerly when I stepped outside. Windsor is no Bay of Islands or Miami, but on the other hand none of those mad buggers called skiers come here. The most astonishing thing about snow is that some people actually play in it.

I managed to avoid fencing in the main. I'd always wanted a big white stag walking across the view from my lounge room windows to skite to visitors — a high-country Moby Dick, someone called it — and I sourced some cheap red and fallow deer for a hobby. The fallow herd is entirely albino now. But I paid a fencer to contain them. The only fence by WV so far is the one around my vege garden. But in truth I did need a tiny patch of hay growing or my hobby would have been too expensive. Neighbours help with equipment and labour. Good neighbours.

I brought all my dogs. I would breed pups and train dogs all day. When a big high-country fellow, used to the general three to four acres to the sheep, showed modest interest in what the old coot was doing with the land, I was able to say I was running 'about half a dog to the acre'. An old shepherd warned me about the pitfall in my plan: 'Never keep two pups, keep one. One will watch the other, and you won't get the full attention of either.' I reared six pups to nine months old, but a lot of them wouldn't follow me out to the paddock without the accord of the pack. I sold them for $100 each, refundable if they didn't work out. Away from the pack environment they all turned out okay. My breeder–trainer idea, however, didn't.

I entertained myself with a garden and invented — I think I invented it — the world's best easy potato-growing system. But mostly I took in animals. I tried pigs, chooks, deer, dairy cows, racehorses, even goats, and various others at different times for different reasons. Nothing ever turned a quid, though some were never meant to. The purebred angora goat I imported from Australia — Muriel was her name — was meant to make my fortune, but $12 000 in costs later, she was a disaster. Heliotrope, my last goat — and I'll never go back on that — was meant to feed milk to my pups. It was one of those great ideas: goats eat less than a cow and why pull four tits when two will do? But she had that goatish Houdini touch and would have won the global goat kick competition. When you did catch her there was a tablespoon of milk from each tit.

There were immediate compensations though. Ima was happy and near medical attention. I was 50, fit, active, and had 10 dogs and all the other animals we had brought from the high country — the lorry driver said it was like shifting the Ponderosa Ranch.

Fiona's pony Gypsy did not enjoy Windsor for long. Fiona had ridden and groomed Gypsy, and loved her 'to bits' as she put it. Gypsy enjoyed Fiona's love a long time, old place, new place. Perhaps the pony licked some old Dieldrin poison, or ate rhubarb, two possibilities; whatever, she dropped dead. Ima visited the boarding school to tell Fiona and her tears were commensurate to her Christmas joy years before.

Fiona was a realist and knew little beyond the high country. 'If you want to use Gypsy for the dogs, you can.' But I told her how I got busy with a back hoe and buried Gypsy. Yet although I had never got much into the Presbyterianism to which I was born, I share with them a distaste for waste. Gypsy quietly and discreetly sustained as deserving a pack of dogs as she could have wished for, passed off as 'beef' to Fiona. Fiona always knew I lied, but said nothing.

But something was niggling me. Paul McCarthy, once a bit of a protégé of mine, asked me to give him a hand lamb marking over Ngapara, seven or eight kilometres away. Then someone else heard about me, and asked me to do something a bit further away. Before I knew what was happening, I was back up the Waitaki Valley with my dogs. I went there for a three-day job once and got back 43 days later.

After one big walking day, out of the mouth of a babe came a truth. I must have been a bit slow coming to the gateway and a young whipper-snapper asked me, 'Why do you get invited here every muster?'

I fixed him with the steely blue. 'My dear boy, because I've got the best team of dogs in the Waitaki Valley and probably in any valley in Central Otago. That's why.' But it was a sign, unmistakable.

With the pressure of ownership off, a bit of security and freedom, I was to range more widely in my — laughable description — retirement than I'd ever done. And there were dog trials.

When I got back after the 43 days away, Ima and Billy were watching TV. 'Gidday. Any important mail for me?' There wasn't. 'Phone calls?'

None. Soon after, Ima went down to Invercargill to look after a crook relation, and came back after a record 44 days. I didn't hear her come in until she opened the lounge door where I was watching TV. 'Gidday,' she said. 'Any important mail for me? Any phone calls?'

'I'm supposed to say that,' I said. Fair indication of our good relationship. Ima and I knocked around dog trials together for a bit, but trials are not a good scene for a diabetic who must eat and sleep at rigidly regular times, so I travelled solo after that. People would ask, 'Is he married?' over drinks in motels. 'Yes, he is,' a bloke would say. Or a woman who'd met Ima would say, 'Married to one of the loveliest women I ever . . .' If a bloke fancied a bit on the side, dog trial society surely cut him off at the pass.

I totted up recently: I gave 340 days of my roughly 28 000-day life, over one per cent, to dog trial judging, counting travelling time. Time to give judging away, I decided. When it was good, it was great, but I noticed that I was getting more cranky and taking more liberties as time went on.

John Harris, a hard doer, was sending his dog off for the Long Pull at the Waitaki club grounds, one of the nation's biggest hills for the sport. Trouble was, his dog kept coming back down the hill to admire its owner, ignoring the sheep. (On the third occasion, a hare he spooked looked like taking him to the sheep, but didn't.) It was getting too much and we had a full card to get through.

'John, it's taken most dogs three minutes to run out. You've got under 2½ to complete everything. How about stuffing off?'

'How many points will you give me?'

'10, for starting.'

'20?'

'I'll split the difference. 15.'

'It's a deal.'

And he missed the trophy by one aggregated point!

The judges' quarters varied a lot. Caravans were best, the most comfortable option. Still, you might have your head out in the rain, as I did, from a car, at Burke Pass one day. 'There's idle caravans sitting all over this town. Surely to gawd . . .' There were four there next day.

I'd retired from judging more times than a vain opera star but one year, about 1980, they were stuck at Tarras so I succumbed when asked. Indeed, it was a real community effort that year. The president had pulled in all those who were able and willing to help out, like a working bee at school, not just dog men. The Tarras trials are late in the season, and a chance to get those last-chance qualification points for the Big One, the New Zealand Open. On the blackboard for draws — a bit like booking a snooker table in a pub — I wrote: 'Qualification points for sale, $5. WVK.' I had long decided being pedantic over poor runs was a waste of judging time; anyone scoring 85 or under these days has no show. Competitors shouldn't ask the judge what their score is, but do. I had taken to writing 'G' alongside a flat 85 and putting the real thinking into top contenders. When they asked what the G was for, I'd say 'Guess'. It didn't matter.

One aspect of the community day out was that Frothy Davidson brought out a heading dog he kept presumably for its smile, and did all right. But then he said he had a huntaway. Back he went and got the thing. The marshall pointed out that the dog, having had an operation to remove a tumour from its throat, may not actually be *able* to bark. Huntaways *have* to bark, just as a sparrow must fly and a trout swim. I pulled a butcher's knife from under Bronze's seat: 'Marshall, if that dog doesn't bark, it might have another operation, and never bark again.' Frothy's Forgeddit ran about for a bit in a silent clueless display of enthusiasm. I couldn't stand it a second longer. Big Bertha, my .303, was in Bronze and I pointed it — no shells — up the hill. 'Marshall, can you get that competitor to stop that dog a moment, please.'

No one's asked me out of retirement to judge again.

I nearly met my match in bullshitting when I ran into a shearer called Jock. Peter Clulee and I were having a nightcap when we heard the shearers drive into El Dorado, so we waved them in to join us. Two girls and two men. Jock was a global shearer, working around the world at his game, in Scandinavia, his native Scotland, Australia and here he was, with a glow on. He claimed a narrow escape that night. 'A foockin' great big brown trout leapt out at oos while we woos crossing that wee bridge over the creek joost doon thar. Hooge bogger. Could have been nasty if it haad hit oos side-oon. As it woos, it narrowly missed the windscreen.'

'You didn't hurt it, did you?' I asked in alarm and concern.

'Nay, what do you mean?'

'Did it have rope burns in front of its fins?'

'Rope burns? What are you talkin' aboot?'

'Phew! That's okay. It's my personal fish. If it's a warm evening I use it to go waterskiing up and down the river.'

Jock was to later tell his boss, Sam Boynton, 'I've bin all roond the worrld and I thought I was the best foockin' liar there woos, but that foockin' old mate of yours at El Dorado took the cake.' This admission was a great comfort to me.

When cut-out day — the finish of the shearing — rolled around, the staff and owners were due to have drinks in the shearers' quarters. I briefed Jock about Mrs Eason: 'She's a very nice, refined lady and doesn't like rough talk, so keep the fruit out of your language, eh?' Jock understood perfectly and behaved like a visiting vicar. As Mrs Eason and her daughter were taking their leave, Jock stood and thanked her: 'Mrs Eason, let me joost say those foockin' savouries were the best foockin' savouries I've ever tasted.'

'Why, thank you, Jock,' she said, smiling. The high country is a broad-minded enough church to contain Jock, and everyone was the richer for his sojourn on our shores.

It had been years since I'd been on the soil conservation committee. But we'd stopped the situation whereby three Soil Con guys and a runholder went up a gully and they overpowered him. Hearings were heard in a public place, which was good, and I thought that was an end to my contribution.

I helped Tim Innes muster and burn on Dunstan Downs, and when he asked me to burn the other end of the block, including a patch of awful scrub and rocks that had often annoyed me, I was delighted to toss a match into it.

But Soil Con sued Mike Thomas and Peter Patterson for exceeding the area of their permit, and Tim for the same plus burning a protected area.

Tim called me and his father George as expert witnesses, and hired a lawyer. But rumour had it that Tim had had an altercation with Joe Cameron, chairman of Soil Con, in the pub one night and cut Joe's tie in half. Tim denied it when questioned, but it was too late — the lawyer withdrew because of a conflict of interest; he was Joe's family lawyer. Tim hired another lawyer from Timaru.

We arrived at court just as the new lawyer was leaving. The court had a criminal matter to attend to and there would be a delay. 'Good,' said Tim. 'We'll go across to the pub and have a booze.' The black-gloved retiring lawyer offered some free advice: 'If you're drinking, drink vodka, because if this magistrate smells booze, you're goners.' So while the court attended to a criminal matter two very sober musterers drank tea.

A Christchurch professor testified that a rare mountain pine charred by the burn wouldn't regenerate. Well, this was the stuff a bush lawyer dreams of. I'd told Tim to get on up there and get a twig off the damned pine and give it to his lawyer. It was singed. But it was growing.

George Innes and I travelled down together to one hearing and something was bothering George under his suit. 'I've got to pop into Dalgety's.' Later: 'I've got to see that accountant.' Eventually we called in at a Cobb & Co restaurant to see Tim and Jeeva. George said, 'Can we get a drink here?' Triples. He later admitted he had spent most of the day in the pub, building up Dutch courage. Give him a horse breathing fire, George'll tame it, but put him in a suit in a courtroom . . .

The magistrate gave this witness a dispensation: I was allowed leave to sit in a chair, presumably on account of my age! George had to stand for his evidence. At one point the questions weren't going anywhere, and I said of the spread of the fire, 'Look, it's happened before and it'll happen again.' I also criticised the professor's evidence of the fate of the poor wee pine and general destruction. Their lawyers produced photos, and asked me if I could not see the damage. Ruffled, I said I'd walked around the old fire scene, stood a metre off the pine, and there was nothing you'd worry about burnt at all. I added I'd not sat down on the tarseal with a telephoto lens. 'Thank you, Mr Kerr.' Then Tim's lawyer produced the *pièce de résistance*, the twig.

A month later, in Oamaru, we attended to hear the decision. The proud magistrate said, among other things, that he'd taken Exhibit A home, put it in a bottle of water and it was regenerating, 'still growing' as he put it. He added that George Innes and I (surely two of the Upper Waitaki's worst reprobates) were 'two experienced, staunch citizens'. He quoted the words of one, 'It's happened before and it'll happen again.' The Soil Con case was dismissed.

You'd think retirement would rule a bloke out for a feud, but it didn't. I blame certain genes Princess Diana and I share through the Ferniehurst

Kerrs. You'll recall how the English stormed Ferniehurst Castle, beheaded every bloke and raped every woman. Utu was called for, but first we had to get the castle back.

The Ferniehurst Kerrs, awfully important and with a few bob at the time, got in hired help for the storming, a French general named Delamont. He besieged the English garrison in our castle, blew a hole in its wall and we went in. The captain of the garrison rushed up and said he'd surrender if Delamont would protect his troops from Kerrs. Delamont didn't get a chance to reply before a Kerr whose wife had been raped came up and cut the Englishman's head off. Well, you would, wouldn't you?

Delamont wrote:

> . . . with such great force, the poor captain's head rolled a good five yards from his trunk. The hundred Scots present were so pleased with this they began to throw the head around, shouting with joy as though they had taken the City of London. Their thirst for blood now aroused, they now engaged in a horrifying massacre, emasculating, dis-embowelling and decapitating the Englishmen who fell into their hands, competing with one another to see who could display the greatest address in severing limbs before inflicting a fatal blow. I even offered to buy English prisoners from the Frenchmen who had taken them. I sold one poor fellow to the Scots for the price of a horse. They immediately stripped him naked, staked him to the ground and four Scots officers took it in turns to ride over him.

The Martins owned a sheep run up in Danseys Pass, running about 4000 perendale ewes, and I used to go there every muster. They bought a farm down country near Duntroon, sold the run house and woolshed and a bit of land around it, intending to drive the stock to the new place for shearing, drenching and the rest of it. To avoid a three-day drove around the Danseys Road Martin gained access through a Martin Dangle's property to a dead-end county road. This route took about an hour's mustering, and all was most convenient for a few trips until Dangle, for some unknown reason, denied access.

Martin tried some other neighbours, the Coys. The boss Coy said no, and that's when an old-time feud started in the valleys.

Martin discovered from some old maps that a paper road went from another dead-end county road, through Coy's property to his boundary! These paper roads were drawn so no property could be 'landlocked'. The 'road' was surveyed at Martin's considerable expense and two-metre-high surveying pegs 10 chains apart marked the chain-wide road. (A chain is about 20 metres.)

The next muster was the weaning muster. Out the boundary gate into no-man's-land, which it was literally and figuratively, came 4000 ewes and their lambs, hill perendales handled about three times a year. 'Keep them between those bloody pegs,' came our instructions. Tough call, but we had six top dog men and everything was going good.

Then over the ridge like Red Indians on the warpath came the Coy mob: Coys, Buttons and Saddams, wives, mothers, children (one Coy had a baby in a backpack). They kept at a discreet distance, having been warned it was illegal to interfere. A policeman watched from another ridge. They followed our progress with abuse and accused us of going outside the pegs. One wife asked me, when I wouldn't reply, silence being golden, 'Are you deaf as well as blind and stupid?' Good for the blood pressure during a tricky manoeuvre. They took photos for evidence that we were out of bounds. Maybe we were at odd times but you try confining that mob to a chain width, no fence. I'm prouder than Punch we got close.

It went on for a couple of years. The only compliment we got was when we were taking the ewes minus lambs back to the run block. At over 60 I was one side of the mob, George Innes was 70-plus on the other, and Don McPherson was giving 80 a fright behind it. A woman county councillor joined the policeman and a Coy on the law's ridge to get an on-the-spot assessment. We guided the mob up through the pegs, heading dogs winging them, an old dog in the lead. The cop later told us the county councillor had said, 'That was as magnificent a piece of shepherding as I've seen.' (Her husband was a farmer.) Coy said, 'So it should be. If Martin had advertised the length of New Zealand for the three best shepherds in the land, he couldn't't've got better than those three old buggers!' We were quite flattered and felt he was more than likely right. Flattery from one's enemies is the best kind. 'Magnificent' — have you got that?

After one especially stressful, unpleasant trip, when we nearly had a smother caused by the Coys' protest, George Innes turned up with a new dog, a bull mastiff cross bigger than a pony.

'What's this, George?' I asked.

'Aw, he's my duck dog.' I went to put out my hand and he snapped. I got the message. Duck dog! If George had cut that dog loose at the protesters, they'd be ducking all right.

During one drove, when tensions were hotting up, the Martin boss had a casual labourer driving the truck, not a dog man. Built like Mike Tyson, and about as erratic, he was told to go with me alongside the mob for a bit 'in case WV needs help lifting ewes out of an under runner'. A weak excuse: he was to be my minder if things got rough. 'Keep him on the chain, WV,' the boss said in private.

The operation was going peacefully when over the ridge came the Indians. The old chieftain of the Coys came tearing down across the top side of the mob, bald head flashing in the sun, bandy legs pumping, balloon shorts blowing, false teeth clapping. 'You're on our land!' he yelled. I told him, 'Settle down, old man, you're out of order.' Then the chain nearly tore my arm off as Tyson towed me uphill in his attack. The old chap saw danger and sensibly retreated.

Tyson's job included going back to pick up a Toyota and going around to the Martins' HQ to get smoko for us. He was confronted by a barricade: a truck across the road through two sets of yards set well away from the homestead, for convenience on the block. There were a dozen protesters and the local cop, all arguing. Tyson had had enough. 'My orders are to go and get those old gents a cuppa tea. My truck has strong bull bars and if you don't shift I'll go straight through your yards.' The roadblock cleared in a hurry, while the insipid cop stood about looking pathetic.

After another stressful trip I was tying up my dog team one night when my Scottish ancestral memories came to the fore. As the Archbishop of Glasgow once cursed the Kerrs, so I would curse the Coys:

By the word of our sovereign Lord,
Truly religious men, wives and bairns,
Baulked, washed and redeemed
By the precious blood of our Savior, Jesus Christ,
Are murdered, burnt, harried and reft.

And under silence of the nest,
Beings — common traitors, reevers, thieves —
Are dwelling in the sooth part of this realm,
Such as Teviotdale, Ayrsdale, Littledale and Annadale.

Therefore my said Lord Charge of Glasgow
Has talked expedient to strike them with the terrible blow
Of Hellicut.
And has charged me to denounce and declare them openly
As generally curséd at this market cross.

Do here hear me proclaim, I curse:
Their hed and every hair on their hed,
Their face, their mouth, their tongue, their teeth, and their craig,
From the top of their head to the tips of their toes,
And every part of their body, their stomach, their back, their arms,
their legs, their feet
and every part of their body, I curse them in this marketplace.

I curse them ganging, I curse them riding,
I curse them standing and I curse them sitting,
I curse them eating and I curse them drinking,
I curse them waking and I curse them sleeping,
I curse them at hame and fray hame,
I curse them within the hoose and I curse them withoot the hoose
I curse their wives, bairns and servants,
Perpetuating wiv them in their deeds.

And finally I condemn them perpetually,
Consign them to the Deep Pit of Hell
To remain with Lucifer and all his fellows.
And their bodies to the gallows of the bottom muir,
First to be hanged, swung and rugged
With dogs, swine and other wild beasts, abominable to all!

The range war eventually ceased. Maybe it was the futility of it, maybe the mounting legal bills or the threat of expensive fencing and roading, maybe common sense finally prevailed; whatever, peace, tranquillity and co-operation settled in the valley of Marawhenui. I think my curse did it. My old father didn't give out a lot of advice but he did say once: 'Son, never fall out with a neighbour — you never know when you'll need him. Don't live at the top of a county road or the bottom of a water-race.'

Another reason to muster is to audit flock or herd numbers and value them when a property is sold. It's called a 'delivery muster'. John Stokes rang me when he sold Cloudy Peaks about 1986 to live a life of ease in Wanaka. He and I and a local went out to do the job but a fog blew in, so we stomped around his garage and he pulled out a bottle of white magic, aka gin. Time passed and rather than bother going back for lunch, John pulled out the barbecue and a couple of steaks. More white magic, then the fog lifted, to be replaced by something that looked a bit like scotch mist. We decided we'd have a day for the queen — no work, full pay — an old mustering convention. We eventually got everything in the holding paddock the next day, but the delay proved unfortunate. My hut was near a dry creek bed and I heard noise that night. At breakfast next morning I said, 'That creek ever come up?'

'Yeah, but there's got to be a lot of rain.'

'Well, there's a lot of noise . . .'

When he came back from taking a look John said: 'It's the biggest disaster since Dunkirk!' The bridge was washed away, and agents with town shoes were piling in to the property to value the stock. With some long uncomfortable detours and white magic application, all was eventually well.

John didn't enjoy much of Wanaka's life of ease but I saw him at dog trials from time to time. He told me he'd have liked to have put me up at Wanaka but he had to go into Dunedin Hospital for 'chest tests'. So I was surprised to pass his car going out when I drove in. Our faces were about a foot apart, window to window, when I asked what he was doing there. 'WV, they sent me home. I'll be dead in three months. Cancer.' He'd been co-opted into being barman at the booth, and cast a pall of misery over everyone he met. Luckily, George Innes called in, and when he got the treatment, said: 'Aw, f'crissake, John, five of my mates have had that chest thing. Just get a bit of altitude in a tent, get some air into your lungs. You'll clear it all up.' John's mood changed immediately. He was going to get a tent and peg it halfway up Mount Cook. But the doctor was spot-on: three months later John Stokes died. I asked Innes if it was true about his five mates. 'Fairly true. One bloke didn't die of it. Fell off a ladder. Broke his neck.'

I was Stokes's only North Otago mate at the big Wanaka funeral, for which John himself had set the tone. As he lay dying in Cromwell Hospital Vic Davidson, who was going to a Lodge meeting, visited him in his evening rig-out. 'Christ, Vic, you're a bit early with the suit,' said John.

Young Rodney McLennan, one of Gordon Lucas's former workers, was taking out one of John's two attractive daughters, whom he later married, and he'd been deputised to drive the car with the chief family mourners. PL — Peter Anderson — heard I'd brought 11 dogs over in my vehicle and tied them up locally. 'WV, this is ridiculous — coming to a funeral with a heap of dogs. You should hire a boy to look after them.'

'Gordon hired that boy there once,' I said, nodding toward Rodney. 'Let's see how he goes, PL.'

Rodney went all right — better than the undertaker's assistant, who threw the trolley on top of the coffin to go to the cemetery — but when the hearse moved off Rodney in the car behind must have been a bit toey with the accelerator because there was a distinct *grrr-grrr-grrr-bang*! — blue smoke, a buck or two, then a leap, before he was off.

I fixed PL with my steely blue. Say no more.

CHAPTER EIGHTEEN

The Concentration Camp for Boys

What man of you, having an hundred sheep, if he lose one of them,
doth not leave the ninety and nine in the wilderness, and go after that
which is lost, until he find it? And when he hath found it, he layeth it
on his shoulders, rejoicing. And when he cometh home, he calleth
together his friends and neighbours, saying unto them, Rejoice with
me; for I have found my sheep which was lost.

Luke 15: 4–6

M OST YOUNG SOUTH ISLAND MUSTERERS HAVE A NATURAL
curiosity about working in the North Island, and I was no
exception. We'd heard tales from blokes who had, of punching big mobs
of romneys, the predominance of huntaways and the beauty of Maori
women. The few northerners who ventured south, in my limited
experience of them, didn't impress: they didn't like hard-walking country
or free-running merinos, and had big sloppy huntaways with no flair for
handy work. Few stayed. They could shine at dog trials — and did — but
not, it seemed, on the hill. Marriage, management and ownership had curtailed my freedom to roam and I'd never joined them and never thought
I would. But retirement wasn't as retiring as I thought it would be.

We were at the New Zealand championships at Lowburn, near Tarras,
in the early 1980s and Alf Boynton had been pumping me all night about
who was up who in the kennels of this bloke and that one. I was getting
sick of all this interrogation, drinking whisky, watching Norman Boyton
pull rotisserie chicken legs from one side of his picket-fence teeth to exit
with a bare bone in one flowing movement, and I expressed the regret of
my youth.

'Come up for the docking,' said Alf, who managed Otairi Station, near

Hunterville. Docking is Northspeak for marking, but wherever it is you have to muster the sheep, yard them and do unspeakable things like dagging, drenching, earmarking, tail-cutting and a considerable amount of castration. 'Starts 22 September,' Alf continued.

All good things must come to an end, this excellent night being one of them. Making our farewells, and having forgotten about his casual invitation, I said, 'See you next nationals.'

'No, 22 September.'

As September rolled around I was as apprehensive as the virgin who'd been told he would still respect her in the morning if . . . So I decided on a silly opener for a phone call. Pompous. Affected. Something easy for one or both of us to pull out of. 'Further to our conversation of 14 June at Lowburn Collie Dog Club grounds, are you still expecting me at Otairi on the twenty-second?'

Silence. He never expected this call, though he hadn't forgotten it, that's for sure. 'Do you want to come?'

'If I'm welcome.'

'Okay. Be here on the twenty-second.'

I loaded up Big Bronze, the Falcon ute, with three heading dogs and six huntaways, and four reared pups ready for work that I wanted rid of.

I hate lots of water and I hate towns, and Cook Strait, Christchurch and Wellington were in my road. I conned a young student friend, Dick Bell, to drive me in Big Bronze from Christchurch to the hold of the ferry at Picton.

'How am I going to get home?'

'Catch a bloody bus.' Do you have to do all these young people's thinking for them?

One of Ima's in-laws, one of the engaged holidaymakers we'd put up at Glenaray who I figured still owed me, was to meet me in Wellington. He'd retired from some TV thing and grew orchids in the 35 years since we'd last seen each other. I was looking about when a dark-suited fellow walked up and said, 'Gidday, Snowy.'

'How'd you know me?'

'With that high-country walk? For chrissake, Snow.' I'd never thought we did anything but blend into the crowd. He took me to Upper Hutt where he lived, gave me a bed and feed, and had even visited the butcher for two dog tuckers. Next morning my truly perfect host drove in front of me until we reached the first sane part of State Highway 1 and my nerves had stopped jangling. Pretty soon I relaxed, started to look at all that new country.

> I'm free as the breeze
> What will stop me on high?
> I will do as I please
> Open road, open sky . . .

Don't recall singing on the way back, but good tenors are fat and I'd lost 10 kilograms.

Alf met me, told me to settle in. He had water in the fridge, he said, and I was ready for a whisky but as usual he couldn't contain his curiosity about my dogs' feeding and breeding, age and stage. I met five young shepherds who came to see the visitor from outer space who'd judged New Zealand trials. Unbeknown to me they'd been psyched up by Alf — don't let your dogs bite sheep in front of WV; don't let a dog run through the middle of a mob while WV's about. With all those youths eager to impress me, I felt things would be pretty easy. Any lingering doubts about my ability to cope vanished as I sipped Alf's whisky and turned in early.

Then I was in Africa: a mad elephant was bearing down on me and I wished someone would shoot it.

'You awake, WV?'

'What the —?' Some rude idiot was clumping about when everyone had just gone to bed. Some of us had to be up early!

'Time to go.' *Clump, clump, clump.* Alf's normal tread. 3.30 a.m.

I watched him eat cornflakes and fruit. I tried it for three days — the doctor had said only one egg a week. But my skinny frame couldn't be fuelled on those rations. I requested eggs, two soft boiled, every day and Alf got quite good at them in the finish.

'Good of you to come up.' These good words, down at the stabling yards, were the first the head shepherd, jockey-sized Alan Nimmo, uttered to me. Made me feel right at home. Here was a realist.

'Well, I don't want any concessions. If I can't keep up, I'll go home. Except one. It's not that I can't handle a hard horse, it's that at my age, I don't bounce any more.'

'Take that one.' There were 25 horses careering about in the yard. 'Just keep your eye on him. Fix him.' That's how I met Alien, Nimmo's top horse.

That day we mustered 18 sheep. Nimmo, Alf, five musterers and I spent a hard day on that block to yard 18 sheep and mis-mothered some lambs doing it. The South Islanders I talked to later couldn't follow it; nor could I then, except that was the way they'd always done it. Only Nimmo and I thought the effort-to-result ratio, not to mention the economics, daft. I still think so, but there were payoffs in Alf's madness.

Another day Alf, an impatient man, yelled to me, 'Get the dry dries, the wet dries and the late wets.' Then he was gone behind a ridge. When Nimmo came by me, I asked him to translate. The first were fat barren ewes destined for harder territory, the second were those who lost their lambs destined for harder territory, and then he too was gone, but I figured 'late wets' were late lambers who'd want a wee spell before their lambs were docked.

Next morning — *clump, clump* — it was 3.30. It seemed to be 3.30 for three weeks.

A description of Alf Boynton and his country will take you some of the way to understanding it.

Alf not only walks like an elephant, he's got a memory like one. Encyclopedia Man, he'll give you the breeding of any particular collie you care to name. I was with him at the Levels trials and he asked Chris Cochrane, 'Still sell your calves at Balclutha?' Chris said, over a beer later, 'Jasus, WV, we haven't had cattle on the the Ranch for 15 years.' But he isn't shaped like an elephant; he's a fine-looking bloke, olive skinned, stocky, broad shouldered, fit, mid-sixties now and keen eyed, though he often seems distracted. Like Churchill he has the ability to catnap on cue anywhere. While his wife Mary told me about the gutsache one of the kids had at school, Alf would catch 40. But the phone would bring him to his feet first ring.

Walking down the road, smelly from dagging and sweat, Alf would ask, 'How's that Jean breeding?' You'd tell him about the South Island huntaway bitch's sex life, while he'd cross your path, pull out his knife from the 'medals pouch' North Island blokes carry — belt with notepad, pencil stub and knife — and dig out a bit of stinkweed on this side and that. But he'd know Jean was carrying on with Ben, although he appeared to pay no mind when he asked.

I've got mixed feelings about his leadership technique — I felt he ought to do more explaining and delegating. He led by example, always taking the newest shepherd, or the youngest, or the weakest close by him so he could look after the bloke and teach him. He had very capable men and boys. They'd habitually dig out stinkweed too.

The stock and the place itself were a credit to him. His stock management couldn't be faulted. His big heavy romneys heard dogs bark every day and were good to work, climbing well in the early morning and getting a bit scratchy in the afternoon. But by then men and dogs were usually on bulldozed tracks and things were easier. I've nothing against his neighbours, in fact I'm on their side if this is the cost, but his weed control superiority was obvious to even the untutored eye. He was cunning and not a minute went by where he was not either finding things out or communicating them or pushing his boys. Otairi had a second woolshed in its backblock and Alf got sick of toast and marmalade so he pinned a scone recipe to the inside of a cupboard of the cookhouse there. Not a boy on the place quibbled if Alf asked him to bake a batch.

'That Innes place, Dunstan Downs, how big's that?' Alf avoiding unnecessary words, bending over something, busy as hell.

'Well, the bottom block's 10 000 acres.' What was he up to? (Otairi had a total of 11 000 acres.)

'How long they take to muster that?' Now I got it.

'About four or five hours.' North Island boys wouldn't have any idea of big open tussocky alluvial flats where you set up a bark and the sheep move across it in huge lines. TV would be their only clue. I was being set up as straight man to Alf's joker, the object to goad boys on to further excellence.

'What are merinos like to muster?' asked one astute boy.

'Well, they're God's own sheep. Not like these slobby gobs,' I said. Merinos can walk the legs off other sheep; the comparison held incomparables.

For my two bob's worth, the two most dedicated managers I've known are Alf Boynton and Bill Pinckney.

Otairi taught me the difference between gullies and ravines like no other place. Otairi was steep, steep country to a man to whom steep country is, well, country. The underlying rock was black volcanic pappa. Central Otago and the Lindis is full of a nasty rock called schist, but schist crumbles under pressure and the worst of it can be picked from a horse's leg. Pappa is unyielding. We've got razorback ridges in the south too, but Otairi's were grassed, hell in the wet. Alf put the yearlings — year-old horses — on a steep block for a year. Some cut themselves up and died, or fell over a ravine. He put the two-year-olds on a steeper block for another year and broke the survivors. Alien was one such. He knew more than I did and I knew it, let him have his head most of the time. At a brow he'd spread his feet sideways and go straight downhill. Pull him sideways and he'd topple, and I knew it. A couple of times I tried to force him down at a spot that looked good to me. He'd baulk, spread his lips and snort *Ppp-ppp-fff-rrr,* then walk off to his own place to scuttle across. I swear his belly was raking stones. I know his legs were out at 45 degrees like brakes. Any South Islander would have dismounted and walked his horse across it, but up there you'd fall behind if you did. It was worse when it rained, which it did every third day. It was huntaway country where you lifted sheep onto a ridge out of bush before you could walk them anywhere; totally different to the South Island's general chase-them-downhill-an'-move-them-along-the-flat.

Alien and three well-trained heading dogs saved me from total humiliation. Otairi's huntaways were used to lifting sheep; mine to slewing from above. I used heading dogs to get below them. Their shepherds had a heading dog and maybe four huntaways; I had three headers and, for Otairi, dumb huntaways. But there are always tight spots on a muster, places where a heading dog can shine, and Otairi was no different.

Even hands-on Alf couldn't be on the hill every day, and he was busy with paperwork one day when Nimmo was absent as well. It was just the boys and me that day. I had some status but no role in the hierarchy. The boys were like boys always are: tired, hungry and gullible. They were surrounded by excellence. They did things different, looked different in their shorts, knife and notebook, leggings — 'chaps' in wild west fiction, and the way they conducted themselves. But they were getting a unique education. That day we were under the second shepherd; from a management point of view they were on their own, led by one of their own.

Lloyd rode in for lunch at the back woolshed. The second shepherd asked him, 'How'd you get on with those four ewes?' In the South Island we spill more than that.

'Got two of them.'

'Well, you know the rules here, Lloyd. We muster the lot.'

Alf heard the two-of-four story and at lunch next day said, 'Lloyd, catch a horse and get those two ewes and two lambs.' It was a 90-minute ride out, but at 6 p.m. Lloyd brought two ewes and two lambs past a gate I opened for him.

'Lloyd,' I said, 'you can fool some of the people some of the time, but you can't fool me. You rode out of sight, had a kip under a tree and cut these two from a handy mob, didn't you?' (I would have.) Lloyd turned white at the thought. 'Christ, no!'

Later that day Alf and I were looking at his poddies — lambs not doing well. He'd drenched, crutched and trucked them to greener pastures for a spell and they were looking good. 'Good day, today.'

'Gawd, Alf, you sent poor Lloyd out on a fool's errand and the rest of us had to work harder in the yards. Six hours for two ewes. What's the sense in that?'

'Two today, four tomorrow, six the next . . . Place'd get untidy otherwise. Lloyd'll try harder next time.'

Next day Alf and Lloyd were dagging ewes. I heard Alf give Lloyd advice on a young huntaway Lloyd had, in a gentle fatherly tone: 'Go soft on her. Just keep doing what you're doing. Don't try any fancy dog trial stuff on her. Let her grow up . . .' This was a fine if complex working relationship.

Much later I rang Alf from home, asked how the boys were.

'Lloyd's gone.'

'Oh?'

'Got disobedient. I told him, "You do as you're told and go left or you can always go right." He went right.' Left to the men's quarters, right to the exit gate at Otairi.

'He's a conscientious bloke, Alf.'

'Jesus, WV, I know that. He'll be a top man some day.'

At the next nationals, Lloyd arrived and he and Alf talked animatedly, not a whiff of their previous animosity. Two big-hearted men.

I eagerly awaited the last day on Otairi. I was bushed, sick of bouncing over pappa and looking at sheep's arses; looking forward to Ima's cooking, a full night's sleep and being dry every day. At the end of each day, after the last cup of tea, Andrew McLeod's voice would boom out like a locomotive whistle with a dead hawk in it: 'Oh well, Day Twelve ends and Day Thirteen begins.' Nothing sums up the conveyor-belt nature of work on Otairi like Andrew's resigned observation.

The last day looked good for a sweet afternoon. There were a couple of cuts and some yarding, a breeze. Common humanity would play its part: the boys had a 3.30 a.m. start elsewhere the next day.

'There's a couple of thistle patches up there and there you missed,' said Alf. 'Get back up there and powder them.' Variegated thistle is a big tough weed; even tough-skinned horses won't brave its thorns, and Alf's boys carried powder weedkiller to counter it. A South Islander would have told Alf to get stuffed after a hard day. I'm stuffed if I know who was right, either. But two riders retraced their steps and got back about six o'clock.

I'd had enough of my North Island adventure, but like women say about the pain of childbirth, you forget. Early September rolled around again, and I got — it sounds quaint already — a telegram:

DOCKING IMPOSSIBLE STOP NEED YOUR HELP STOP ALF

I was considering it when, next day, another telegram arrived:

NEED YOUR HELP STOP GET BIG BRONZE HOTTED UP STOP
THE SHEPHERDS

What's a man to do? I closed the tailgate, kissed Ima goodbye, rolled out onto the tarseal, and had my sixtieth birthday on the inter-island ferry. At the back woolshed that year I took a photograph of the shearing crew, and a cheeky young Maori bloke came up to me and said, 'Now you can tell 'em you've been to South Africa.' (Nelson Mandela was still on Robben Island then.) Things I like about New Zealanders of Scottish descent and Scots immigrants, their hospitality, material and social generosity, love of the land, eating, drinking, and storytelling I found I liked about Maori also. Nimmo was there. Boynton was exactly the same: impossible, a bit crazy, difficult and wonderful.

I did five seasons at Otairi. The boys came and went, fine young men most of them, and top blokes. Mary's cooking seemed to just get better. I can understand why New Zealanders have a burning desire to go overseas, but I don't. My son John knew the weakest point in my implacability, a trip to southern Africa to see gazelle, zebra, lion, buffalo, impala and that unbeatable wildlife combination. All I had to do was get myself there and back; the rest would be organised by him at his expense. I was tempted, but a tussocky ridge and the Southern Alps at my shoulder was enough and I never went.

But, except for Wellington and Auckland, I love the North Island. Mustering and dog trials took me all over it, even unto Northland's north.

On each Otairi trip, during a two-week gap between docking and shearing work, I went to Ngakuru and Waikate, 20 kilometres south of Rotorua. Two good mates, Ray Hamblin and John Rothman, a former Otamatapaio Station shepherd, had drawn ex-Lands and Survey blocks there. On my first trip I detoured through Tongariro National Park to mate a bitch to a class dog of John Journeaux. The country did not impress. Awful eerie and empty, I felt.

Nearing the end of my journey, I called at a farmhouse for directions to Rothman's. The windscreen was pretty fogged up and it had been raining. The distance between the gate and the house frontage was black. I thought how sensible this North Island idea was: tarseal, no lawns. I swung Big Bronze sideways and up but didn't get far — I was bogged. The front door opened and an elderly man screamed, 'That's a bloody new-sown lawn you're on!' I backed off, apologised profusely and offered to return, rake in hand, seed under my arm — as you'd do. Turned out the old man was only caretaking for the weekend but he was worried about his owner son-in-law's reaction on returning. When the Rothmans told locals at a party that night about my lawn-wrecking, everyone thought it hilarious but I didn't. I pointed out to them the South Island habit of a few pegs and a bit of white tape could've avoided the whole thing. Honestly, I'm sure a lot of those North Islanders do their courting standing up in a canoe on a choppy lake, the hard way.

I spent a week with each of my mates docking — free bed, food and two or three whiskies a night. It was good to catch up with them and for them to catch up on Waitaki doings.

On my last trip a recently widowed neighbour of Ray's had two well-bred black-and-tan huntaway pups from her late husband's crack bitch to give away. Ray and I agreed to take one each, then fought over who got which one, but he let me have the agreed-upon best one. On the long trip home I called at Tim and Jeeva Innes's and they persuaded me to give it them. Six months later I called back and asked how the pup was going.

'Come with me,' Jeeva said. There, standing on the kennel, was a big dog, a prick-eared half-Alsatian. The dog became a guard dog in Wellington I heard, but I was sure glad he'd not been reared on my meat and milk powder.

Margaret Anderson, John's widow and now sole runholder of Ben Ledi, a substantial property in the Waitaki Valley, came to the door of her lounge room and asked her sons Ian and Don if they would like some ice cream. They stared at the television oblivious.

'Would you like some ice cream?' again. She looked very tired. She had 15 men on the place — breakfasts, smokos, lunch, teas to provide as well as the usual mother's load. The pause lengthened.

'Aw, yeah.' Boys were still glued to some soap opera.

'What kind? There's vanilla, raspberry and lime.'

Some teenage girl on TV was getting cross about her girlfriend's lack of common humanity in the matter of the latter's attitude to the lout with the earring who was the subject of all the drama. The boys heard her out while their mother waited. 'Vanilla.'

'You want vanilla too?'

'Yeah.'

I had been behind a newspaper, listening with gritted teeth. The house was old and Margaret had to go outside into the cold to the freezer. While she was out, I leaned forward: 'You know, ice cream isn't very heavy.' And an idea took root.

I waited for a couple of years — 17 was a bit young for Stalag Otairi — but at 19 it was time, and Alf was keen to have them. Their grandfather Ian was a renowned dog man, after all. Margaret wasn't so keen: she'd heard Boynton was a hard man. When she asked me what she could do for them, I said, 'Teach them to make scones.'

On my last year there we were eating Ian's scones out at the back woolshed. There was only one left. 'No one touch that,' I said.

'Why's that, WV?'

'Because I want to wrap it up and take it to Ian's mother.'

The signs of men emerging from boys were already up on the board. I was on the phone to their mother after they returned from their first incarceration. 'You wouldn't believe it, WV. They're way out on the spur spraying nodding thistle. Never done that before. On their Christmas break, too!' Now, where would they have got that idea? Same place they learned to break and shoe a horse, use a handpiece for dagging and much, much more.

Donald and Ian junior put in two and a half seasons each on Otairi at different times.

Ian won a national championship event — Straight Hunt — and Donald was placed in a heading event not long after.

CHAPTER NINETEEN

Retirement? What Retirement?

If I was honest unto myself I would have to admit I hate bloody hills.

Doodle by Duncan Anderson,
found in his office after his death

T HE IDEA AGE MAKES YOU PLACID IS NONSENSE — LIKE THE IDEA two can live as cheaply as one. You get grouchier.

I'd been mustering around the Ahuriri, but came home for Christmas 1978. The phone rang before I'd scratched anything familiar. Ron Williamson was stuck. Shearing was held up. He needed someone to give him a hand to get the yearling cattle out of the Dingle. And the sky was falling, Chicken Licken.

Ron's Birchwood Station was high up the Ahuriri, in the Southern Alps. His neighbour and pal Ian Sargeson owned the Dingle Station on the Hawea side. Both worked the Dingle Valley. The Dingle runs into Lake Hawea, not that it matters a bugger where the bloody thing goes.

My dogs and swag were still in the vehicle while we talked. Some Christmas break. On the other hand I'd never been on the Dingle, in the valley where Ron kept his yearlings for a bull-free 12 months, up near the little-fenced reaches close by Hawea. Few people had. Said to be fisherman's heaven too. People raved on about the Dingle's beauty, uniqueness, perfectness, all that palaver. 'Any fish up there?' I asked.

'WV, oh, the fish!' he said, like he had a fish plague of Egyptian locust proportions. 'You've got to hide behind the matagouri to tie your minnow on or they jump out and take it from your hand!'

Hmmm.

We fished all bloody day, Ron, two boys and I. No joy.

Ron wanted to look at a pakihi, a swampy clearing in the scrub, for cattle, see if they'd drifted down that far. 'Henry, take Mr Kerr to that hole over by Sandstone Cliff. He'll get one there, no worries.' Sandflies as big as leeches, buckets of them. No fish. When we got back Ron said, 'Gis that rod,' and rode — he had crook legs — up the Dingle, that fisherman's Shangri La, casting left and right beautifully from the saddle all the way back to the hut. Truly awesome perfect casts, every one, better than my best. But no fish.

Getting the cattle was easier and more rewarding. At least they were there. I rode Jet, a 21-year-old mare.

We wound up at the Williamson homestead. Jennifer brought morning tea into the sunroom for us. 'Well, Bill, what do you think of the Dingle? Isn't it the most beautiful valley?'

'Don't think so. All I saw were two paradise ducks and one young one, and a hare. Looks to be starvation country to me.' She changed tack, clearly taken aback by hard words about a spot she clearly loved.

'How did you find Jet? Isn't she a beautiful mare?'

'Can I buy her?'

'Oh, sorry, Bill, we'd love to retire her to your place, but we're only half owners, you see, and . . .'

'It's not that. She's the worst horse I've ever ridden. She nearly rolled over on me three times. Wanted her for the deep freeze.'

Such scorn is usually a good way to get the scones and the beer cut off in the high country, but next year Ron rang again. He was stuck again and I was back in the Dingle, like some old song's refrain.

Henry, Ron's schoolboy son, and I went over the saddle into the Dingle Valley's bush, then rode down the valley to collect the cattle and brought them back to the headwaters. We would stay in the Forestry Department's Dingle Hut overnight, pick up the cattle in the morning and take them over the saddle into the Ahuriri Valley the next day. I was then going to a previous engagement with George Innes, and was to return for another muster on another block. Ron had given us the key and passed on permission to use the hut's food. By the time we'd settled the cattle and got to the hut, dark was descending fast. The horses snorted. Knowing how young fellas love drama, terror and a challenge, and preferring it to boredom myself, I said: 'Don't like the look of this, Henry. Might be somebody dead in there. You go look.' He'd gone about 10 metres when I added, 'If there's a deadie in there, I bags his watch.' But the problem wasn't deadies: the foresters had changed the key to the tucker store. We edged it open with the blade of an axe. Then Henry couldn't get the fire started, so I advised him to put an old rug that was lying about over the front top three-quarters of the fireplace to draw oxygen in from the bottom. He managed. Good boy. The tinned tucker was tops — big blue plums so good I took the label for Ima's shopping list.

We pulled out next morning, but a minor misadventure with a horse slipping its reins meant we left hurriedly, with half a tin of peas out on the table. That night we discussed the next muster. 'How many yearlings recorded in the diary?' I asked, an important question as there isn't much sense looking for cattle that don't exist. But Ron wasn't a diary man; he recalled 82 or 83 but said there might have been two or three deaths over the winter, so around 80. (We got 83 and a cow and a calf; Ron was chuffed, but that was later.) Then I laboured for that old ingrate George Innes down the Ahuriri for three days. A southerly blew up while I was away from the Dingle. A real wicked surprise attack of a storm.

I picked up the mail at Birchwood's gate — a high-country custom townies could well emulate when visiting busy stations — and walked noisily into the kitchen so as not to frighten or embarrass anybody. Jennifer cut me off at the pass. 'WV, none of your funnies, mind. Jonathan Elworthy's had a few personal problems to sort out and has been in the hills to get within himself.' George Innes had talked Ron into seeking a bit of political help from Elworthy — 'Jonathan knows the ropes'. Elworthy was a former Minister of Lands, and half the high country was hopping mad about steep rises in rents and rates. The astute reader will realise I know when to shut up.

I walked into the sunroom, surprised to find Elworthy prone on Ron's favourite couch. He shook my hand without much energy and his story unfolded.

Jonathan had been staying with Ian Sargeson on Dingle Station and decided to trek up the Dingle River to Birchwood. Ron got a ring from Sarge to see how the troubled fella was. He hadn't turned up. The big southerly was cause for further concern, so Ron, not able to walk over tussock though a superb horseman, went up his side of the mountain to survey the track over the saddle with his son Henry. They came up to another forestry hut. 'Henry, look inside. He may be asleep in there.' Henry dismounted and walked 10 metres, then stopped: 'Dad, if he's dead, bags his watch.' They were about to turn back when Jonathan, wearing shorts and shirt, carrying a groundsheet under his arm, walked down the track.

He'd got bushed by a side stream of the Dingle and followed that instead of the main river. His swag had been washed over a waterfall and he'd not been able to retrieve it — entirely understandable in that rough country with steep rapids and falls everywhere. He'd lost his parka, sleeping bag and a change of warmer clothes. He'd stopped in the Dingle Hut — recognised my name from the visitor's log — but couldn't get into the food cupboard or light the fire. (He was going to talk to the Forestry Department about that.) He'd eaten the half tin of peas we'd left, but escaped ptomaine poisoning. He'd not seen cattle marks, though we'd taken 80 head through. Perhaps that'd been a good thing: if he'd tried the saddle we'd taken the cattle over and got caught in the southerly, he'd have been a goner.

Ron had papers strewn around, some with Lands Department letterhead, so I knew he'd been lobbying to get Elworthy on side. He cut to the chase: 'Well, Jonathan, what do you think about these rises? You gonna help us?'

'Certainly not. From what Sarge tells me about the prices you fellows are getting for merino wool, I think they should be higher.' Ron was speechless and furious. Elworthy indicated The Outside with a languid wave, and changed the subject. 'Gee, it's amazing how the bush is regenerating in the Dingle.'

'Yeah. They used to blame my cattle but it was the bloody deer.' Like a lot of places, venison shooters had cleaned the Dingle out, made deer extinct locally.

Young Henry's eyes were out on stalks at this adult drama but he was self-possessed enough to give me a nudge and say quietly, 'Good watch, Mr Kerr.'

Jonathan's son arrived from Oamaru to pick his father up. Jennifer had had a quiet but firm word with Ron and Ron saw him off with all the grace he could muster, but returned ears red with rage. 'Did you *hear* that bugger, Kerr?'

'Yeah, that's the bloke you and Innes were going to get to fight your cause.' But Ron wasn't listening. I might as well have howled at the moon.

Politics: dark, dirty, dangerous business. Someone's got to do it. But it ain't me, babe, it ain't me you're lookin' for. New interests were taking me more often to the city. Like owning Pakistanian Lad, the racehorse.

Ian Anderson and I drove to Wingatui in my Ford Falcon utility with the fibreglass floor and a flash new custom-made dog cover over the tray, with a wee gap for dogs' noses out the back. We were going to see the horse run. About Moeraki Ian said, 'Now, Kerr, I don't want to be a nuisance, but I've got a bit of a problem.'

'What's your problem?'

He'd seen an ad in the *Otago Daily Times*: Black Douglas whisky was going cheap at the Bowling Green Hotel, and some cash in his pocket was rapidly deteriorating under the weight of galloping inflation. I offered to go halves. Six bottles would have been the biggest purchase of whisky I'd ever made. 'No, Kerr, I thought a wee bit more than that.'

We pulled up at my son Johnny's place. He was a varsity lad then, studying accountancy and camped out in one of those old brick houses in Dunedin. We got him to drive us to Wingatui, and back. But first he shouted us a whisky. I said to Ian: 'John'll know the drill; he used to work at that pub as a barman.' We put Ian's modest proposal to him. 'Leave it to me.' He rang the pub.

'No,' we heard him say, 'that can't be right. The way I estimate it, this bloke wants about 12 dozen.' They had to break it out of bond and when Johnny pulled in close to the loading ramp that Saturday morning, a bloke on a forklift asked him to move out of the way. John noticed the words 'Black Douglas' printed on the cartons and said, 'No, this is where it goes.'

He did a meticulous accounting and supervised the loading while we went in and squared up. The bar room was a barn of a place, the bar itself the shape of a U forming the bottlestore as well. There were old ladies stopping in for a half of sherry, idle drinkers, punters watching the TV and Ian in his old gaberdine overcoat and the brim of his hat turned up. A bloke in a white shirt and his mate behind the bar were working the register and scratching away with pen and paper when Ian reached into his pocket, pulled out his tight roll and whipped the rubber band off.

Notes sprang all over the bar. Heads turned. The bloke totting up was completely thrown out — he had to go away to another room, sit down and start again.

We set off in the Falcon, loaded to the gunnels with booze, and this story nearly took a bad turn. There was a godalmighty bang: the tailgate had slipped open going up one of Dunedin's famously steep streets. It was a miracle the load didn't slip straight out over the back and onto the road, but it hovered on the lip, not a drop lost.

It was quite cold at Wingatui but Anderson took off his overcoat and tucked the thing around the booze so no robber would spot the stuff through the gap, and froze. About then Johnny, who had been distracted, was adding up x x 750 millilitres, y x 1.5 litres and z x 1125 millilitres. Then he announced there had been a mistake, told us to go place our bets, and drove the ute back into town. There he showed the Bowling Green Hotel the error of their calculations and extorted a promise to have the quantity brought up to full weight when they found some more booze. Anderson's $2000 booze order seemed to have cleared the city of Black Douglas.

We'd been invited to call in on George Innes on the way back from the races. He asked what we'd have. 'Whisky,' I said.

'Whisky, if you would, George,' said Ian. 'If I had known we were going to call in, I'd have brought a bottle.'

Back in the ute I told him I thought he was a bit rich saying that when he had umpteen gallons in my vehicle.

'Bugger Innes,' said Ian. 'It's good to drink *his* booze. *He's* drunk enough of mine in the past.'

I was going to Dunedin a while later and offered to pick up the balance of the booze, about two dozen bottles, from the Bowling Green, but he declined my kind offer. The suspicious old miser loaded up Betsy's little hatchback until the two of them looked like a liquor ad on wheels.

A lot of old high-country men are funny about money. Bill Hazlett used to have a tin of taxable loot buried in his garden. He was making a deposit or withdrawal once and saw the curtains move — his old housekeeper snooping — so he changed the spot in the middle of the night. Ginger Anderson was mowing the lawn at Ben Omar long after the old chieftain had shifted into retirement in Omarama and suddenly there were dollar notes everywhere, a tin Ian had forgotten.

George Innes is a good man at a funeral. He goes to everybody's.

When Gunner Collins, Omarama's longtime storekeeper, died, Bernard Thomas of Killermont made up a carload of mourners to go to Waimate and see Gunner off. Percy Kelland, Innes (wearing singularly inappropriate yellow socks) and I joined him. George said, 'Aw, we'll skip the service. We'll go to the pub and have a booze. See them afterwards.'

'Like bloody hell,' said Bernard. 'You're going to do it my way. You're going to do it right.' George was an example to all at the service, carting flowers out of the church and draping them on Gunner's coffin in the hearse. At the graveside he said, 'Christ, now we're away to the pub?'

'Like hell we are. Lotty's invited us around for a cup of tea and that is where we are going,' Bernard insisted.

Old Mrs Collins was looking a bit sad until George sat beside her and asked, 'And what'll you be doing for sex tonight, Mrs Collins?' She laughed out loud.

Charlie Collins was a marksman, hence the nickname, and a Boer War veteran. The commander of a dawn raid on the veldt is said to have asked, 'Is Gunner Collins here?'

'Yes, sir.'

'Then let battle commence.'

Fair enough. That's what New Zealanders are for. Gutting Springboks.

I didn't attend Ian Anderson's funeral. Couldn't. I'd have fallen in with him.

His grandson, young Ian, rang from Oamaru, looking for a bit of moral support perhaps. His mother had gone up to Omarama township to be with Betsy, Ian's second wife and now widow, and wanted young Ian to come up too. I plugged on up that familiar road determined not to show my heavy heart — Ian was still young.

'Bill, Betsy's got Grandad in the house. He made her promise not to leave him in the morgue.' Ian had died in Oamaru Hospital at 85. He wasn't keen on crowds, even in death, apparently. 'It's a hot day,' I said. 'Hope they put plenty of preservative in him.'

At Betsy's — for the time had come to think of it as hers — nephew Tim Wallace had flown Betsy's sister over from Wanaka and they needed someone to pick them up from their helicopter's landing spot. Ian volunteered and the widow and I were alone. 'Bill, see what you think of this.' I thought we'd open the coffin for a last look at the old fella, but she directed my attention to his pipe and tobacco taped on the lid. I thought of what Betsy told me about their world tour: she was willing to bet Ian was the only man in the whole of Disneyland wearing a hat and smoking a pipe. It seemed fitting. 'He always had it with him; he might as well take it with him,' she said.

'Poor old fella won't have a drink up there,' I said, thinking of the time I'd said, 'You'd be an alcoholic, Anderson. When was the last time you went a day without a drink?' He pulled on some aromatic weed and claimed a dry day the previous year in London. Betsy had been there too. Her brow had knitted: 'When was that?' He reminded her of a visit to some teetotal relatives. 'But I had to put the car away at our hotel and when I got to the room you were drinking whisky,' she said. He reminded her that that had been after midnight. I remembered how he couldn't comment on my observation that the last inch of a bottle of whisky gets sour after a week or two 'because,' he said, 'it doesn't last around here.'

She got one of those tiny bottles and taped it on the coffin as well. Then she added his dog whistle.

I was about to go back home when Betsy, with funeral business to attend to, persuaded me to siphon mourners from the house. The pub seemed to be appropriate. George Innes, Rick Aubrey and others gathered there, leaving the widow her time alone. At the pub one thing led to another. Rick's next stop was Ben Omar to see Ian's son Ginger. I went with him. Condolences were exchanged — I think Ginger understood I'd lost my best mate, and Ian loved his son, so Ginger shouted for us, which is what you do.

Back at the pub a good many of us had a lot to drink. The publican, Peter Casserly, was once a shearer for Ian, and he shouted a feed of bacon and eggs at 11 p.m. — it was not only free, it was compulsory. The contrast with another publican was refreshing.

At home next morning I had trouble making it out of bed, but dear Ima and Fiona represented the family. I fed my dogs and thought of the hills Ian and I had climbed, the spots where 'good water for dogs' existed wherever Ian was thirsty, Ian's victories and disasters at dog trials from Kaikohe to Invercargill, his appetite for life, dry wit, love of the sound of bagpipes and, with guilt, the dog men asking, 'What happened to Kerr?' at the funeral.

I need not have worried. Ginger's wife Sylvia said, 'Bill was here yesterday and very nice it was of him to come.'

The idiosyncrasies of bosses have been an amusement for 70 years, and retirement offered me plenty in the way of owners, managers and head shepherds to choose from. 'Idiosyncrasy' is a word I have only recently come across, but it's the best word in the language. There's a heap of things that have seemed strange to me, but they are idiosyncrasies. My next retirement job is to learn how to pronounce it.

Dick Bell came out of Lincoln to manage a property up the Awatere Valley in Marlborough. Dry, hard country with a good merino flock, and they'd never had a footrot problem, but Dick thought he detected it. Would I, he asked, give him the benefit of my learned wisdom and come up? We tipped over the whole flock and found two that might — *might* — have had symptoms. But something *was* spreading: fear. A neighbour stopped his kids catching the school bus at Dick's gate. He brought over some old books, 20-year-old Ag. Department manuals on eradicating footrot and, when Dick told the fellow three of his stragglers were await-ing collection, he said, 'Cut their throats, don't bring 'em over here.' I joined a conversation between them and heard the profoundly modern environmentally sensitive eco-farmer explaining how he'd mixed up a footbath of formalin to disinfect his gumboots before coming over and he'd be in the trough when he returned. It was too good to resist: 'What about the ducks?'

'Ducks? Ducks! What do you mean "ducks", Mr Kerr?'

'Dick's feeding out grain here and there's a hundred or so paradise ducks feeding on the remnants. When they've finished, they could fly over to your place.' He went white faced at the thought of it. 'They could have the germ on their feet.'

That got rid of him. Next morning he was up early, blazing away, clearing the ducks off his property half a mile away. The rare protected teal wouldn't have had butter's chance in a red-hot frying-pan. His kids were going to get awfully sick of duck on access weekends too.

I played offsider to Dick Bell at Criffle near Wanaka once. Dick's the bloke who put Richard Prebble crook about the Wool Board mucking up his deal with the Italian wool buyer fellow a year or so back. The place hadn't been run too well, and the sheep were weak. When we shedded up for the shearers each night, a few animals died. We packed them more loosely but still a few died. Each morning the rouseabouts, reasonably, got the dead ones off the gratings and threw them out the windows of the shed. 'Shall I get a truck and cart those bloaters away, Dick?' I asked.

'No, we'll do it tomorrow,' he said. But 'tomorrow' didn't come in the three days I spent there. We went to the shed one afternoon and he started picking up teabags the gang had thrown out the door. 'If there's one bloody thing I can't bloody stand, it's bloody teabags lying around everywhere.'

He and I brought a mob up from Luggate to a block near Criffle, road traffic a pain, and three escapee lambs getting into side paddocks on the way. We plugged back in the Toyota to get them, with Queen, Dick's white heading bitch, the only dog with us. Good thinking, Dick, I thought. A lamb will think that white dog is its mother. Dick can outrun a hare and he did this day, around and around, sweating and lunging for frisky lambs. When I'd enjoyed the farce long enough, I pulled the lambskin cover off my seat, drooped it over a big thistle and went '*Maa-maa*.' Got one, then the other two and put them in the truck.

Which puts me in mind of Mike Thomas. On Dunstan Peaks I had a rat problem. Ken Anderson said he could get rid them. 'Can you?' We poured a gallon of petrol down the holes, lit it and stood back with shotguns. Every now and then there'd be a *whompf* and rats would come out, a few burning, and run up trees. He lived at Killermont at the time and Killermont's owner, Mike Thomas, was most impressed with our success. He poured 20 gallons down his rat holes and blew up his motel kennels.

Mike called on me down country when I had a few pigs — a passing enthusiasm. 'There's a few bob in pigs, Michael,' I told him. He got into them, and put a heat bulb over them like I had over mine. Must have been too close to the straw, though. 'There's a fire over there, Michael!' someone yelled as they left the house for the muster. They did what they could, but as Ken observed, it seemed Michael had started up a new market for rotisserie pigs. Trouble was, he didn't kill them first.

At Windsor I showed Mike my high-tech low-labour spud planting method too. You run a shallow furrow, drop the spuds in it and cover them up automatically as you push the overburden off the next furrow onto the last one. What could be simpler? But he set his blade about a metre below the surface and of course the poor sprouting spuds never made it to the surface for light. I tell these fellows less is more, but do they listen?

John Stokes and I got on well, but he wasn't free from idiosyncrasy. He had two houses on Cloudy Peaks, a quite satisfactory one on a rise and a better one down below the terrace. Sharing a drop of white magic one day I asked him why he lived up here, not down there. 'My father told me, "Always live in that house. Then you can see what the employees are doing down below yer."'

He had two hard doers working for him, Doug Still and Jack Patterson. They reported in and John told them to repair an implement and tidy up the workshop just below the woolshed and John's house. John knew a peephole in the woolshed and used it to see what they were doing, but he was a chain smoker. At a telltale wisp of smoke Doug said to Jack, 'He's there again. Your turn with the hammer.' A mighty blow on the anvil sounded like Thor was belting out a lightning storm. Jack threw down the hammer and sauntered back to his seat. 'My deal . . . spades trumps.'

Doug and Jack were working tractors, a harrow and a grubber, around and around a paddock when Stokes came up to have a yarn to Doug. He waited on the leading furrow until Doug came around, but Doug, looking behind his shoulder at his handiwork revealing itself beneath the harrow, didn't see him, and Stokes had to sidestep pretty smartly to avoid being run down. After that, Doug's concentration was Hollywood intense. He knew full well Stokes was standing directly in the tractor's path. This time Stokes had to leap for his life into the dirt. 'John! Didn't know you were there!' No wonder Stokes felt he'd had enough and opted to sell up for a life of ease in Wanaka.

He traded in the beaten-up old International 4x4 for a flash new 4WD to take prospective buyers, four a time, out on the mountain tracks. On a top he'd fire up the barbecue and apply the Gordon's white-magic treatment to loosen tongues — his nips were fierce. That night he'd ring his stock agent: 'Put the pencil through that one, he's got no dough. And that one, he's got the dough, but . . .' PL, Peter Anderson, Stokes considered so unlikely he didn't even rate a steak. PL was trying to sell up his down-country place near Milton and get back around Tarras–Cromwell. Peter felt he was so far short of the money being talked, he didn't even attend the auction in the Tarras Town Hall, though the Milton deal was nearly through and Cloudy Peaks was what he was looking for. His agent went, but left his wallet behind and cashed two cheques — $8.50 for fish and chips and $15 petrol — in Alexandra from his new chequebook. Then he bid $475 000 and Cloudy Peaks was knocked down to him. Those two paltry butts made the auctioneer very suspicious when he paid the 10 per cent deposit, and he rang PL that night to tell him what it went for. 'Did it? Ohmigod! Who bought it?'

'You did.'

Tim Innes's special expertise was labour relations. The shearers' union rep came around and grilled Tim about the station's shearers' quarters. The shower was okay but you couldn't stay in it to dry yourself off. You got wet from pipes spraying in all directions from frost-popped pipe leaks, and had to step out on the grass outside to towel down while the Mount Cook bus passed — 'Look, Mum, funny men in the nuddy'. But Tim thought the accommodation was okay. He called the union rep 'a big fat ugly communist old bitch' and told her to get off the place in the way any New Zealander will recall. Blacklisted pronto.

The more I think about bosses I've known the more I'm sure I'm completely alone in being totally rational, consistent, fair, clear and responsible. It's the idiots I've had to work with who made all those mistakes. I have always known exactly what I wanted and have never scrambled the message. All those balls-ups were at the other end of the chain.

I was having a whale of a time being 'retired', but changes were sneaking up on me. Mustering for Gordon Lucas through Tarras way, punching 2000 lambs short of water, getting in the river, I was generally having a long, hot, hard day of it. Sitting back over a whisky that night I told Gordon and his missus, Spin, I'd felt a bit woozy, nearly passed out and fallen over the bank at one stage. 'Noticed that, WV,' said Gordon. 'Spin and I talked about you. You've lost your old vault-over-the-sheepyard action.' This account of a noticeable decline of vim and vigour rang too true. 'Why not have a check-up with my doctor, Dr Pezzaro, in Wanaka?'

'Oh, can't stand doctors. Waiting rooms full of pregnant women, their bellies rattling all around me.'

'I know this bloke pretty well. I'll phone him.' Things were getting out of hand. Next thing he was on the blower, quoting my prejudices word for word. When he came back he said, 'It's all fixed up. You can go at a quarter to nine, before he opens up.' I was a bit toey about it. 'You and him will get on fine. Bet the two of you yarn away for an hour.'

The Kerrs have one physical weakness: skin cancer. Half them have died from it. I'd learned to recognise cancer spots pretty well by then. So when I fronted the nurse, I presented my hand, thinking this new lesion might as well be fixed up, seeing I was there. I asked her to take my blood pressure too. She took it three times, sitting, standing and lying down. 'Dr Pezzaro's going to have a very serious talk with you, Mr Kerr.' In walked a short, dumpy fellow in shorts, who grabbed my hand and the nurse's notes without ceremony and announced, 'This hand is the least of your bloody worries. Where'd you say you where staying?'

'Gordon Lucas's. Mustering.'

'Just as well. If you were sitting where I am, behind this desk, you'd be dead.' I knew the bloody mustering game had to be good for something, but this was small comfort. But he had barely begun to get stuck into me. 'Sugar?'

'Yeah, like my sugar.'

'How much?'

'Two teaspoonfuls every cup, one on my pudding . . .'

'Out.'

'But I thought sugar was good for energy.'

'You don't *run* around the bloody hills, do you? Out. Salt?'

'Like my salt.'

'Out. You get enough in cooking. Salt's out. How many feeds a day d'yer have?'

'Two at least. Three usually.'

'Smoke?'

'Yes.'

'How many?'

'Fifteen a day.'

'Hmm. I know how hard it is to give up smoking. Five. You've got to do this if you want to live. Alcohol?'

'I like a couple of whiskies at night.'

'One, two, three or four?'

I hesitated.

Bissaro didn't. 'One, two, three or four?'

'Two.'

'Two of Gordon Lucas's house nips. That's about bloody eight. Who's your local doctor?'

'Don't have one.'

'Well, get one, and give him this.' He swung around to scribble a bad report card. I figured he was perhaps Jewish and thought every tall blond bugger who came into his surgery was a Nazi and he wanted to punish us for killing his parents. His hand was covering a lot of paper. I stood up, a bit sick of him. 'Now that you've taken most of the good things of life away from me, how about sex?'

He looked up. 'Go for your bloody life. If you can.'

I called in at the Tarras store on my way back to Lucas's. 'Gidday, WV. Your usual?' said Joe as he reached for a carton of Matinee.

'No, thanks. Carton of chewing gum, please.' I'd had a fright, a big fright. And I had a bone to pick with Spin and Gordon Lucas. 'By Jesus, so much for your bombastic little Idi Amin over there who was going to yarn to me about dogs and things for an hour. He only knew one word: "out".'

I got the Lucas kettle going on the doctor's envelope but couldn't read a word. It was in a medico–Yiddish–Ugandan code. But old Pirate knew a codebreaker: Tim's wife Jeeva used to be a nurse, but even she couldn't read it. Well, if I couldn't break the code, I could smash their network. The bloody note would stay in my pocket.

The next job was on Michael Moynihan's Loch Lomond, where we drove up to about 4000 feet pretty quickly. I had a team of big heavy red huntaways, toey as hell. I stepped out of Michael's Land Rover and found myself struggling, whanging the dogs to keep them under control, wincing at the sound of the bark-up. The medical showdown couldn't be put off much longer. I said to Michael and Robyn, 'I've got to go to the doctor and get a big check-up. There's a new lady doctor advertising she's started up over Glenavy, Seven Mile Road. I'll give her a go.' I was only joking; dyed-in-the-wool male chauvinists like me from the wombs of '25 do not go to female doctors. But Robyn Moynihan called my bluff. She set up an appointment.

Dr Goldrick had married a farmer, fellow called Anderson, and I fronted the farmhouse. It said SURGERY on the door. All the people in Millers Flat I knew who went to hospital died. I feared death and I feared doctors more. I suppose the discerning reader has picked up by this stage that I come from a long line of cowards. But I breasted the door, took a deep breath and opened it. A big dark girl, heavily pregnant and in a state of undress, was standing with her mother beside a small woman in a white coat. That was enough for me. I shut the door, strode off to my car, and was intent on heading for my beloved back country among the distant peaks when Dr Goldrick caught me and told me to wait in the car for a bit; she'd call me in.

She gave me the most thorough examination of my life: every part of me was checked. And I was astonished to find I didn't feel the slightest bit embarrassed. I told her the whole story about Dr Out the Ugandan, personal details, bad habits, even told the truth. It felt really beaut to be in the hands of someone so thorough, and to be looked after. I'm with her still 20 years later, though I do her the courtesy of removing my tobacco from my shirt pocket and sticking it in the glove compartment when I call on her. And she's had a waiting room for ages, too.

I altered my life. Cut whisky to two or three a night, cigarettes from town ones to 10 or so roll-your-owns a day, and waged a successful war on salt and sugar.

I've learned to take it easy at last, though I hide this as best I can. Stewart Eason rang me at a considerate 11 a.m., bragging about his new phone. 'These cellphones are beaut.'

'Yes, they are. But hang on a minute while I tie up my horse. I'll hear you better then.' In fact, I'd been enjoying a siesta. It's taken too many years, but I've finally adopted a motto inconceivable not so long ago: 'Never do today what you can put off until tomorrow. And don't do it tomorrow if there's a chance of getting some dumb bugger to do it for you on the third day.' No one is impressed by all the work you do, whatever century it happens to be.

CHAPTER TWENTY

The Times, They are a-Changing

There's a bridle hanging on the wall,
A saddle in an empty stall.
You asked me why the teardrops fall . . .

Unknown Country & Western lyric writer

THE SOUTH ISLAND HIGH COUNTRY HAS SEEN A LOT OF CHANGE, but surely never so much in so little time as it has during my life. I was born in 1925, making my generation only the third, arguably the fourth, Pakeha generation there.

In my sixties I headed Big Bronze, my ute, to Glenaray Station, where 40 years before I had been casual musterer, shepherd and half a married couple, for a reunion. I knew time had woven a new world there, as throughout the high country. But how different was it?

A call at the local pub while a puncture was repaired gave me an opportunity to find out. It was, as I knew it would be, full of musterers from the district. I asked one young musterer what I should say if I was asked to say something. His reply caught me by surprise. 'Ask them,' he stammered, 'why it is that a rous-rouseabout can arrive in the back of a contractor's truck wearing jandals, smoking a marijuana cigarette and with all his gear in a sugar bag an-an-an' gets $12 a hour, an-an-an' a mus-musterer with all his d-d-dogs and his ute and th-that only gets $40 a day.' He wasn't joking, either. Attitudes had changed like everything else.

His query didn't go down well in the after-dinner speeches with the old hands, but the young ones nodded agreement.

Boys are always wrong. They're either bolshie — anti-authority, kicking against the flow — or bullheaded — too willing to learn, running before they can walk. Most get over it, but some never do. Sad but true. You can't train boys, but you can guide them. I try to accentuate the best that's in them, and I reckon I've done all right as a teacher. This boy, though, had a valid point. Let's look at the shearing workers' story as a comparison.

Shearers are not pigs who sleep on straw, though straw mattresses they used to get. The union, whatever its faults, did right in fighting such things. Contractors have fixed most of that, without the union's pettiness about rules, and that's good too. A runholder bloke I know was asked by a shearer what he'd do after he quit the game: 'Oh, go shearing and take it easy for a while.' Another runholder firmly believed that, when a man took up a pair of blades or a handpiece, he ceased to be a man. (He was referring to the unreasonableness of union rules that, say, demanded knock-off at a prescribed hour when another hour would finish the mob entirely that day, to everybody's benefit, including the sheep and shearer.)

There's a clash of cultures between a unique breed that crazily get up at 2.30 a.m. to climb a mountain, and men who are governed by the clock. But the idea that shearing isn't hard work is ridiculous. A good shearer doesn't struggle with his sheep, but pulling 100 of them each day onto the board and clipping them, or perhaps 300 in a machine shed, and sending them down a chute is no picnic. Today, it's better than it's ever been; tomorrow, a shearer's lot should get better.

I believe there are more blade shearers working today than at any time since the introduction of machines, and this trend surprises many people. But it has come about because of the tremendous flock losses in the high country when machines were embraced with enthusiasm. The enthusiasm was understandable enough — machine shearing effectively doubled the rate of woolfelling and halved the time sheep spent in holding paddocks and yards. But these days it's getting back to blades, which simply leave more wool on the beast. Hector Munro, a blade shearer himself, was one man down on his board and brought in his son Walter, a blade man, to help shear a mob. It was Hec's first shearing with machines. Exactly 700 hoggets went down the chutes, 96 of them down Walter's. A storm blew up that night and one of Walter's tally died. All 604 of the others did. But stock safety isn't the only factor in the regrowth of this seemingly antiquated method.

Percy Kelland of Glenbrook near Ohau was good at calculation and he figured he gained one clip in five shearing with blades. Regrowth of wool isn't as severely checked. As an overly severe pruning of a fruit tree will retard new-wood growth, so too wool fibres.

Thirdly, there is more pre-lamb shearing done now, as early as August, encouraging the accent on safety of animals.

And no less important, the whole shed can enjoy the cricket (or the football) on the radio without those noisy machines roaring. 'Hadlee's coming to the crease. He acknowledges the crowd's applause and encouragement . . .' and there's a soft *chew, chew* from down in the fragrant lanolin, unmixed with lube oil and motor fumes.

Flock numbers have grown but shearers, machine or blade, still take about the same time to separate fleece from animal. There's more work for them than ever.

Musterers' numbers have been steadily dropping during the latter half of my life, and it's a better life today in many ways. Much toil has been done away with, and only a madman would nurse any nostalgia for the old walking days. When Ian Anderson bought Ben Ledi he command-eered us to muster his wether block. It took me 18 hours to go right around the outside. We tried running things from a hut, using a 4X4 army truck along neighbours' tracks, walking in from the top of Danseys Pass and just leaving the homestead for work, in order to make the musters shorter and easier. Nothing worked well, but we always got them in. Recently Ian's grandson got me to drive his men to their beats there and pick them up on bulldozed tracks. The 99 kilometres on the odometer that day was mostly walking saved, much of it uphill. And there was two hours spent bashing Anderson's credit card — a good musterer doesn't carry cash on the hill — in the Danseys Pass pub.

High-country farmers embrace scientific and technological inno-vations they think or are told will help them. HJ Wardell was on the Omarama Rabbit Board in the early 1950s and told me: 'Know what they're doing in Marlborough, Bill? Putting poisoned carrots out of aeroplanes!' That spread like fire in gorse, and top-dressing with superphosphate and seeding followed. It is no longer noteworthy. A very recent visitor, a much younger man than me but no spring chook, felt rabbit calicivirus was the greatest single change in his lifetime, and the best!

The effect of bulldozed tracks and the many years of fencing that's gone on, making smaller and smaller, more manageable blocks or paddocks, is a major factor in the declining numbers of high-country musterers. Morven Hills up Lindis Pass used to have three to four permanent busy men. Glenaray was a village once. On Nokomai there was one truck, an old 12-hundredweight thing, and all it ever did was get in stores. Today many musterers start their day getting into a truck or 4WD. On lower suitable country a four-wheeler motorbike can scoot over territory a lot faster than a horse. Trailbikes seem to me to be able to go pretty well anywhere it is useful for them to go, although there is land they can't get across. But why bother? The helicopter can lift men to their beats and out at will. It can view paddocks and let men on the ground know not to bother sweeping up a certain area because there are no sheep there. It can direct sheep in its own right. Morven Hills is now mustered by one man — owner Richard Snow, with two dogs and a helicopter. Nokomai has its own private copter. A professional photographer, Andris Apse, took a photo on a tussocky mountainside of a man and his stick, man and horse and pilot and helicopter, which reminded me of sail giving way to steam. But there were still plenty of dogs in the frame, and always will be until a computer can grow wool.

The generation that follows me does have new opportunities, exciting ones too. They're different, though. Because of the gruelling daily schedule and lack of transport for my generation, we never had the leisure to develop the skills they have. The new generation skis, climbs mountains for their summits, rides horses constantly, flies helicopters. They become ski instructors, mountain guides, trail-ride leaders (with 'horses on valium' one told me), and scenic flyboys. Tourism offers the big occupational opportunities, and that includes managing too. Stations offer homestays and folk seem to enjoy sheepwork, strange as it sounds to a bloke like me.

But though ways have changed, fundamental high-country values seem to have adapted but stayed intact. When a barbecue salesman called on a place I was working on, an older man than me observed, 'They used to shit outside and eat inside. Now they shit in and eat out.' A lot of high-country life had been dedicated to the proposition that what could be done inside should be done there, and our generation welcomed sewerage, electrification, the flush toilet, cabs on tractors, air-conditioning and anything else offering convenience and comfort and warmth. (I think the microwave oven is civilisation's highest attainment so far; it's turned me into a top heater-upper.)

Back to musterers. One incentive to take up the trade — that of getting land of your own — is getting harder and harder, sadly. Everybody seems to want a bit of the high country now. A big Otago place sold for over $2 million recently, to an Australian concern, and they go for more sometimes. A Southland man on downs country made a packet and put his son on a high-country place. The Department of Conservation is buying up land in a fit of madness. Tourists seem happy enough with 100 metres either side of the highway, a gape at Mount Cook and a couple of lakes, and a run down a ski slope. Seems a rare case where you can have your $9 billion tourist cake and eat more of the $22 billion sheep cake. Most musterers are runholders' sons today, gaining experience on the properties of others, and the educational aspect of the game is a primary function.

Glenaray had 1000 steers in its back country in 1948. Now there are none. Cattle hooves were damaging peat bogs, it was decided. I certainly fail to see how those bogs are anything but a pain for man and beast, and no tourists are going to climb up and admire them. Lake Wanaka they ain't. As to the environmental damage, anybody who knows those bogs can see that trailbikes are the problem, making drainage ditches. Far too many academic fanatics leave their computer screens and come up in shorts with a notebook on a summer day to treat local knowledge with contempt. They're seldom nocturnal, seldom winter visitors.

Muldoon's Think Big programme was important for the high country, and I still don't know what I think about its value. The general taxpayer didn't know how much of their money was poured into farms in the form of attractive government loans for top-dressing, seeding, irrigation and the like. A lot of those loans got wiped by Wellington. And it is not only government lenders who let mortgagees off the hook. Back in the 1930s a Lindis man sold a property near Tarras and bought another, leaving £5000 on the old place. The buyer got into trouble and the government wiped the debt. New car for the buyer, hard times for the seller. Walter Cameron held a mortgage on Dunstan Peaks years ago, and used to say,

'How's my place?' whenever he saw me; he'd invested money on the property for Arthur Munro, and the government of an earlier era wiped that. At the time of writing a Central Otago property is being sold up at tender because of the owner's financial difficulties; one tenderer, $80 000 less than valuation. I don't know the answer, but individual sellers and buyers and the taxpayer seem too often to lose. On the other hand, Think Big improved the productivity of many lucky owners three- and four-fold, thus the value of their land and leases.

There's one last high-country phenomenon to deal with.

After the quiet time of winter the plovers would return to our paddocks. From that sign we knew that soon, on the first warm spring afternoon, other migrant species too would return to the high country.

Waitaki Soil Conservation officers, Lands Department officials and MAF agents, having shed their winter coats for shorts, light shirts with at least three pencils sticking out and carrying attaché cases, were eating fresh cheese scones and cold merino mutton and salad for lunch.

One morning after heavy rain Omarama Creek flooded. It was a big one: three floodgates were washed out, the new-sown lucerne blocks badly scoured and there was a good bit of repair work to do. Just then an *Academic fanaticus* turned up to look at the water gauge which was, in fact, under two or three feet of water. He asked me for an estimate of cusecs. In a sarcastic tone I told him to find out how much water was going over and through the Waitaki Hydro Dam and halve it. After deep thought, he said he reckoned he could get data on his way home to his roost down country. But they're not all stupid.

In the 1950s there was one soil conservator who handled the whole Waitaki Valley and Mackenzie Country, handing out permits to burn and subsidies for shelterbelts and the like. Ross Maxwell was the most dedicated civil servant it has been my privilege to know. He worked all hours and his office was a hut in Kurow. After he retired, to farm in North Canterbury, I heard he was still planting trees on roadsides as he did in the Waitaki.

Then a strange thing happened. A mating pair in Kurow must have got busy, because they multiplied to become 45, with leather chairs, varnished tables and motel-like quarters. Then a virus, like the rabbit calicivirus, must have struck. The whole set-up just disappeared overnight, their niche occupied by a new species, DOCs, who can be sighted in riverbeds in summer, looking for the black stilt, or kneeling over outcrops of schist with a magnifying glass looking at lizard droppings. I've never seen the stilt or the God's own lizard but thousands of dollars have been spent stripping willows to make the braided river channels nicer for them, not to mention increasing the risk and severity of flooding.

When a fella sits on his lounge chair these days and looks at Mount Domett, which these days is about as close as I want to get to the alps, and a white stag passes by the verandah, a bloke these days gets to thinking. You can't help yourself, any more than you can help saying 'these days'.

I punched sheep for a crust, and want no appellation beyond 'musterer' on my grave. 'Shepherd' is okay too. What the blue blazes will I care anyway?

I wasn't born with a silver spoon in my mouth, but I've enjoyed the challenges — there've been a few. But they all say that, don't they? There's a few other things they all say, but they're true. Ima has been a good wife to a difficult husband. I think I've got better and cannot understand why she can't agree.

Now and then these days people from my past walk through my head at night.

High-country people seem to be invisible to town people, their way of life registering zero on the understanding scale. Some Oamaru people in the Omarama pub were cock-a-hoop about their adventurous day: they'd climbed Mount St Cuthbert, which was real nice for them and I'm glad they got a buzz out of it. Who'd be the sort of mean soul who'd tell them Maurice Haye climbed it often, in the dark, in 90 minutes, and when he did, he signalled for the day's work to begin? Went around the Cuthbert 43 times myself.

'Still going?' I would ask Ian Anderson whenever I called on him at Omarama in our retirements. And he'd know my dogs had howled in the night, a sign a dog man's spirit had departed his body. Ian'd take his pipe from his mouth and say mildly, 'I can definitely say it wasn't me.'

One day it was. He lived 85 years. I knew him for over 30 of those. We're not a demonstrative lot, but I miss Ian.

I've six grandchildren, but Billy's three are Collinses and Fiona's two Reeds. Five-year-old John Mackenzie William, the spitting image of me, a handsome child, carries on the Kerr name.

I still dream of that silver tray. My big black-and-tan huntaway Rambo has the bark of Cerebus. Maybe next year I'll emerge from retirement and give him a run.

On a warm afternoon these days you might find three old gents in my six-hectare dog-training paddock. They'll be Don McPherson, George Innes and me, dubbed the last of the summer wine by a local lady. You'll note a pen for sheep and three chairs. One will be standing, having a run, while the two others reminisce and talk of life.

Donald will tell of his father, who owned Fairlight Station, and how he and his brother Duncan owned Lorne Peak Station, a place in Southland between Kingston and Garston, and if you don't know where that is, never mind. He'll tell of trials and tribulations. You've got ask. 'Would you do it all again, Don?'

'Yes, I would.' Now it's his run.

George, a much more vocal chap, sits and tells of his father's days on Haldon Station in the Mackenzie Basin, of a young shepherd, of a soldier in Cairo, of being the toast of the showring in equestrian sport and of being owner of Dunstan Downs. 'Would you do it all again?'

A long pause.

'Yes, I would.'

'Rambo. Sit. S-iii-t. Good boy. Good boy . . . Wayleggo!'

The sun went and so did they. I retired to my leather chair, microwave, spa bath and liquor cabinet, the small luxuries 70 years' punching sheep have brought me. An albino fallow deer walks past the window, followed by some red ones. I think about the men, dogs, horses, sheep, cattle and mountains I knew, snow-capped Mount Domett there to keep me focused and realistic.

My mind travels back to a time I drove up the Waitaki Valley at Christmas time, passing caravans, boats, trailers, expensive 4WDs loaded with camping gear. The Omarama camping ground was full of tents, just a few metres apart. Some even had scrim around them like fences. To keep the kids in? To keep neighbours out? I'm not sure. These people had waited and worked and saved all year for a fortnight in the paradise I'd lived in all my life. When their time was up they went back to their quarter-acres, little offices and factories, the noise and fumes of the city. Would I do it again? Sure I would.

Index